When **GOD** *Becomes a* **Drug**

Understanding Religious Addiction and Religious Abuse

Book I

Father **Leo Booth**

SCP Limited

SCP Limited
2700 St. Louis Avenue
Long Beach, CA 90806

© Copyright 1998
Leo Booth

When God Becomes A Drug
ISBN: 0-9623282-9-4

Dedication

This book is dedicated to all those who shared their stories of religious addiction and religious abuse—also to those too numerous to mention who made valuable comments.

CONTENTS

Acknowledgments

THIS BOOK IS the culmination of many ideas and opinions expressed by my family, friends, and colleagues over the years—far too many to list accurately. But it is important to me to acknowledge that these insights into religious addiction and religious abuse are the collective awareness of a variety of people, particularly those who shared their personal stories with me.

Having said this, special mention needs to be made of Kate Russell, my researcher and editor. When I originally self-published the central theme of this book under the title *Breaking the Chains . . . Understanding Religious Addiction and Religious Abuse* (Emmaus Limited), I knew that more was required to establish religious addiction and abuse as a separate and distinct dysfunction. Kate tirelessly researched much of the material and helped rewrite and adapt this revised version. The result is a much more precise account of how people become addicted and abused in the name of God.

Special thanks goes to Jeremy P Tarcher, for his vision and support, without which this book could not have become a reality. I am deeply indebted to Connie Zweig, for her invaluable editorial guidance and patience. I also express my appreciation to John Bradshaw for his foreword, and to all those who reviewed the manuscript and offered their encouragement.

Foreword

I WELCOME THE OPPORTUNITY to write this foreword to
Father Leo Booth's *When God Becomes a Drug*. It takes great courage
to write such a book. No addiction is more toxically shaming and
soul-murdering than the religious abuse that flows from the actions of
religious addicts.

My definition of addiction is the following: a pathological
relationship to any mood-altering person, thing, substance, or activity that
has life-damaging consequences. Father Leo makes it perfectly clear that
the insidiousness of the religious addict is his delusion about the
life-damaging consequences of his behavior. There is no addiction that
covers up the addict's core of toxic shame better than religious addiction.
The religious addict stays delusional by saying things like: "Are we not
supposed to give our all in relation to God? How could one be doing
something wrong by giving his life to God? By taking care of others? By
sacrificing one's life for God?"

Like Father Leo, I've been in this state of mind. I've felt the
exhilaration and righteousness of a four-hour prayer session and the
goose-bump thrill of humbly following my spiritual master. I've often
thought of writing about my addictive religious experiences. In a sense,
I've been afraid to do it. God's penetrating eyes of judgment turned my
conviction into procrastination. Father Leo has risked it and I'm grateful to
him. One has the best chance of being heard if one has been there. Father
Leo is an insider who dares to question everything religious. He has
theological credentials. He knows about that of which he speaks, especially
the power and control possessed by those who have religious authority.

Beyond the theological aspects of this problem, one must have a
thorough grasp of the addictive process and how it is rooted in family
dysfunction. Chapters 1 through 4 are the products of a man who knows the

dynamics of addiction. To my knowledge, no one has ever outlined the etiology, stages, and symptoms of religious addiction in the manner of this book. This work is pioneering. Without a clinical knowledge of the addictive process, one risks doing exactly what the TV evangelists do to the addictionologist.

In addition, Father Leo is very respectful of healthy religion. He sees religion as the frame of developing spirituality. If spirituality fails to emerge, religion becomes religiosity.

The sections on spirituality are eloquent. For Father Leo, spirituality is the power "to discover and use one's own unique specialness." To my mind that is the essence of true religion. It supplies the supportive community whereby one can find a unique sense of self.

Moses was told by God that his name was "I am who I am." Every child is born with a sense of "I am who I am." The job of the family and the church is to orchestrate life so that the sense of "I am" can grow and expand. Chapter 5 painfully outlines how children raised by religious addicts have their "I am"ness ripped apart—how their sense of wholeness is split. This is a far cry from religion's promise of at-one-ment.

Father Leo also offers a thorough and practical step-by-step guide for healing the wounds of religious addiction and religious abuse. The chapter on breaking the chains is especially good. There is an insidious quality about religious addiction and the abuse it spawns. The denial of religious addicts is the most delusional denial of all addiction. Delusion means "sincere denial." Religious addicts are generally rigid. They live with a barrage of thought-terminating clichés. Lionel Trilling called this the language of non-thought. The simple, easily memorized, and oft-repeated phrases create mental restrictions, a shriveling of awareness. This state of mind is comparable to a trance state. Breaking out of such delusional certainty is a mighty challenge, and Father Leo takes it on with great insight and persuasion.

Finally, we need to know what healthy spirituality is. I am in agreement with Leo Booth's position concerning spiritual awakening and spirit growth.

This book is groundbreaking. It is a must for all because religious education has been a major force in most people's development. This book is especially important for professionals who are uncomfortable with religious belief. Often therapists fear confronting clients' religious statements. I hope this book gives the clinician permission to intervene in the life-destroying shallowness of religious addiction. I further hope many people can break through their denial and see just how damaged they've been by religious abuse. As Freud pointed out in *The Future of an Illusion,* one of the assumptions of dysfunctional faith is that one loses faith by questioning faith. It takes courage to go against the terrors of hell and judgment that our wounded child fears. Only by questioning our faith can we emerge with a mature faith.

I encourage you to follow Father Leo Booth's model. He is courageous, maybe even a rebel. But after all, Jesus was put to death for being a rebel. I've always known that the more I risked being Christ-like, the more dangerous it would be. Father Leo has taken that risk. I urge you to read this book.

John Bradshaw
April 1991

When GOD *Becomes a* Drug

Understanding
Religious Addiction and
Religious Abuse

PREFACE: *Leo's Story*

My name is Leo. I'm an alcoholic. A codependent. A religious addict and religious abuser. I'm a recovering priest.

THIS IS HOW I introduce myself when speaking at meetings. I have been a recovering alcoholic for more than fourteen years, but only recently have I recognized the extent to which I am also a victim of religious abuse, have been a religious addict, and have abused others. Although I've called myself a recovering priest for years, recognizing my religious abuse revealed another dimension of my condition.

Some years ago I first heard the statement, My name is . . . I'm an alcoholic, drug addict, child of an alcoholic, and a *recovering Roman Catholic!*

The room filled with laughter. I chuckled because it was the first time I had heard such an expression. Many people in the meeting room, however, were nodding their heads with approval, obviously identifying with that part of the speaker's self-description. Since then I've heard that expression thousands of times—over coffee, in Twelve Step meetings, at lectures, in therapy groups.

Of course, the term is not peculiar to Roman Catholics. Any rigid, controlling, and oppressive religious structure or belief system fits: I'm a recovering Baptist . . . recovering Orthodox Jew . . . recovering Fundamentalist . . . recovering New Ager. . . . Beneath the laughter and chuckles that always greet these admissions is a deep pain and an awareness that religion can be dysfunctional—an awareness that people can be abused in the name of God.

This religious abuse has not been sufficiently explored in public, and the laughter merely serves to cover the shame and embarrassment of one's having been abused by, of all things, the concept of God. So in religious abuse, the highest source of love is used to create guilt, shame, and, ultimately, self-hate.

After I first heard the expression recovering Catholic, I began to consider seriously the staggering prevalence of religious addiction and the abuses that result from it. Religious addiction entails using God, a religion, or a belief system as a means both to escape or avoid painful feelings and to seek self-esteem. It involves adopting a rigid belief system that specifies only one right way, which you feel you must force onto others by means of guilt, shame, fear, brainwashing, and elitism. Thus religious addiction nearly always results in the abuse of someone else in the name of your beliefs. Considering the number of people this could involve, I wondered if I had uncovered a hidden epidemic of religious addiction and abuse.

I began to pay more attention to how often I was hearing about these issues. I wondered if these religiously oriented problems were as widespread as they seemed, or if there was something about me which invited such confidences. My work involves educating people about the spiritual aspect of recovery from all kinds of addictions and about the effects that addiction has on families. I do this via lectures, workshops, and seminars, and by serving as spiritual consultant at hospitals and treatment centers, where I often counsel patients. I try to teach people that spirituality is the process of becoming a positive, creative person and that spirituality is separate from religion. Perhaps my beliefs—the fact that I am a priest who respects other faiths and beliefs—and my own experiences as a recovering alcoholic made people feel safe in talking with me about religious issues.

Perhaps the confidences surfaced because I was talking about how spirituality—not religion—is necessary in Twelve Step recovery. I was clearly saying that people can be spiritual without being religious—and religious without being spiritual. Religion is a belief system organized around a prophet, teacher, or set of human precepts. Spirituality is the ability to discover and use our own unique specialness, and religion does not always help us do that. I was inviting people to share why and how they had left organized religion, not to pass judgment but to help them find the sources of their own pain.

Perhaps it was inevitable that I would hear an increasing number of accounts related to religion and its various abuses. A priest or minister today cannot talk to alcoholics, food or drug addicts, or adult children from dysfunctional homes without at some point discussing religious guilt, shame, and fear of God: "Why did God allow me to be sexually abused?" "How could my family fight all week and go to church pretending to be the ideal family on Sunday?" "How could God allow my little girl to die?" "How could I believe God loved me when He didn't stop the beatings . . . stop the drinking . . . stop my eating?"

And perhaps such confidences were coming up because I had been subconsciously struggling with these issues myself for years. The story of religious addiction and how it helps create religious abuse was *my* story. Unbeknownst to me, my questioning, my lectures on spirituality, my discussion of the clear distinction between spirituality and religiosity were all leading up to the point at which I could give my religiously abused inner child and religiously addicted adolescent permission to emerge.

It began, as it always does, in childhood. I was born in Manchester, England, in 1946. I grew up in a home divided by religion. My mother was Anglican (Episcopalian); my father, Roman Catholic. Although both are Christian denominations, they are not the same. Religious prejudice and put-downs between Catholics and Protestants are just as common in England as they are in Ireland. It didn't help that my father's heritage is part Irish.

As a child, it always seemed to me that people who were Roman Catholic were viewed as foreign, even though their families had lived in England for centuries. Protestant tracts, often pushed under the front door, reminded us that the Roman Catholic church was controlled and determined by a foreign power, an alien nation. To many Protestant people in England during my childhood, simply being a Catholic was cause enough to be viewed as a political traitor—one who owed allegiance to the Pope, not the Crown. For this reason, I was baptized and brought up an Anglican; that is, a member of the Church of England.

When Mother had an argument with Father, all the historical prejudice and venom were unleashed. My sister, who is ten years older than I, tried desperately to protect me from the shouting—the raging quarrels that often ended in physical violence. My mother would hit my father. My father would push my mother. Then the fighting would begin. It always ended the same way: My father would avoid hitting my mother by physically hurting himself. Often he would bang his head against the wall until it bled.

Only recently have I begun to understand how witnessing those incidents made me a victim of physical abuse. I remember trying to separate my fighting parents. I remember hiding my head under the pillow to make the screams go away. I remember seeing my father covered in blood because of his self-mutilation. All this was done by Christians, to Christians, in the name of God. I remember telling my sister that God was destroying our home.

The next significant chapter in the story of my religious abuse began when we moved to Wythenshawe, in greater Manchester. I was thirteen years old. To meet new friends, I attended a church youth club. There, I met Father Ronald Croft. He was an extreme high churchman in the Church of England, and he was to have a dramatic influence on my life. He was always called Father Croft and would have considered being addressed as Father Ronald an insult—much too intimate. He was strict. Controlling. Authoritarian. Arrogant. Demanding. Selfish. Ignorant. Masochistic. Yet very, very funny. A priestly Benny Hill! He made me laugh.

Father Croft took an interest in me and encouraged me to do well in school. From ages thirteen to eighteen, I was his disciple and he was my priest, my idol, my hero. His mannerisms, attitudes about worship, prejudices against Protestants, love of Roman Catholicism, and, I'm ashamed to say, ridicule and religious put-downs of women became my own. (I will deal with this issue as well as the special problems of other minorities in some detail later in the book.) Eventually I debated religious issues with him, often seeking to be even more extreme than he was, but always he was The Master.

Let me explain a bit about Anglo-Catholicism, which is a segment within the Anglican communion, or Church of England, and is sometimes described as Catholicism without the pope. When Henry VIII broke away from Catholicism, many English Catholics wanted to remain as true to the historic Church as they could and yet not get in trouble politically. Thus, although Anglo-Catholicism does not look to the Vatican for governance, in many other ways it differs little from European Catholicism.

Anglo-Catholicism retains a belief in the validity of the priesthood and sacraments but allows Anglican priests to marry. The High Church, as it is called, believes that God has passed his Word from St. Peter down through the line of bishops, which is how the Church claims its authority. Anglo-Catholics also believe in the importance of the Virgin Mary and the saints, as well as the dogmatic need to follow the teachings and precepts of the creeds and early councils of the Church. Although no longer governed by the Vatican, Anglo-Catholicism emphasizes unity with Rome and, like Roman Catholicism, does not recognize Protestantism as a bona fide faith.

So Anglo-Catholics carry much of the same zeal and prejudices as do their Catholic brethren; in fact, in their rigid adherence to dogma and ritual, they are in many ways more fundamentally Catholic than Roman Catholics! Some Anglo-Catholics—and I was one of them—take a sort of snobbish pride in their faith, feeling quite superior to the people who follow the traditional Protestant faiths.

Today, I am able to understand that the drama of church ritual—which, as a male, I was privileged to carry out—became my first drug of choice. It provided me a safe place where I could escape my dysfunctional home life. I was being molded for the priesthood. My self-esteem depended on my being part of an authentic remnant within the Church of England, solemnly observing the strict ceremonial of the Mass, attaining purity through sacramental confession, and not tainting myself by associating with Protestants, the nonreligious, or girlfriends. I became Father Croft's blue-eyed prodigy. I had already decided to study theology and philosophy at the university, and during my first year at King's College I was accepted for the priesthood. The sick cycle had begun.

When interviewed for the priesthood I was asked why I wanted to be a priest. I answered, "Why, to wear those beautiful clothes, of course." The interviewer laughed loudly and decided I had the necessary sense of humor for the priesthood. But such jokes often foreshadow tragedy: I enjoyed wearing the ceremonial robes and vestments largely because they made me feel superior.

During this time, the seeds of my alcoholism were being sown as well. The Anglo-Catholic movement in the Church of England is affectionately known for its love of the Blessed Virgin Mary, incense, and a good gin-and-tonic. I think I'm being too kind by implying that order of priority. After Mass, including the evening Masses during the week, the priests would gather at the local pub. Surrounded by their male acolytes, they would laughingly recount stories about bishops being set on fire by confused incense swingers, or church pilgrimages during which unsuspecting English villages would be surrounded by crusading Anglo-Catholics singing *Ave Maria.* These social groups were preparing me for the priestly all-male club I was about to join, which was fueled, or should I say, well-oiled, by gin-and-tonic.

My five years at King's College and St. Augustine's College resulted in a defense of the rigid religious principles that had earlier been taught to me by Father Croft. I learned to manipulate scripture and church history to substantiate my dogmatic churchmanship.

I argued that only Catholics were proper Christians and that people who were not baptized as Catholics were not members of the church. Thus members of other Christian religions were not worthy of receiving Holy Communion. Moreover, women could never be ordained to the priesthood because Jesus called only men as his disciples. Women could give service by keeping the priestly garments clean, arranging the flowers, and attending Mass in the pews. I believed that celibacy was the ideal state for priests and felt sad that some priests in the Church of England were married.

As you can see, I have had my days as a dogmatic religious fundamentalist. So I do know what I'm talking about when I say that it is possible to change.

Here I must mention my flirtation with the Jesuits at the Church of the Immaculate Conception in London. As an Anglican seminarian at King's College, I approached the Jesuits for instruction, intending to leave the Church of England and become a Jesuit priest. I studied with the Jesuits alongside my theological studies at college and for two years worked under the firm guidance of Father Michael Nevin, S.J. He was strict, authoritarian, and persuasive, and I sought to imitate him—as I had Father Croft.

I was just about to jump into the arms of Mother Rome when the pope released the encyclical Humanae Vitae, which addressed the issues of sexuality and birth control. Although I was rigid, dogmatic, and obedient to the creed of faith and liturgy, like a number of my Anglo-Catholic friends I was remarkably lax and uncertain when it came to ethical morality. My alcoholism was progressing. I remained unmarried but was by no means sexually abstinent. In short, I was a hypocrite. Despite my hypocrisy in some areas, I had genuine differences with the Catholic Church over the issue of birth control, and after many discussions with Father Nevin I ended my formal association with the Jesuit community.

Why did I really want to be a Jesuit? I was attracted to their power image: intellectual giants, storm troopers for Jesus, shrouded in mystery. Coveting that elitist image I continued a quasi-Jesuit life-style in the Anglican tradition.

In 1971 I was ordained to the priesthood in the Church of England. The Right Reverend Ian Ramsey conducted the ceremonies at the Anglican Cathedral in Durham City. Here, alcohol nearly got me in trouble. I went out the night before to celebrate the occasion with a few swift gin-and-tonics, only to find myself the next morning confused and suffering the first of what was to be a priestly ritual: a whopping hangover. In my stupor that morning I mislaid my Bible, which I was supposed to carry with me in the procession following my ordination. Instead, I grabbed a book of similar size and appearance—the complete works of Oscar Wilde. I'm sure I am the first priest in the Church of

England to receive ordination to the priesthood while clutching such a secular tome. Perhaps that explains my rebellious spirit!

From 1971 until I was hospitalized in 1977, my priesthood was characterized by periods of ritualized religious addiction, followed by shameful episodes that resulted from my alcoholism. Perhaps the more I drank, the more extreme I became in my religious practices, medicating my guilt with ritual and dogma. I could blot out my guilt and my growing awareness of my religious hypocrisy with alcohol. Long before I had tasted alcohol, however, I had used religion to escape loneliness, low self-esteem, and fear of reality. Anglo-Catholicism was my first drug.

I also regularly abused every church and congregation I worked with prior to recognizing my religious addiction. In my rigid, dogmatic adherence to Anglo-Catholicism, I somehow missed the charity and compassion that should also characterize a priest.

For example, I taught my Catechism classes that only Catholics were real Christians. I made the students learn the Ten Commandments and Seven Sacraments; if they could not remember them in a spot test, I would clip them behind the ears or humiliate them in some other way.

I was relentlessly dogmatic in my insistence that my congregations follow the teachings and rituals to the letter. I told them they could not be forgiven for their sins unless they came to sacramental confession. Confessing their sins to God without seeking absolution from a priest (meaning me) was a cowardly way to God. Attending Mass each Sunday was mandatory; missing Mass was a rejection of Jesus' invitation to the Last Supper. I used this guilt trip as a means to increase my Sunday congregations—and to control, to feel superior.

As I look back now, my prejudice and intolerance astonish me. I regularly preached that those who did not accept Jesus were simply pagans and heathens, and that those who did not believe in the Catholic tradition were not promised salvation. Often from the pulpit I would make sarcastic references to the Baptists, Methodists, or Congregationalists—indulging in a caustic wit patterned after Oscar Wilde to make my congregations laugh at their fellow Christians. I actually forbade my congregations from attending unity services with other faiths, preaching unity only with Rome.

I set up the Church (meaning myself) as the absolute authority on all aspects of life. Only the Church could give an authoritative interpretation of biblical texts, and these opinions were binding on all Christians. I all but forbade people to ask questions, think for themselves, or doubt the Church. I inferred that priests and nuns were at a higher spiritual state than so-called ordinary members of the Church and, therefore, should be obeyed without question.

I had continued the tradition of Father Croft. Indeed, after I became a priest, we became a sort of team. Together, we celebrated Mass, went on pilgrimages, encouraged young men to become Anglo-Catholic priests, and warned congregations of the imminent dangers created by the Women's Ordination Movement. We also, of course, got drunk on gin-and-tonic together.

Nobody seemed concerned about what was happening; nobody questioned my attitudes and behavior—as if it were natural to have a priest who was either drunk or hung over most of the time. Even today, few seem concerned about the number of priests in similar situations with similar pain, abusing themselves and their congregations.

Then came my drunken car crash in 1977; it was the natural intervention that put me on the road to recovery. I call it my "moment," and describe it in fuller detail in my book *Spirituality and Recovery.* Struggling to quit drinking, I had been dry for about three months. I went to a party at which I intended to drink tonic water. I drank tonic water all right—laced with liberal doses of gin! I drove home with no problem, celebrating my supposed control of drinking, only to discover I'd left my wallet at the hotel. When I went to get it the next day, the hotel manager invited me to have one for the road. Little did he know how prophetic that was. I proceeded to have several at a succession of pubs until, by three o'clock in the afternoon, I was drunk as a skunk. I drove my car into a tree. I stumbled out of the car—dazed, drunk, and bleeding—and sat down on the curb to await the police. There, on that curbside, I had my moment of clarity. I saw what I had become and did not like it at all.

That moment led to my treatment for alcoholism at Warlingham Park, in Surrey, England. For three months, I was hospitalized, my clerical duties suspended. For six months after that, I lived in a recovery home. I was just plain Leo: no black suits, no saying Mass, no being the-one-who-knows. Although it was never called religious addiction and religious abuse, it was suggested that I had used God and the Church to avoid facing my real pain. The little boy who had buried his head under the pillow and wished the world would go away was slowly being encouraged to face reality.

I began to work on the First Step of Alcoholics Anonymous and began to trace in detail how I was truly powerless because of alcohol, how my life had become increasingly unmanageable. I knew, then, even though I had no idea how my life would unfold, that it would never be the same. My God and the trappings of my religiosity had become a disabling crutch. My sobriety would depend on my rejecting religiosity and becoming a spiritual person.

As a major part of my treatment, I had to make amends to those I abused when I was drinking. At the time, though I didn't know it, I was confronting my religious addiction. It was never put that way, but in seeking out people I had hurt in my various congregations, I was showing them I was not perfect. I did not have all the answers. I was as confused as the next person and had hidden it behind my clerical collar and my booze.

I left the hospital with a changed outlook on life, determined to be a different priest. Church ritual, the priesthood, the use of scriptural texts—I had scrutinized them all, and my attitude toward other Christians and those of other religions was changed forever. I had severed my connection to the tradition of Father Ronald Croft. My treatment for alcoholism had created a spiritual intervention. Leo-the-person was separated from the priestly Father Booth and his dysfunctional religiosity. Today, I accept that I am an ordinary man with a series of compulsive behaviors.

The self-help support groups in England, as they do in America, helped me discover a God I could understand. I learned that spirituality consists not in what religion you practice, but in the acceptance of your own humanity—your limitations as well as your strengths. I learned that spirituality means developing a relationship with the God-within. I saw how I had never truly had a relationship with God; what I thought was a relationship with God was really a relationship with the dogma and rituals of religiosity. I had used those things to keep God at a distance. People who shared their thoughts and feelings at these support groups, who often had no theological or college education, spoke from the heart about love, forgiveness, and the need to be open-minded. They said we are all children of God, and we need to begin the slow and often painful journey into self-acceptance.

For the next three years I worked on changing my inner self and becoming a priest who was willing to discuss in public how people could be religiously abused in the name of God. I found myself telling large, public meetings that I was a recovering alcoholic priest. In doing so, I was shattering cherished beliefs about religiosity and the priesthood, but I was teaching people that priesthood does not mean perfection, that God does not magically take our imperfections away. I was learning that I could be much more effective by admitting that I am not perfect than by holding myself up as a perfect example, as the authority. I also discovered a feeling of freedom in saying, I don't know.

I was helped in my ministry by a loving bishop, the Right Reverend Colin Docker. He stood by me when many in the Church said I was a disgrace and ought to be defrocked. He recognized that I had a talent to educate people not only about alcoholism but also about the spiritual insights that often accompany a personal crisis. With enthusiasm, I threw myself into a new ministry. In 1981, after a series of lectures I had given in Chicago and Los Angeles, I was invited to come and work full time as the spiritual adviser at the chemical dependency treatment center at Memorial Hospital in Long Beach, California.

I have since held a number of positions at hospitals and treatment centers, working with people who have a variety of addictions. During the past ten years, I have seen the study of addiction develop into a diverse series of model programs that seek to educate, treat, and provide on-going support for a variety of compulsive behaviors: alcoholism, drug addiction, eating disorders, codependency, sex and love addiction, gambling—and for adult children of dysfunctional families.

Equally important, I have seen the insights and resources of the Twelve Step program applied to such psychiatric illnesses as depression, anxiety, paranoia, and post-traumatic stress due to sexual and other physical and mental abuse. I have seen more psychiatrists willing to accept and treat the dually diagnosed patient—someone with both a systemic mental disorder and one or more addictions. For too long, many of these patients were denied the benefits of full recovery, and I am happy to see them now being successfully treated.

Most important of all, the use of spirituality, rather than religion, in the treatment of addictions, compulsive behaviors, and psychiatric disorders has gained wide acceptance. Now there is greater emphasis on self-acceptance, honesty, forgiveness, willingness to change, humility, and the discovery of a God, or Higher Power, who is involved in our lives. People are beginning to recognize that spirituality flourishes with mental, physical, and emotional well-being.

There is, moreover, the dawning recognition of the devastating effects of dysfunctional religious messages—that religious addiction and abuse *do* exist; that they can and must be addressed in treatment, in therapy, and among the Twelve Step support groups.

For some of you, my position as an Anglican priest may seem particularly privileged and remote from the difficult daily experiences of women, minorities, and homosexuals. I recognize that my upbringing and religious education was filled with what Americans call a "WASP-ish" air of moral superiority, to which I clearly acknowledge I was very addicted. I am also aware that, no matter how many people I counsel, how many stories I hear, I cannot pretend to know from personal experience the pain of everyone I meet. Yet I can certainly acknowledge and validate it. I cannot undo the abuse I myself perpetrated, except by recognizing it and seeking to change it.

Further, I need to state again that while I am a Christian priest and a recovering alcoholic who believes deeply in the Twelve Step approach, I do not wish to imply that recovery from religious addiction and abuse can only happen in a Twelve Step context. Just as I would never insist that any religion is the one right way, I do not wish to foster the idea that Twelve Step programs are the only right way to recover. Recovery, like spirituality, is uniquely individual and special.

Many people come to me and thank me for identifying religious addiction and religious abuse. Others come with sincere questions. The religiously addicted come armed for combat, spoiling for debate. I generally make it a practice not to enable them to *use* by arguing with them. I am aware, too, that many other people will take what I say as gospel, without questioning, which I find just as alarming as those who seek combat. To paraphrase the closing used in A.A. meetings, the opinions expressed in this book are those of Leo Booth and do not represent those of the Church (or of God). Take what you need and leave the rest.

The purpose of this book is not to dispense with God, but to stop an abuse of God; not to destroy religion, but to discover the challenge and adventure that religion can provide in the here and now; not to ridicule discipleship, but rather to encourage the development of a creative relationship with God that allows for personal responsibility and change, enabling one to discover the Power that exists within each of us.

Chapter 1

Sin, Shame, Fear, & Control:
The Roots of Religious Addiction

> I hate God. And I also love God, Father Leo.
> When I hear you talk about God being loving,
> forgiving, nurturing, and involved in my life, it
> bears no resemblance to what I was taught as a
> child. The first words I remember as a child were
> "God is going to get you." And it went downhill
> from there. God was always to be feared. An
> *angry* God. A God who punished you and your
> family with sickness if you broke the rules. A
> God who was against laughter and fun.
>   Father Leo, a part of me loves God. But a
> bigger part of me hates God.

THESE WORDS WERE spoken by a woman in a treatment center where I lead a spirituality group. It is tragic, but this woman's love-hate relationship with God is not uncommon. Time and again, during the course of my work as a priest, as a counselor for people with addictions and eating disorders, and as a recovering alcoholic, I have encountered people struggling with grievous issues related to their religious experiences. These are people from all walks of life: lay people, clergy, fundamentalist and mainstream Christians, Orthodox

Jews, atheists, agnostics, Buddhists, Muslims, New Age disciples, and Twelve Step junkies.

They all share a common experience: In the name of God, they have been made to feel fear, guilt, shame, and anger. In the name of God, they have emotionally, physically, or sexually abused themselves or others. In the name of God, they have brought themselves or others to the edge of financial ruin. In the name of God, they have judged and condemned themselves or others as worthless and inherently bad.

As a result, their unhealthy beliefs about themselves and God poison their lives. They use religion as a means to acquire power and control, especially to gain money or sex, or both. Their only means of gaining self-respect or self-control is to lock themselves into rigid, intolerant perfectionism, harshly judgmental of others who don't follow their rules. They use God, religion, or their beliefs not to liberate themselves spiritually but to escape emotional pain. Eventually, however, their relationships sicken; their self-esteem withers and dies. Desperate to feel better, they then fall prey to any substance, person, or belief that promises relief.

Such behavior creates an insurmountable barrier to authentic spirituality and, worse, to a healthy, creative relationship with that inner Power I call God. As a recovering alcoholic trying to help others work a spiritual program, I find this tragic. As a priest, I find it unacceptable.

My experience in the treatment centers clearly illustrates how shame fuels addictions. More and more, I have seen that much of the shame comes from dysfunctional religious beliefs. Dysfunctional religious messages about sin, about sexuality, about God as an angry judge or Cosmic Fixer have created these toxic beliefs—from which people have tried to escape by means of addictive practices.

TV EVANGELIST SCANDALS

I had just begun to fully explore the relationship between shame, religion, and addiction when the TV evangelist scandals first made news. Fascinated and slightly amused, I followed each new episode: financial embezzlements by Jim and Tammy Bakker at PTL; Jimmy Swaggart's sexual escapades; Oral Roberts's outright blackmail of his flock in demanding millions of dollars or else God would call him home. My fascination turned to horror, however, and my amusement burst into outrage as the media's reports of the infighting revealed the magnitude of the tragedy of religious addiction and abuse. These supposed men of God had betrayed people's trust; they had taken people's sacred belief in God and made a mockery of it. Yet many of those who had been abused, betrayed, and bankrupted never seemed to question what was happening. They remained faithful. How could that be? Why? How could they not see the abuse?

My tolerance snapped.

I am not one to keep quiet about my views. I hold degrees in philosophy and theology, and I love a good debate over theological issues. I broke with the Roman Catholic Church over the issue of birth control, though it meant giving up my goal of becoming a Jesuit priest.

Today, the challenge of differing ideas stimulates me, moves me ever closer to my God. My faith is built on the freedom to doubt, to question, for it is in questioning and exploring that my faith is affirmed and deepened. The spectacle of so many people being blindly betrayed without questioning, coupled with the tragedies and pain I was meeting in my work with addicts, catapulted me into action. I began to speak out. Loudly. I began to write this book.

What I read and heard in the news reports concerning the TV evangelist scandals echoed what I often heard in the treatment centers and in Twelve Step meetings:

- God will keep me from drinking again.

- Jesus helped me get thin.

- I don't need the Twelve Steps. I just have to follow the teachings in the Bible . . . in the *Course in Miracles* . . . in the Talmud.

In these dogmatic statements, I saw black-and-white thinking; I saw refusal to think, doubt, or question; I saw obsessive thinking. In short, I saw addiction. Taking away the scripture quoting, the praying, the sacrifice, the rigid devotion to rules, and looking solely at the attitudes and behaviors behind them revealed the same kind of attitudes and behavioral patterns long identified as those of alcoholics and addicts, and of codependents. I saw a family of God as dysfunctional as any family of an alcoholic I have ever met.

It was staggering to realize that many children of God have grown into adult children of . . . of what? A dysfunctional God? Not possible. But the *messages* they have received about God are dysfunctional, or at least create dysfunction. Whatever they experienced in the name of God molded their beliefs about themselves and about God. Here is the source of the religious shame, the insurmountable wall that separates so many people from a loving, creative relationship with God.

The more I examined the idea of the dysfunctional family of God, the clearer it became. In the excessive tithing and giving I saw the same compulsive urgency I've seen in gamblers. In the dedication to church ritual I saw the sex addict's need for ritualizing. In the glazed, hypnotized look of a woman quoting scripture at me, I saw the drugged stare of addicts after a fix. In the staunch loyalty of the Bakkers' followers, I saw the same denial I've seen in an alcoholic's spouse. The TV evangelist scandals now appeared in a different light. I started looking first at the churches involved in the scandals and then at all religions and belief systems for the sources and symptoms of the dysfunctional messages.

It is typical that adult children of dysfunction—any type of dysfunction—nearly always believe a negative, unhealthy message about themselves. Rarely do they ask if something is wrong with the *message*. They assume that there is something wrong with *them*. Each time I dug to find the reason for this curious dynamic, I struck a bedrock of unhealthy religious beliefs and messages from which seemed to spring all kinds of abusive, addictive behaviors.

I believe in a loving, caring God who delights in a creative relationship with the human race. How could this relationship, which I view as special and precious, have become so grievously distorted and dysfunctional? More important, could it be healed? I had to look back across the history of humankind and trace the patterns of our relationship with God as set down in the development of the various religions in order to find some of the answers. What I found was an increasingly addictive and addicted society desperately searching for a fix. In the patterns of how religion has shaped society, I found that religious messages which teach that we are inherently bad, powerless, and weak—and must therefore look to God to make us good and strong—are at the core of this addictive behavior.

A short look at how this unhealthy cycle developed will help us understand how the messages we received about God can lead to dysfunctional behavior, and how those messages laid the foundation for much of the shame and guilt that so deeply afflicts so many in our society today.

GOOD OR EVIL: HOW RELIGION DEFINES US

The question is not one of religion or not? but of which kind of religion?—whether it is one that furthers human development, the unfolding of specifically human powers, or one that paralyzes human growth.

Erich Fromm

In his book *To Have or To Be,* Erich Fromm describes religion as "not necessarily having to do with a concept of God," but as "any group-shared system of thought and action that offers the individual a frame of orientation and an object of devotion." As Fromm suggests, religions and belief systems seem to be divided into two camps: those that believe that human nature is essentially good and focus on our innate dignity, and those that maintain that humans are inherently evil and base.

This corresponds with my own definition of religion as being essentially a set of man-made principles about God, focusing on a teacher or prophet, in contrast to spirituality, which is the process of becoming a positive and creative person. Moreover, this definition allows us to look not only at organized religion but also at any group or belief system that either generates dysfunction or is used dysfunctionally.

When those beliefs inspire us to develop our creative potential, whether spiritually, as individuals, or culturally, as a society, those beliefs move us forward and may be seen as healthy. When they limit or paralyze us, are used by ourselves or others to oppress and victimize us, they can be regarded as unhealthy.

Increasingly, I believe that many of the religious messages we have received, not only in the Judeo-Christian faiths but also in most of the world's religions have been twisted, misinterpreted, or misunderstood to the extent that, far from bringing us closer to God, Allah, Buddha, or the Great Spirit, they have created a spiritual void, a vast chasm that separates us from God. Our desperate search for something to fill the void, bridge the chasm, fix the problem leads us to addictive, compulsive behavior. In this book I explore some of the reasons and sources for such misunderstandings and show how they create the dysfunctional beliefs and behaviors that lead to addiction.

From Original Sin to Original Blessing

Many Christians perpetually struggle to reconcile the concepts of sin, pain, and suffering with the concept of a loving, forgiving God. It is hard to imagine someone who loves us allowing us to endure pain and tribulation. We must have done something wrong to deserve punishment, only we're not sure what we did. If we could find out, we would fix it and be loved again. The messages and teachings concerning the concept of original sin offer the explanation that we were born bad, and only by following God's rules can we overcome this inherent blight. The negative effects on self-esteem and spirituality created by this concept, and how it contributes to religious addiction and abuse, warrant some examination.

While I may be the first to label the dysfunction and its effects as the disease of religious addiction and abuse, I am by no means the first to point out the negative effects that traditional religious teachings have had on our spiritual growth. In this century alone, I am but one of many who has observed that something is wrong with the interpretations of the messages often given by organized religion, and that the resulting dysfunctional message has created dysfunction in us.

In *The Varieties of Religious Experience,* William James quoted in 1902 from a letter written by the eminent Unitarian minister Edward Everett Hale.

> *A child who is early taught that he is God's child, that he may live and move and have his being in God, and that he has, therefore, infinite strength at hand for the conquering of any difficulty, will take life more easily, and probably will make more of it, than one who is told that he is born the child of wrath and wholly incapable of good.*

Hale is pointing out the effect that messages of guilt and shame have on the way we cope with life. James quoted this passage in a chapter called The Religion of Healthy-Mindedness, in which he noted a growing movement away from a focus on hellfire and damnation toward a more positive, affirming theology: "We now have whole congregations whose preachers, far from magnifying our consciousness of sin, seem devoted rather to making little of it. They ignore, or even deny, eternal punishment, and insist on the dignity, rather than the depravity of man."

This search for the dignity, rather than the depravity of people is reflected in much of the pivotal religious movements and theological writings of this century. Increasingly, there is an awareness that the idea that we are born bad, evil, or inadequate has had a negative effect on our self-esteem, and on our relationships with God and our fellow humans. With that awareness is a sense of how these negative messages form the core of all addictions, to which I now add religious addiction.

In the early 1920s, *Père* Teilhard de Chardin, a Jesuit priest and noted geologist, shocked many orthodox Catholics by rejecting original sin and espousing a theology that strove to reconcile physics and Darwin's theory of evolution with Christianity. *Père* Teilhard saw life as pure energy, expressed in both physical and spiritual domains, at once interconnected, yet independent. According to his theory, our physical and spiritual sides are two halves of a whole; we are incomplete if we deny one, or exalt one side over the other. The human task, as he saw it, was to build a bridge between our physical and spiritual sides so that the two energies could be mutually enlivened.

Père Teilhard explained sin, or evil as he preferred to call it, as "diminishments" that come from both inside and outside us and hinder our ability to unite with God. The diminishments from within, for example, might be our own human weaknesses—our attitudes and attributes. Diminishments from without are such phenomena as poverty, natural disasters, disease, or the effects of someone else's behaviors or illnesses. He believed that anything obstructing or sapping our physical and spiritual energies keeps us from the source of all energy: God.

One can see, in *Père* Teilhard's philosophy, some of the seeds of what was later to become integral parts of the Alcoholics Anonymous Twelve Step program. In his description of sin as diminishments that keep us from God, we can see the A.A. concept of *defects of character,* which perpetuate addictive behavior. My understanding of spirituality as encompassing the mental, physical, and emotional aspects of humanity owes much to Teilhard's explanation of how our physical and spiritual sides unite to create a whole.

Writers from William James and *Père* Teilhard in the early part of the century, to Matthew Fox, M. Scott Peck, and John Bradshaw today, all chronicle and explore a growing awareness of the spiritual emptiness felt by many people—the alienation and shame produced by the negative messages religion often gives.

In *The Psychology of Religion,* psychologist Wayne E. Oates examines the effect that the idea of sin has had on self-esteem and our relationship with God. Describing sin, he says that "the realistic acts of wrongdoing of a person—as the person perceives right and wrong—do produce a sense of guilt. When that guilt is felt to be in relation to God, the guilt is concentrated into a sense of sin."

The end result of this sense of sin, Oates says, is alienation from other humans and God. He says that

> *sin as alienation from God and man is the composite and end result meaning of sin. Idolatry alienates one from God and those persons and/or things that are put in God's place. Shrinking back from participating with God and man in the demands of growth in personal and corporate life alienates one's relationship to self, others and God.*

So we have the idea that sin means breaking rules or violating a code of ethics, which produces guilt and, ultimately, stands in the way of our relationship with God and others. This corresponds to *Père* Teilhard's concept of sin as diminishments, which weaken our ties to God. It also applies to William James's description of religion as either a search for truth, or a means to avoid error.

Recently, we have seen renewed attraction to metaphysics, and the rise of New Age philosophies. The issues of women's rights and their place in the church have led theologians such as Matthew Fox to seek a feminine and nature-oriented theology, in which God is as much Mother as Father. This movement away from traditional religion reflects a new kind of search for an explanation of the existence of pain and suffering—one that is not based on the premise that humans are inherently evil and deserve to suffer.

Fox makes a natural bracket, at the close of the twentieth century, to *Père* Teilhard. Both are priests, both seek to blend the spiritual and physical worlds. Fox, too, sees humankind as an expression of spiritual energy drawn from and back to its source. Like *Père* Teilhard, Fox has been forbidden by the Vatican to teach his theology of creation spirituality, which promotes the idea of original blessing as a counter to original sin.

In an interview in *Psychology Today,* Fox said:

> *I also object to original sin as the starting point of religion because of the tremendous psychic damage it has done. People are already terribly vulnerable to self-doubt and guilt, especially members of minority groups—women, blacks, Native Americans, homosexuals. The whole ideology of original sin increases one's alienation and feeds the sado-masochistic energies in the culture—the sense that one is not worthy.*
>
> *If you start with the notion that you were born a blotch on existence, you will never be empowered to do something about the brokenness of life. In creation spirituality, we begin with the idea that each of us is born a unique expression of divinity, an image of God. Teaching our children this is the only way to build the pride and security our culture needs so desperately.*

So we have come full circle, from Edward Everett Hale in the 1890s, to Matthew Fox in the 1990s, saying the same thing I am talking about: A belief system that tells us we are depraved from the outset victimizes us and limits our spiritual growth individually and as a species. Moreover, in explaining why he refuses to leave the church, Fox echoed my beliefs: "Even if the church is a dysfunctional family, it's my family and I would rather see it healed than abandon it."

In these theologies and philosophies we can see reflected the same themes: rejection of the shame-based messages traditionally taught by the major religions because of the spiritual damage such messages inflict, thus an abandonment of God as traditionally represented. Alongside this, we see the search for personal dignity and self-respect that, when it arises out of a lack of a Higher Power, leaves a spiritual hunger, a yearning, a restlessness. "We are restless til we rest in God," St. Augustine says.

It is this restlessness and yearning that tell us we are in need of that power in our lives. The negative teachings and dogmas that often cloak God also hide God from us and propel us into unhealthy behavior. Once we can separate God from the dysfunctional messages about Him, God comes alive, ever inviting us to become positive, creative people.

The Roots of Religious Addiction and Abuse

Clearly, the idea of original sin—of being born inherently weak and inadequate—has had a negative effect on us as individuals and as a society. I am often asked why God would tell us that if it weren't true. I suggest that perhaps God never said so. I recognize that I am treading on the core beliefs of those who depend on a literal, fundamentalist interpretation of scriptures. I would never deny anyone the choice of interpretation of the scriptures of any religion or belief system. However, certain changes occurred in Christianity and in the way the Bible evolved that leave room for many interpretations. My objection has never been to fundamentalism; rather, it is to the insistence that I or anyone else is eternally damned for believing in a different interpretation.

Religious addiction is built on absolute, unquestioning, uncritical acceptance of a set of teachings. On this foundation abuses are committed in the name of God. The key ingredients are fear, shame, power, and control. No matter what the religion or belief system, fear and shame are manipulated by those wanting power and control. Those abuses extend even to changing or twisting the basic scriptures or writings, and I believe Christianity is no exception. As a Christian and thus most familiar with that faith, I will use it as an example, but the dynamics I will explore apply to any religion or belief system that is used abusively.

First, let me reiterate that I am a priest, actively practicing and teaching my Christian faith. I believe in the historical Jesus, that he existed, that he was divine, and that in his teachings are to be found all that we need for spiritual growth and nurture.

I believe, however, that a literal, absolute, and dogmatic interpretation of scripture opens the door to dysfunctional religious messages and behaviors. While I accept the historical Jesus, I also recognize that much of the teachings about him—the dogma and doctrine central to Christianity—came from people who were interpreting what the messages in the Gospels meant to them. These interpretations are often the source of today's dysfunctional messages. In contrast, a healthy religiosity permits us to distinguish the religious teachings from the spiritual message. An unhealthy, rigid religiosity limits Jesus, the Church, and us, for it only serves to separate and alienate us from God. How did we get the idea that God told us we were bad? How did that process put us on the road to all addictions, especially religious addiction and abuse?

Matthew Fox has observed that "there were nineteen billion years of history and God's creative activity before human beings appeared on the scene and invented sin." Ever since Genesis was first handed down, great theological debates have raged over the issue of sin: What is it; are you born with it, or do you acquire it along the way; and what do you do about it after you've got it?

The theories and doctrines concerning sin are many and varied, but some predominant ideas about it are common to both liberal and fundamentalist theologies. Sin results in alienation from God and others, and this has its roots in the biblical story of Adam and Eve. In the Judeo-Christian context, most theologians agree that the concept of sin was born in the story of Adam and Eve's disobedience to God's instructions. Like Wayne Oates, Erich Fromm says the consequence of that disobedience was alienation from God and from ourselves. The symbolism in the story of the Fall implies that, prior to Eve eating the fruit, Adam and Eve were unified. They were part of each other, as symbolized by Eve having been created from Adam's rib. They had no awareness of each other as separate beings. The curse of Eden, if we want to call it such, was that once Adam and Eve saw themselves as separate, mistrust, doubt, and division entered the world. From that time forth, we would always be struggling to be reunited with ourselves, with each other, and with God.

Thus we have the basis for the fear that underlies so much dysfunction. If we are bad, we will be rejected and abandoned, always struggling to get back into, and remain in, God's good graces. In turn, this leads to a desperate need to be perfect, to do things right so that we won't be punished. This is the avoidance of error William James refers to when defining unhealthy religiosity. It lead to a blind following of the rules, which abrogates all choice.

But who makes the rules? Who decides what is bad and punishable? The literal, fundamentalist explanation is that God made the rules and God metes out the punishment. If that is so, then God must be very busy, to be so many places at once. But the question opens the door to an examination of how this fear of God is used to control and often to abuse.

Erich Fromm, in *The Dogma of Christ,* gives a carefully documented overview of the role religion plays in any society and how that is reflected in the transformations wrought in Christianity in its early days. These changes, he says, provide much of the basis for the underlying guilt and shame that permeate Christian doctrines.

Explaining the role religion plays in any society, Fromm says that it is often used to compensate for the deprivations created either by nature or by the ruling class, and that it also serves as a means for social control. Thus, he says, religion provides a fantasy means of making up for those deprivations, a mental or emotional image in which desires are fulfilled. Moreover, he says that religion, or fantasy satisfactions, "have the double function which is characteristic of every narcotic: they act as both an anodyne [painkiller] and as a deterrent to active change of reality. . . .

To sum up, religion has a three-fold function: for all mankind, consolation for the privations exacted by life; for the great majority of men, encouragement to accept their class situation; and for the dominant majority, relief from guilt feelings caused by the suffering of those they oppress.

How Religion Creates Dysfunction

Modern Christianity holds that God, in the human form of Christ, came to bridge the alienation caused by Adam and Eve. It teaches that Christ is the only means to reunite with God and gain salvation. However, it is unlikely that this was the original belief of Christianity. It came about as a result of tremendous changes in Christianity that occurred in the first three centuries of its existence—changes involving the contemporary social and political climate.

The first Christians lived in a time of extreme economic, political, and religious oppression and chaos. Even during Christ's ministry, there were differences of opinion regarding his role and intent. Some followers believed he was going to lead a political revolt; some saw him as a spiritual leader. This difference of opinion led to many arguments and power struggles within the faith, and the debates still rage today.

Gradually, new interpretations of Christ's identity and the purpose of his mission on earth replaced the original ones. Although he had once been seen as a mere mortal, a Son of man who was adopted by God, Jesus was now seen as God in human form. God became a man, then reascended to His throne. This gave Jesus much more power and authority and, by extension, gave that same authority to those who claimed to speak for him.

To ease the disappointment that the Second Coming was not imminent, there emerged the notion of rewards—not in this life but in the next. The concept of a conqueror who would physically deliver the oppressed was abandoned in favor of a Messiah who had brought them salvation in the next life—if they followed the rules in this one. This gave the ruling classes a means of maintaining control without constant fear of revolt and allowed them to salve their own consciences about their abuses. Partly to justify this change and partly to soothe the oppressed, the tradition of the Messiah as the Suffering Servant, as described in Isaiah, was restored. Thus, for the poor, the Messiah was still one of them—a servant suffering just like them.

Ultimately, this interpretation is what allowed Christianity to flourish, keeping it from being an obscure and quickly forgotten sect of Judaism. At the same time, it provided a foundation for new interpretations about the source of authority. Continuing the theme of adoption, the fourth-century Church used Paul's teachings, especially in Romans, to prove that the Church had been anointed as the arbitor of conscience. The scriptures were no longer the authority; that power now rested with the bishops as Christ's vessels. This made the bishops divinely authorized to speak in the name of Christ; only later came the concept of the Pope as Christ's vicar on earth.

The changes were firmly entrenched from then on: The itinerant teacher who referred to himself as the Son of man had been transformed into the Son of God, the Savior whose sacrifice was the salvation of the world. The message that would free the oppressed became, in the hands of the power-hungry, the means to keep them in submission. In many ways, God and Christ now began to be used as weapons.

Perhaps, in these changes, lie the seeds of Christian guilt and shame. The shift to a "suffering servant" Messiah who was sacrificed for our sins brings with it an inherent message of shame: We were so bad that God had to sacrifice His son in order to save us.

Also, I believe the Christian idea of God becoming a man in the person of Jesus, of the Word becoming flesh, and coming down to save the human race reinforces the idea of original sin and our inherent badness. It seems to have predisposed us to confuse our physical acts with our spiritual being, so that today we cannot distinguish between *making* a mistake and *being* a mistake. More important, it conditions us to avoid taking responsibility for changing our behaviors and to look instead to something (such as grace) or someone (that is, God) to fix us.

The controlling authority of the clergy was maintained in part by the power structure of the Church and the lack of education among the lower classes. Until well into the nineteenth and even the twentieth century, the clergy was the educated class, assigned the task of teaching and interpreting religion. This is true of the ancient religions that existed prior to, and alongside, early Christianity, and of other faiths in the world today. For centuries, the general populace did not have the knowledge or skills needed to study and examine religious teachings on their own. They were totally dependent on their priests, mullahs, rabbis, or shamans for guidance. Thus religion was used as a means for social control—often abusively.

So for thousands of years, human beings have been accustomed to living under an authoritarian theocracy in which the few, the chosen, and the called control the many. This divinely appointed power group claims not only to speak for God but insists that it is also the only way to God. From the cradle on, we are trained to look to someone else to tell us what to do, when to do it, and what will happen if we don't. So it is that people allow themselves to be abused in the name of God.

This power group can manipulate scripture to create doctrines and dogma designed to keep people in submission, fearful of error. They make the rules and say the rules are God's, so that questioning the teachers or teachings equals questioning God. Those rules, those messages have been, still are, often dysfunctional and abusive.

Teaching the concept of original sin—that people are born bad—and keeping the focus on avoiding error, which religious addicts equate with sin, makes people slaves to following rules and prevents them from the spiritual freedom of truth. Promising heavenly rewards as compensation for suffering and deprivation in this life conditions people to escape into magical thinking and denial of reality. Teaching that acceptance of Christ (or any prophet/teacher) is the way to absolve sins leads to rationalization and the inability to take responsibility for one's actions. This is the foundation of religious addiction and abuse: We are bad, and God will magically fix us if we do what someone tells us is God's wish.

TV EVANGELISM: GOD THE PRODUCT

Those who saw this belief as abusive and spoke out against it were for a long time a silent and much-maligned minority. The TV evangelist scandals, however, brought this version of religious addiction and abuse out of the closet and onto the six o'clock news.

Much has been written about the rise of consumerism in today's society. For a culture that is conditioned to have someone else tell us what we want and need, we should not be surprised. As Erich Fromm noted:

> *We are eternal consumers, receiving, receiving, receiving. . . . in our leisure time . . . we are completely lazy, with the passivity of consumers. . . . We consume cigarettes and cocktails and books and television; we seem to be looking for the big nursing bottle which would provide total nourishment. Eventually, we consume tranquilizers.*

Such consumer passivity allows us to be manipulated and subliminally seduced into thinking we must buy this product, that having it will cure whatever ails us. Anacin will stop our headaches; a BMW will win us the respect or envy of our neighbors and probably improve our love life.

Religiously, politically, socially—as a species and as individuals—we have grown accustomed to someone else telling us what to do and when to do it, what is good for us and what isn't; what rewards await us when we obey (buy), and what punishments lie in store if we don't. Those doing the manipulating are always careful to let us think they have our best interests at heart and are equally careful to assure themselves that we won't dare to question.

In the dynamics of TV evangelism, we see all the components we have just explored in the evolution of religious dysfunction: power and control, fear, guilt, passivity, and magical thinking. Again, we can find this reflected in almost any religion or belief system that is used dysfunctionally. Since the evangelists' scandals bring the issue into sharp focus, they illustrate how religion can be used addictively and abusively.

At its worst, the Electronic Church combines television's blatant consumerism with evangelism's hellfire-and-brimstone tactics to become probably the most powerful marketing agency in the world, and the most shamelessly manipulative one. The services, music, and testimonies are carefully designed to grab emotions—especially fear and guilt. Dangling the promise of heaven, televangelists threaten the fires of hell for unrepentant, nongiving sinners.

God, Jesus, and the Church make up a neatly packaged product, marketed to convince people they cannot live without it. Every day, at any hour, you can see preachers telling you how to find God, conducting services in which those who are sick seem to be healed by faith, where the promises of eternity and prosperity are within your grasp. Put your hand on the television and pray with us, they say, while you reach into your pockets and send that little bit of money to speed your prayers along. And if your prayers aren't answered, it's because you weren't good enough, didn't give enough. So send more. That appears to be the message of so many televangelists. So skillfully do the God-mongers manipulate that the vulnerable actually believe they can be healed by placing their hands on a television screen, while a woman sobs her way through "Nearer My God to Thee."

These are the trappings with which they cloak God: the glitzy sets; the preachers in their polyester suits spouting oversimplified scriptural platitudes; the (usually overweight) women overdressed and overly made up; the crocodile tears; the appeals for more and more money to help continue their mission. And hidden within these trappings are guilt, fear, and shame.

The witnessing and testimonies from those who were apparently healed physically and/or emotionally by claiming to accept Christ are designed to lend authority to the preacher and to keep people hooked with magical thinking. Some of these people, of course, by developing a deep spirituality and faith, do make profound improvements in their lives. There is a vast difference, however, between genuine miracle and magic, between genuine Christian charity and charlatanism.

When the TV evangelists' scandals first broke, many people thought they revealed merely religious trickery and con artistry, but ultimately, the excesses were on a scale sufficient enough to cause a hard look at the ways those ministries were run.

Time magazine reported that, from 1984 to 1987, the Bakkers received $4.8 million in salaries, bonuses, and other compensation. In an article on Jimmy Swaggart, *Newsweek* noted that he spent less than 10 percent of $2 million raised for a children's fund on that specific charity. The rest, *Newsweek* says, was spent on Jimmy's $1 million dollar home, his son's $776,000 house, and an air-conditioned treehouse for his grandson.

Still, in an era in which the Pentagon was caught with $600 toilet seats, people were numbed to financial finagling—or maybe so accustomed to it that they scarcely questioned. Oral Roberts's plea for $8.5 million or else God would call him home was largely treated as a circus sideshow, as was the revelation of Tammy Faye Bakker's compulsive shopping. When Tammy was quoted in *Newsweek* as saying, "There's times I just have to quit thinking, and the only way I can quit is by shopping," people were amused; Tammy Faye jokes abounded, and few people seemed to recognize the symptoms of addiction she was revealing. Money continued to pour in to the various ministry coffers, even after Roberts claimed to have raised the dead and the Bakkers were indicted. The faithful saw nothing wrong and remained loyal; cynics told more jokes; few saw addiction, pain, and abuse.

Then Swaggart's sex scandal broke. *Time,* reporting on his televised confession, quoted Swaggart's explanation: "I do not call it a mistake, a mendacity. I call it a sin . . . I have no one but myself to blame. . . . I have sinned against you my Lord, and I would ask that your precious blood would wash and cleanse every stain until it is in the seas of God's forgiveness, never to be remembered against me anymore."

This illustrates much of what I have discussed so far. Here is a man who could not distinguish between *making* a mistake and *being* a mistake. This is a man who, having been raised with the belief that he was born a blotch on existence, had not the resources to cope with the brokenness within him—a man desperately seeking dignity, struggling to find self-esteem within a belief system that told him he was depraved. Trying to find that self-esteem by progressively abusing power and control, he immediately invoked the God-will-make-it-better magic when called to account for his abuses.

Looking at Swaggart's abuse of power, sociologist William Martin observed to *People* magazine:

> *I thought [Swaggart] was one of the most honest and sincere preachers I had ever met. But I've seen him change over the years. He really seems to have been seduced by the power and the fame.*
>
> *I think what happens to this kind of person is that he begins to think, "I couldn't have come this far if not for God." Then he begins to say, "Well, if I have this idea to build a Bible college or a mission, it must come from God." Next he starts to say, "God told me this. God told me that. . . ." And the next step from there is that he says, "I think what God meant to say was. . . ."*

Martin has succinctly charted the progress of religious addiction: It begins in low self-esteem, becomes a dysfunctional means of finding self-worth, and ultimately ends in magical thinking—in delusion.

The Roberts, Bakker, and Swaggart scandals created a national intervention that served to interrupt the progress of this unhealthy phenomenon. What had previously been viewed as fanatacism or zealotry increasingly began to be called religious addiction and religious abuse. People began to talk publicly about being addicted to a church, a concept of God, a TV evangelist, or a rigid interpretation of the Bible. Some related how the evangelist scandals made them see how their religious behaviors and attitudes were similar to the way they had sometimes behaved with alcohol and drugs. Some realized they had simply changed addictions or added religion to their list of compulsions. Still looking for a fix, they became hooked on religion.

Finally, people were asking questions, were acknowledging dysfunction. Both the abusive preachers and their passive, abused flocks came under examination as more and more people began to question how the preachers got such power and control.

How *did* they get such power and control? Part of the answer to that question lies in the way that religions have been used in society to ease or explain deprivation and suffering, which often results in escape into magical thinking. Although our society has increasingly been in search of a healthy spirituality that might enhance our self-esteem, the conflicts and sources of guilt and shame within Christianity have left us vulnerable to victimization by those who would abuse the power we give them.

When we overlay this cultural profile with the dynamics of addiction, it will become clear that both the abusers and the abused have been motivated by a force over which they were powerless. The patterns that have molded society for thousands of centuries, coupled with the patterns of obsessive thinking, compulsive behavior, and addiction are the twin patterns that lead to the despairing cry I hear so often: "Father Leo, I love God, but I also hate God."

Chapter 2

When God Becomes a Drug:
The Stages of Religious Addiction

SHORTLY AFTER I began to speak out about religious addiction and abuse, I received a letter from a woman describing how she became painfully aware of her addiction to religion and its effects on her life. She wrote about her compulsive quoting of scriptural texts and her obsession with her own religious convictions, which led to arguments with family and co-workers.

She described her eventual isolation from the people she loved and her near-bankruptcy caused by excessive tithing. She told me how she tried to escape feeling lonely, angry, depressed, fearful, and guilty by increasing her religious activities. The more she pursued her obsessive religiosity, the more helpless and isolated she became.

She had tried numerous times to stop her compulsive behavior by not going so frequently to church; removing statues, crucifixes, and incense burners from her home; not watching religious TV; hiding from members of her congregation; not returning telephone calls from her pastor; and by canceling subscriptions for numerous religious magazines. Each time, she relapsed into more severe religious addiction, causing greater guilt and shame.

She finally sought counseling and eventually entered a treatment facility where she could undergo "religious detox" in a safe environment. I still hear from her. Today, she is recovering from her religious addiction and is developing a healthier kind of spirituality.

What she described was the classic progression of an addiction. We could substitute alcohol, cocaine, or food, and the pattern would be the same. If I had any doubts about religion being addictive, being used as a drug, letters like these have washed them away. Religious addiction does exist; it is a disease like any other addiction; and it can and should be treated by the same methods used to treat other addictions.

I define religious addiction as using God, a church, or a belief system as an escape from reality, in an attempt to find or elevate a sense of self-worth or well-being. It is using God or religion as a fix. It is the ultimate form of codependency—feeling worthless in and of ourselves and looking outside ourselves for something or someone to tell us we are worthwhile. Thus it is an unhealthy relationship with God. It is using God, religion, or a belief system as a weapon against ourselves or others.

In a sense, religious addiction has very little to do with God or spirituality, just as food addiction and alcoholism have less to do with the substances involved than with the way in which they are abused. Religious addicts use the accessory items of religion—rituals, dogma, and scriptural texts—to reinforce the dysfunctional message that all humans are evil, stupid, or incapable of merit. Thus, far from enhancing spiritual development, religious addiction stunts or paralyzes spiritual growth and creates a barrier to a healthy relationship with God.

The great lie of addiction and codependency is that something external, beyond us, will make life better. Something beyond us will make us feel good, acceptable, lovable, and worthwhile. The more we believe that an outside source will fix or rescue us, the more dependent we grow on external things to make us better.

This is especially true for religious addicts. Because most religious addicts believe themselves inherently worthless and powerless, they look outside themselves for some religious authority who functions as a go-between, an intermediary who tells them what God is like and what God wants them to do. Thus religious addicts never experience God firsthand, never truly get to know God. They only know what somebody has told them about God. If what they are told about God is dysfunctional, then their relationship with God becomes dysfunctional.

Eventually, this unhealthiness shows in their lives. Just as other adult children of dysfunction mirror the unhealthy beliefs and behaviors of people who were their role models, so the family of God reflects the dysfunctional messages and beliefs handed down from religious go-betweens. Perhaps you've heard nutritionists say "you are what you eat." Similarly, religious addicts become what they believe: The God they experience is reflected in their behaviors and attitudes. Religious addicts feel judged by God—so they learn to judge. Religious addicts feel that God sees them as dirty and sinful—so they make others feel dirty and sinful. Religious addicts feel like victims of God's whims—so they victimize and abuse others.

In religious addiction, as with other addictions, denial runs rampant. After all, the whole purpose of an addiction is to escape from reality. So addicts will be looking for a way out. Religious addiction, like alcoholism, springs from a reservoir of low self-esteem, a sense of inadequacy, shame, guilt, and the desire to escape, fix, or numb these feelings.

Often people tell me that they can see how religion can be unhealthy and dysfunctional, but they still cannot quite understand how it can be an addiction—much less a disease. Many of you might be familiar with the disease process of addiction. You may be recovering from one or more addictions and want to see how you might be using religion addictively or may have been religiously abused. For others, this may be your first introduction to the concept of any addiction being a disease. So let us look at what addiction is, what its patterns are, and what makes it a disease.

TRYING TO CONTROL THE UNCONTROLLABLE

There are many excellent descriptions and definitions of addiction. Craig Nakken, a chemical-dependency therapist and addictionologist, describes it as being a progressive relationship with either a substance or event that is designed to control the environment and/or produce a desired mood change. In his book *The Addictive Personality,* he says:

> *Let's start with a basic assumption about most people: nearly all human beings have a deep desire to feel happy and to find peace of mind and soul. At times in our lives, most all of us find this wholeness of peace and beauty, but then it's as if it slips away and is gone, only to return another time. In many ways, this is one of the natural cycles of life. It's not a cycle we can control.*
>
> *Addiction can be viewed as an attempt to control these uncontrollable cycles. When addicts engage in a particular object or event to produce a desired mood change, they emotionally believe they can control these cycles. And at first they can. Addiction, on it most basic level, is an attempt to control and fulfill this desire.*

Wayne Oates, in *The Psychology of Religion,* expands on this when he describes obesity, alcoholism, and drug addiction as "forms of nonverbal communication of rebellion against one's situation in life, or of protecting oneself from the unwanted responsibilities of life by incapacitating one's self through the compulsive use of food, alcohol, and drugs." These descriptions include the key elements of all addictions: control, escape, and progression.

Much of addiction is about control. Many of us grew up amid the chaos of a dysfunctional home; our addictions and compulsions have grown out of our attempts to make sense of or bring order to something we never knew was beyond our control. Never having learned how to express or cope with feelings appropriately, we fear them—go to great lengths to deny or avoid them. In order to win approval or escape abuse, we become people-pleasers, over-achievers, perfectionists—rigid and intolerant of our own and others' mistakes.

Another way to control our situation is to simply give up—to become a victim of life. We function under the illusion that we have no control over anything, that we have no choices in life. We wallow in self-pity. We become passive. We allow ourselves to be controlled by others or by circumstances. We give our power away, incapacitating ourselves with the belief that we can't change. Our mottoes, our excuses are: I can't . . . You just don't understand . . . Yeah, but. . . . This is what Erich Fromm means when he says addictions create a deterrent to an active change in reality. We believe we are helpless; our addictions make this belief come true—they create a self-fulfilling prophecy.

Yet we rebel against this perceived lack of choice—against the perceived inability to take responsibility for our lives. We are angry victims, furious with a world that does not validate our sense of being a victim by indulging us in our self-pity, by fixing or rescuing us. So in our victimization, we become passive-aggressive—doormats that bite. Victims control others by using depression or always being the underdog and by using underhanded aggression and covert manipulation to get their way.

THE STAGES OF ADDICTION

Addiction is a process, with a beginning, middle, and end. No matter what substance or behavior we abuse, there are certain phases common to all. Addictionologists have long been using a chart based on E. M. Jellenik's disease concept of alcoholism to illustrate the downward progressions of addiction. I have developed a chart showing similar patterns for religious addiction. (See pages 40–41.)

In the first stage, the use of alcohol, food, religion, or whatever is fairly balanced. Social drinking, dining out with friends, or going to church are part of our lives; the alcohol, the food, the church rituals are not the focus of our activities.

In this stage, we may be putting in long hours at work to meet an important deadline. Fasting may be part of a religious celebration or ritual. Our friends may enjoy beer and popcorn when we gather to watch videos. We enjoy doing these things, but somehow, the part of us which deep down doesn't feel good about ourselves gets confused about what's giving us pleasure. We begin to associate alcohol with feeling more relaxed around people; crunching popcorn with relieving tension; church with feelings of belonging. We don't realize that these things are giving us the illusion that they make us feel better about ourselves.

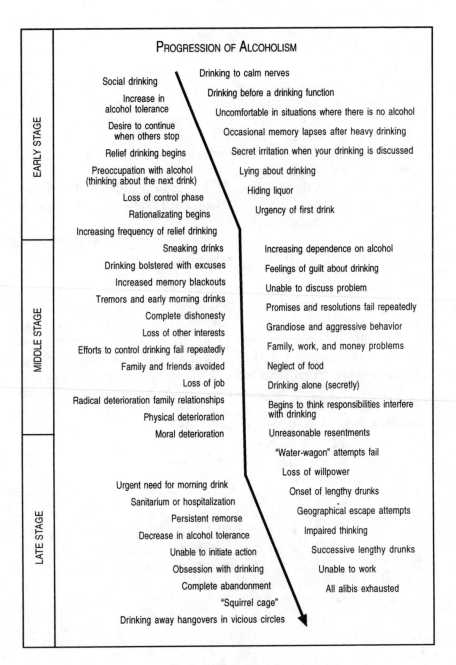

PROGRESSION OF ALCOHOLISM

EARLY STAGE

Social drinking

Increase in alcohol tolerance

Desire to continue when others stop

Relief drinking begins

Preoccupation with alcohol (thinking about the next drink)

Loss of control phase

Rationalizating begins

Increasing frequency of relief drinking

Drinking to calm nerves

Drinking before a drinking function

Uncomfortable in situations where there is no alcohol

Occasional memory lapses after heavy drinking

Secret irritation when your drinking is discussed

Lying about drinking

Hiding liquor

Urgency of first drink

MIDDLE STAGE

Sneaking drinks

Drinking bolstered with excuses

Increased memory blackouts

Tremors and early morning drinks

Complete dishonesty

Loss of other interests

Efforts to control drinking fail repeatedly

Family and friends avoided

Loss of job

Radical deterioration family relationships

Physical deterioration

Moral deterioration

Increasing dependence on alcohol

Feelings of guilt about drinking

Unable to discuss problem

Promises and resolutions fail repeatedly

Grandiose and aggressive behavior

Family, work, and money problems

Neglect of food

Drinking alone (secretly)

Begins to think responsibilities interfere with drinking

Unreasonable resentments

"Water-wagon" attempts fail

Loss of willpower

Onset of lengthy drunks

LATE STAGE

Urgent need for morning drink

Sanitarium or hospitalization

Persistent remorse

Decrease in alcohol tolerance

Unable to initiate action

Obsession with drinking

Complete abandonment

"Squirrel cage"

Drinking away hangovers in vicious circles

Geographical escape attempts

Impaired thinking

Successive lengthy drunks

Unable to work

All alibis exhausted

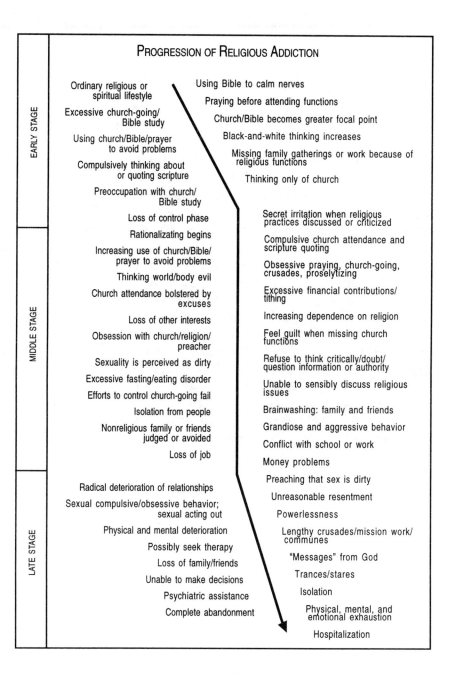

PROGRESSION OF RELIGIOUS ADDICTION

EARLY STAGE

Ordinary religious or spiritual lifestyle

Excessive church-going/ Bible study

Using church/Bible/prayer to avoid problems

Compulsively thinking about or quoting scripture

Preoccupation with church/ Bible study

Using Bible to calm nerves

Praying before attending functions

Church/Bible becomes greater focal point

Black-and-white thinking increases

Missing family gatherings or work because of religious functions

Thinking only of church

MIDDLE STAGE

Loss of control phase

Rationalizating begins

Increasing use of church/Bible/ prayer to avoid problems

Thinking world/body evil

Church attendance bolstered by excuses

Loss of other interests

Obsession with church/religion/ preacher

Sexuality is perceived as dirty

Excessive fasting/eating disorder

Efforts to control church-going fail

Isolation from people

Nonreligious family or friends judged or avoided

Loss of job

Secret irritation when religious practices discussed or criticized

Compulsive church attendance and scripture quoting

Obsessive praying, church-going, crusades, proselytizing

Excessive financial contributions/ tithing

Increasing dependence on religion

Feel guilt when missing church functions

Refuse to think critically/doubt/ question information or authority

Unable to sensibly discuss religious issues

Brainwashing: family and friends

Grandiose and aggressive behavior

Conflict with school or work

Money problems

Preaching that sex is dirty

Unreasonable resentment

LATE STAGE

Radical deterioration of relationships

Sexual compulsive/obsessive behavior; sexual acting out

Physical and mental deterioration

Possibly seek therapy

Loss of family/friends

Unable to make decisions

Psychiatric assistance

Complete abandonment

Powerlessness

Lengthy crusades/mission work/ communes

"Messages" from God

Trances/stares

Isolation

Physical, mental, and emotional exhaustion

Hospitalization

That is what addiction does: It gives us false information, an illusion. We don't know that the need to drink is out of our fear of others; that our hunger pangs stem from anger; that we overwork out of our sense of inadequacy; that we are increasing our church activities more out of loneliness and guilt than devotion to God.

But what happens is that we get hooked because whatever we end up abusing at first seems to solve the problem. Alcohol does relax inhibitions, making us feel more comfortable. A rich piece of chocolate cake does taste sensuously comforting. Cocaine does numb the senses; it seems to bring an exhilarating feeling of power. Starving while others cluster around the doughnut table does bring a feeling of control and superiority. Being in a relationship can make a person feel valued and special. So can a high paycheck. Joining a church does give us a sense of family, of belonging, of being loved.

We become addicted because at first these things work—they work so well that the addict in us wants more: more alcohol, more food, more money, to be thinner, to have that better job, that special person, that special place in church. What happens is that the progressive search for a fix—the persistent need to control—leads to increasing impairment and dysfunctional behaviors. That's where the addiction begins: We grow to depend on that outside source; we have the illusion of being in control, of having found something to fix us.

In the middle stages of addiction, the focus shifts. Now we can't go to a party without having a drink . . . several . . . before we leave the house, so we'll already feel loosened up. We start avoiding places where there's no booze. We used to go out to eat with friends for the companionship; now the focus is the food. Will there be enough? Maybe we ought to eat something before we go or make sure there's a snack waiting in case we're still hungry when we get home. We're not newcomers at church anymore, not getting that special attention. So we do more: join the choir, teach Sunday school, go on retreats, tithe more. Underneath it all there's a growing urgency, a compulsion that says we must do more. We begin losing control.

The loss of control signals the loss of self. What Craig Nakken calls the addict self begins to take over; the attempts to stop and the relapses are signs of the struggle between the healthy and addicted parts of ourselves. Nakken says that the addiction starts to create the very thing we were trying to escape: pain. Thus begins the vicious cycle of trying to stop, relapsing, feeling increasing guilt, remorse, fear, and a consuming shame and self-hatred when we go back out and do it again. Denial sets in. Something tells us we're in trouble and we don't want to believe it. Our problems are somebody else's fault.

We drink or overeat because of our spouse, our job. We starve because we believe we are heavy—we think the scales tell us so, even when our clothes get baggy and fall off us. If people avoid us because we're always preaching at them, it's their fault—they're just heathens. We don't need them anyway. Nobody understands how important our work is—nobody else can do our job as well. So it goes, deeper into denial, deeper into delusion, deeper into pain. Always the pain.

The rationalizing and justification, denial and self-victimization get worse. We're angry, irritable. We become increasingly abusive to family, friends, and co-workers. We're either trying to stop the addiction and failing, or we're in such total denial that we see nothing wrong and keep doing more.

Our lives grow steadily unmanageable, yet we still don't want to believe we are addicts. We're still looking for something else to blame. When we at last face the fact that it's the drinking, the eating disorder, the codependency, the religiosity that's causing our pain—when we can't deny it anymore—we still want to avoid responsibility. We want something or someone to fix us and make us better. We get stuck in hopelessness and despair that we'll never get free. We are powerless; our lives are unmanageable; and we cannot see any way out except to die or go crazy.

Formerly, it was believed that all addicts must reach this bottom, this pit of despair, before any kind of help would be effective. Today, we know that is not true. There are people who are recovering from every addiction who recognized that they had begun the addictive cycle and sought help before they reached this lowest rung on the ladder.

ILL AT EASE WITH LIFE: ADDICTION AS DISEASE

In most cases, what helps people recognize their addiction and seek help is the increasing cultural acceptance of addiction as a progressive disease that can be arrested but not cured. *Newsweek,* in a cover story on support groups, noted that some fifteen million Americans attend some kind of self-help or support group, many of them based on the Twelve Steps of A. A.

There are those who still consider that such problems as overeating, compulsive shopping, compulsive sex, obsessive relationships, and extreme religiosity are immoral actions, irresponsibility, or bad habits rather than addictions. Such compulsions fit Nakken's definition of addiction as a relationship with something we increasingly use to change our mood. As Wayne Oates described, these behaviors are also ways in which addicts victimize and incapacitate themselves. Perhaps, then, people who object to addiction or compulsive behaviors being diseases do not fully understand what is meant when they are labeled as such.

When we talk about addiction as a disease, we do not mean a virus or germ, but rather, a physical, mental, and emotional reaction that occurs in response to abuse of alcohol, drugs, codependency, or other compulsive behavior. Addiction is often described as being a sign of *dis*-ease with life, of literally being ill at ease with ourselves. The word *dis-ease* is the opposite of being *at*-ease. It signals pain and discomfort in our lives that causes physical, mental, or emotional problems.

No matter what the addiction—whether to food, alcohol, relationships, sex, or religion—emotionally you feel shame and low self-esteem, guilt, rage, inadequacy. You are depressed and anxious, perhaps have panic attacks; you may well have an underlying organic depression or mental illness alongside your addiction. Substance abusers, anorexics, bulimics, and overeaters do physical damage to their bodies; sex addicts may contract sexually transmitted diseases.

All addicts, including codependents, gamblers, workaholics, and religious addicts, suffer the physical effects of stress: backaches, headaches, irritable bowel syndrome, metabolic dysfunction, chronic fatigue, insomnia, memory loss. Some battle stress-related diseases, such as asthma or hypertension. I submit that any condition that produces such grievous physical, mental, and emotional symptoms might properly be called a disease. Some people, however, still argue that addicts bring their ill health on themselves, that addiction results from willful misbehavior—from sin.

Is it sin? Is addiction truly a matter of bad habits or depraved behavior, which can be modified (or cured) by accepting God? What if it is willful misconduct rather than a disease? How does that affect an addict's self-image and ability to change behavior? People respond quite differently when labeled sick or sinful. In *Loosening the Grip: A Handbook of Alcohol Information,* authors Jean Kinney and Gwen Leaton observe that how we label something determines our expectations and treatment of it. Labeling a bulb as either a tulip or an onion will affect, they say, whether we "chop and saute or plant and water. Very different behaviors are associated with each. An error may lead to strange-flavored spaghetti sauce and a less colorful flower bed next spring."

Labeling ourselves blotches on existence renders us powerless and leaves us no hope of change, for it tells us we are inherently bad. If we are labeled as tulips, people will water us, nurture us, be thrilled when we blossom. If we are regarded as onions, people will hold their noses and run away lest we make them cry.

So it is with labeling addiction a disease rather than a sin. If we have a disease, we can recover from it. If we are immoral, depraved, misbegotten, and generally bad people, that doesn't leave us much hope of change. The objection to calling addiction a disease is that it offers a cop-out, an avoidance of responsibility. George Vaillant, in *The Natural History of Alcoholism,* defends the disease model of addiction by noting that having a medical explanation for their behavior often gives alcoholics hope that they can change. More important, he points out, success in Alcoholics Anonymous requires taking responsibility for one's recovery and for past errors rather than avoiding it.

All addicts begin by engaging in behaviors that lead to or perpetuate addiction—behaviors that may have begun as perfectly acceptable activities. This is one of the arguments used by E. M.

Jellenik in his landmark book, *The Disease Concept of Alcoholism.* Pointing out that alcoholism often starts with social drinking—an activity that in American culture is acceptable and almost mandatory—Jellenik says that we cannot then call it self-inflicted or willful misconduct. We can consider other addictions in this same light. Eating is a national pastime, especially in churches. The Protestant work ethic is woven into America's national value system; church membership is considered a vital ingredient of upstanding citizenship.

As Erich Fromm noted, in looking for that nursing bottle to comfort us we have become a nation of consumers of almost any substance or product—accustomed to being cajoled or almost browbeaten into buying. We grow accustomed to being told, for example: Come on, you can have just one piece of cake. . . . Stay and have another drink. . . . If you want to be of service to God, you must pray for us and send money to help us continue our mission.

Thus, poor coping mechanisms and other emotional or psychological factors help create a genuine disease. Addiction begins in emotional pain: We hurt and only want something to make us feel better. That is not the willful misconduct of immoral people; it is the cry of souls in pain.

One key to understanding the concept of addiction as a disease may be in making the distinction between acute disease and chronic disease. If we have an acute disease, we go to the doctor or into the hospital and are taken care of until we are cured. That kind of sickness connotes a passivity—a you-fix-me attitude. Yes, addicts would love to have that kind of disease—like the morbidly obese person who fervently wishes for a glandular disorder that would excuse and justify the obesity or else wishes for a disease that will cause effortless weight loss. But a chronic disease does not go away; it may be arrested but never cured. With proper self-care, people with such chronic diseases as diabetes or asthma may live full, productive lives. People with chronic illnesses have a responsibility to effect their own recovery and continued well-being. They did not deliberately catch their disease; but having gotten it, they can learn healthy ways to live with it.

So addiction begins as *dis*-ease: an inability to cope healthily with life. Unhealthy religious beliefs poisoned your life and left you feeling alone, alienated from family, friends, and, most important, from God. People like Charles, whose story follows, write, call, or come in person to tell me how they tried to use religion as a fix and only ended up in worse pain and despair.

CHARLES'S STORY

Charles was in the audience during one of my appearances on the *Oprah Winfrey Show*. My suggestion that some adult children escape into religion after growing up in an alcoholic home hit Charles like a thunderbolt. He could hardly wait to talk to me backstage.

Charles is black and grew up in Chicago in an abusive, nonreligious home. The youngest child of alcoholic parents, he spent his childhood enduring a nightmare of arguments, fights, and beatings. He had two older brothers, and often the three of them would huddle together at night for comfort and protection.

From his earliest days, Charles remembered embarrassment, fear, pain—and the dream of escape. He often thought about suicide. When he was about fifteen, a friend took him to a mission chapel. The preacher's message was one he had longed to hear: He was loved. God loved him. Jesus loved him. He had a home in Jesus. Singing the hymns, he broke into tears of joy and relief that at last somebody loved him. At sixteen, he gave himself to the Lord.

From that moment, he was hooked. He went to other chapels, churches, crusades, baptisms, Bible-study groups. He traveled to hear the big-name preachers and watched the TV evangelists. He could never get enough of it. He went beyond devotion and discipleship to a burning sense of mission. He wanted to create a better world, a better society, more loving families—but they had to be devoted to Jesus. He read the Bible, learned all the scriptures and dogma. Jesus was the way, the truth, and the life. The Bible was the absolute, literal Word of God. Only fundamentalist Christianity was the Truth.

His family grew tired of his preaching and soon rejected him. So Charles took the message to others. He became active in a fundamentalist church in Southside Chicago. There he met Anne, whom he later married. Although she shared his beliefs, she did not practice her faith as rigidly as he did—did not read her Bible every day, pray before every meal, or get high planning the next Christian mission or crusade. Church was part of her life, not the purpose of it. They fought constantly over religion. Charles thought Anne's faith was lukewarm; she thought his was demanding, rigid, fanatical. When she left, her parting words were: "Religion is like a drug to you!"

And so it was. As with other addicts, his drug, which was his narrow and rigid faith, often created conflicts with his employers. He would frequently go on weekend crusades and not get back for work on Monday; he was always preaching at his coworkers, proselytizing on company time. He told Catholics that the Pope was the Antichrist; he told Jews they were beyond salvation unless they accepted Jesus. Co-workers disliked him, and he was fired from many different jobs.

When he became depressed his guilt grew, and he never felt good enough for Jesus. He was always trying to do more, say more, give more, be more effective, convert more people, tithe more—be more perfect. When he failed, he beat himself up emotionally. Along with the depression came periods when he felt besieged by what he felt were impure thoughts of wanting sex and wanting to quit the religious life. The result was more guilt and shame.

About this time he attended the *Oprah Winfrey Show* and began to look at his behavior in the context of his childhood. He heard that many children of alcoholics become compulsive, obsessive, and perfectionistic. Before he saw the show, he had thought that his problematic childhood had impaired his ability to live constructively with others. He had blamed his growing depression on his childhood and on his perceived failure as a Christian.

After hearing about the symptoms of religious addiction, he began to connect his pain and problems with his strict adherence to religion. He saw that he had become obsessive about his faith, but he thought that all good Christians had to be obsessive about Jesus. He recognized that he had real problems and emotional pain, especially in the area of relationships. Despite his church activities, he had few friends. He slowly began to accept that his extreme religious practices had not only caused the divorce from Anne but had also placed a wedge between himself and most people. Charles was as isolated as any alcoholic I ever met.

After a series of conversations with me, Charles was able to connect his escape into an authoritarian religion with the abuse he experienced in his childhood. For years he had said that his brothers took drugs to escape their pain. Slowly, he began to accept that Anne was right, that he was doing the same with religion. Religion was his fix. When we last spoke, he was planning to attend some support-group meetings for adult children of alcoholics and, as he said, just maybe a support group for religious addicts.

Perhaps you recognize some of yourself in Charles's story. You do not feel at ease with God, yourself, your relationships, or your world. You use God, a church, preacher, scriptural text, TV evangelist, holy message, belief system, guru, or mystical vision as a means to escape your discomfort. You discover in this dysfunctional use of religion that something outside of yourself makes you feel good, accepted, or powerful. You get high on being saved. You are hooked on a particular interpretation of the Bible and lack tolerance, charity, and acceptance for those who do not share your beliefs. You are spaced out in your own fantasy world and avoid reality.

God has become your drug of choice. You crave a belief in heaven that will take you away from a living hell. You develop an impossibly high standard of personal purity to ensure redemption. You have become hooked as a true believer, who must convert totally or be eternally damned. Your need to be special leads you to believe that your acceptance of God makes you superior to others.

Perhaps you, like a large number of people who become religious addicts or have been religiously abused, grew up in a dysfunctional family environment. You may have been neglected, abandoned, or abused physically, mentally, emotionally, and sexually. Keeping alcoholism and such physical abuse as sexual assault a secret became a second nature; you learned to hide your feelings in order to stay safe from abuse.

Growing up in the chaos and pain of such a home would naturally create the need to escape—and more than a few of you escaped into religion. You escaped to a God who would take you out of this painful world. You escaped to a God who was gentle, kind, and nonphysical. You escaped to a spiritual power who condemned your abusers to hell. Like other addicts, you did not set out to become addicted. You only wanted to feel better.

Charles's story, and others like it, is typical of what happens to people who enter or adopt an abusive, shame-based belief system, whether it is an organized religion, one of the New Age organizations, or even a Twelve Step group. Many people associate religious addiction and abuse either with fundamentalist faiths or with cults. Addictive people can take a perfectly healthy belief system and use it as a weapon against themselves or to escape their feelings. I see this happen in Twelve Step programs, where some people quote Bill W. and the A.A. guidelines known as the *Big Book* as authoritatively as religious addicts do the Bible. No faith, denomination, or belief system is exempt from being used abusively and addictively.

For example, a woman called my office practically in a panic. "Am I crazy?" she asked. "I don't know if I'm seeing what I think I'm seeing." Her six-year-old daughter has a rare and possibly terminal disease. This woman had joined a support group for parents and families of people with such illnesses, hoping to find help in processing her grief, fear, and rage that her child had to undergo such pain. The group used *A Course in Miracles* as its focus. While she basically liked the message in *A Course,* she did not embrace it fully. After all, she said, she was looking for support, not a religion. She found herself being humiliated and belittled, told she wasn't doing it right, wasn't good enough. The group members were controlling, intolerant, and critical. She was met with a rigid only-one-way approach, which appalled her, especially when she was told that not accepting all the teachings in the *Course* might cause her child to die.

She had been reared in an abusive religious family; as an adult, she had carefully avoided rigid, dogmatic churches. She did not expect to encounter similar abuse in a support group. Instead of healing and comfort, she found more shame and rage than she had ever experienced in her life. Her issues were real: It is agonizing to watch a child suffer; more so to know the child might die. She needed to know it was okay to be angry at God, that her grief, fear, and rage were absolutely natural. She needed validation and support, not guilt and shame.

Was she crazy? Of course not, and I told her so. She was absolutely correct in identifying addiction and abuse. This group had taken a belief system and turned it into rigid, authoritarian dogma. The use was dysfunctional, not the beliefs themselves. The message contained in *A Course in Miracles* was being used not to enlighten and heal, but to gain power and control—to abuse. That is an unhealthy use of a belief system; that is religious abuse.

This story illustrates a point I cannot emphasize enough: Religious addiction and abuse are not limited to churches or sects. People can take a healthy belief system and use it unhealthily, usually with dogmatic rigidity that does not permit any kind of questioning, personal choice, or freedom. I see people who come into Twelve Step programs who never question their sponsors; they memorize the *Big Book* and related materials without understanding what they mean. I see people whose sponsors or therapists are rigid, authoritarian, controlling, and shaming; most of these people are unable to end such abusive relationships because they don't dare challenge the authority figure who supposedly knows the answers. The biggest single hallmark of an unhealthy belief system is a written or unwritten rule that forbids you to think for yourself, to doubt or question beliefs and practices.

What then is healthy spirituality? How do you get through the layers of guilt, shame, and dysfunctional messages and beliefs to a spirituality that frees you to become a positive, creative human being?

First, you must recognize that you are not spiritually healthy. If you do not like yourself, if you believe you aren't good enough for God, that you are a lost sinner and God is going to somehow raise you up and make you better, you are not spiritually healthy. You diminish your ability to be a positive and creative human being if you are addicted to anything—including God or a belief system. So the first task is accepting that your belief system and your relationship with God are dysfunctional. By doing this you can open yourself to a new concept of spirituality.

What does spirituality mean? It is related to the word *spirit*—not a child's concept of a white-sheeted Holy Ghost flying in and out of our lives, but an inner attitude that emphasizes energy, creative choice, and a powerful force for living. It is a partnership with a Power greater than ourselves, a co-creatorship with God that allows us to be guided by God and yet to take responsibility for our lives.

When we hear references to a spirited debate or to our national spirit, we immediately envision vitality, strength, pride. We associate spirit with positive and creative energy. This energy gives us the power to live, work, and create. Spiritual people are positive and creative human beings. They know, deep inside themselves, that they have the power to create the difference in their lives. They have looked within and found what can be called their yes to life, and this yes shines forth in their attitudes and actions.

Recovery for religious addicts and those who have been religiously abused begins when they become able to appreciate the concept of the Big God: discovering God within the happenings of ordinary life; allowing God to be involved in the everyday choices they make. Recovery for religious addicts means discovering divinity in one's own life. It is the ability to see the miracle, see the gift—not as something God gives to us, but something we create *with* God.

Many of us think of God as the Creator without really understanding what that means. God created the world and continues to create in and through our lives—in our relationships, activities, the way we use our minds and hearts. We are co-creators with God, not puppets on a string waiting for something to happen. We make things happen; we create the difference, not in our old dysfunctional pattern of isolated control but in choosing a partnership with our Higher Power—however we define that entity. In our determined choice, the miracle exists. This is our yes to God.

Recovery from religious addiction and abuse is a process. We first accept that we need to change our beliefs and behaviors. Then we learn the symptoms: that which we need to change. Then we learn how to make changes, discovering what tools we need and how to use them.

This is how we ourselves become the somebody who can fix us. In recovery, we appreciate that we are powerful human beings. In that appreciation lies healthy spirituality and a rich, rewarding relationship with God as we now understand God.

Chapter 3

Where Does It Hurt?
Symptoms of Religious Addiction

WE HAVE ESTABLISHED that addictions spring from pain and from our dysfunctional attempts to escape that pain. Where does the hurt come from? Are some people more susceptible to religious addiction than others? How can we tell when someone is a religious addict? What is the difference between faith and fanaticism, healthy religiosity and addiction? As we explore the full range of symptoms of religious addiction—and discuss what types of people might be vulnerable to it—you will begin to answer some of these questions.

Like alcohol and other addictive substances, humankind has unknowingly been using religion unhealthily for thousands of years. Religious addiction starts almost as a cultural bad habit, rather like Jellenik's observation that alcoholism often begins with social drinking. To sum up the patterns Erich Fromm, William James, and others have noted, religion has served several functions in our society:

- To avoid error in order to escape punishment.

- To compensate for deprivations and suffering.

- To provide rules for correct behavior, to be perfect so that the rewards are guaranteed.

- To maintain social control, often by the clergy or others seeking power, and to salve the consciences of those who abuse it.

It slides into addiction the more it is used as a nursing bottle to fix us. Psychiatrist N. S. Xavier, in his book *The Two Faces of Religion,* says that religious beliefs and practices become dysfunctional when they "do not express healthy striving, but are attempts to ward off repressed impulses."

He also makes the very important observation that when an unhealthy belief or behavior is challenged, the result is excessive fear. Anyone who has ever tried to challenge a religious addict's belief system has undoubtedly been met with a hostility bordering on fury. People who are spiritually healthy will not react with fear and anger to questions about their beliefs and practices.

One good test of whether you are addicted to something is to see how you feel when you try not to engage in it. If the result is anxiety, irritability, and moodiness, and the sense that those feelings will go away if you just have one of whatever it is, you are probably addicted. If you react with indignation or anger to someone's questioning how much you drink, eat, or go to church—or how consumed you are with work or significant others—that is a warning sign of addiction.

Healthy spirituality, in contrast, is very freeing; differing beliefs or even outright opposition do not threaten you. The symptoms of religious addiction point to a narrow, restrictive belief system, which limits your spiritual growth and victimizes you as well as the people around you.

THE SYMPTOMS OF RELIGIOUS ADDICTION

Inability to think, doubt, or question information or authority

Black-and-white, simplistic thinking

Shame-based belief that you aren't good enough, or you aren't "doing it right"

Magical thinking that God will fix you

Scrupulosity: rigid, obsessive adherence to rules, codes of ethics, or guidelines

Uncompromising, judgmental attitudes

Compulsive praying, going to church or crusades, quoting scripture

Unrealistic financial contributions

Believing that sex is dirty—that our bodies and physical pleasures are evil

Compulsive overeating or excessive fasting

Conflict with science, medicine, and education

Progressive detachment from the real world, isolation, breakdown of relationships

Psychosomatic illness: sleeplessness, back pains, headaches, hypertension

Manipulating scripture or texts, feeling chosen, claiming to receive special messages from God

Trancelike state or religious high, wearing a glazed happy face

Cries for help; mental, emotional, physical breakdown; hospitalization

EXPLORING THE SYMPTOMS

Healthy spirituality enlightens the mind by broadening the vision; it changes the heart for the better—to be more courageous and prudent—and transforms the will to be genuinely loving. On the other hand, unhealthy religiosity darkens the mind by narrowing the vision, hardens the heart with fear and foolhardiness, and transforms [people] to be selfish and hateful in general, or at least towards people with a different belief system.

N. S. Xavier, M.D.
The Two Faces of Religion

Let's take a look at the symptoms of religious addiction to see how they fit the patterns and behaviors we have discussed so far.

Inability to think, doubt, or question information or authority. This is the primary symptom of any dysfunctional belief system, for if you cannot question or examine what you are taught, if you cannot doubt or challenge authority, you are in danger of being victimized and abused. You miss the messages and miracles God places in your life because you literally do not know how to recognize them.

In refusing to think or question, you hand over responsibility for your beliefs, finances, relationships, employment, and destiny to a clergyman or other so-called master. You are usually told that not thinking, doubting, or questioning is a sign of faith—so you become a religious slave. Often if you use your critical faculties, you are told that this is the devil at work in your life. Faith is said to mean unquestioning obedience. This is how religious abusers control; it is how ministers and leaders are able to financially or sexually abuse their followers. It leads to brainwashing and mind control, for when you have no choices or freedom to decide for yourself, you are not in control of your own mind.

If you are not permitted to think for yourself, to question, you stop your spiritual growth because you do not know how to see the ways God is working with you and through you. When you use your critical faculties to analyze, interpret, explore, and question, you discover new shades of meaning and greater richness in God's truth. Questioning and exploring is a means of having a dialogue with God. To refuse to doubt, think about, or question what you are told is to miss an opportunity to talk with God.

Black-and-white, simplistic thinking. This is one of the predominant symptoms of religious addiction. You see life in terms of right or wrong, good or bad, saved or sinner. You never see the gray areas. Your need for order, perfection, or control is so strong that anything that is not clearly black or white confuses or perhaps frightens you. Those who turn to religion as a means to avoid error are no doubt attracted to the black-and-white aspects of a rigid dogmatism.

The chief danger of this type of thinking is that real life is seldom black or white. Life constantly presents us with situations or choices that are ambiguous or problems that require complex solutions. If you are unable to cope with these gray areas, with complexities, your life is likely to feel forever out of control. People who think only in terms of black or white have difficulty making decisions. You frantically try to fit a difficult issue into a neat, tidy solution, and it just doesn't work. You frequently feel you have no choices, or that God has not heard you because the answers aren't simple. You are forever at the mercy of those who will give you the simple, black-or-white answer.

Spiritually, thinking in terms of such absolutes paralyzes you, for people who think this way are always waiting for the right answer—the clear signal, the burning bush. You sit and wait for the solution that fits your simplistic dogma, even though the answer is often right in front of you. Black-and-white thinking prevents you from being able to find effective solutions to problems and to see when you are being abused.

You limit and stunt your life by rejecting anyone or anything that does not fit into your narrow frame of reference. You become abusive of others who do not share your views because difference, variety, and change all fall into the ambiguous gray areas, with which you cannot cope. Such shades of gray become the uncontrollable elements in life that Nakken says all addicts are trying to master. You increase your pain, he says, by becoming more rigid, harsh, and dogmatic the more you are confronted with situations that fall outside your simplistic views.

Shame-based belief that you aren't good enough or you aren't "doing it right." Like the inability to question and the black-and-white thinking, this is a fundamental symptom from which many of the other symptoms of religious addiction spring. As Matthew Fox observed, people who are taught from birth that they are worthless never have the resources to cope with the challenges of life. Religious addiction, as well as other addictions, is an attempt to escape this pervasive sense of shame and inadequacy.

Shame-based thinking reinforces the belief that you don't make mistakes, but that you are the mistake. Thus it robs you of the ability to constructively and healthily examine your behavior or choices, to learn how you might do it differently. Your black-and-white thinking causes you to label all your beliefs and behaviors as good or bad—mostly bad. So you constantly feel that you are a failure, who has not measured up. This symptom is the seed of codependency, leading to people-pleasing and approval-seeking as a means to assure yourself you've done—whatever the task is right. Ultimately, it creates a terror of what will happen to you if you don't do things right, which makes you vulnerable to many of the other symptoms of religious addiction.

This type of thinking also cheats you of the opportunity to discover and nurture you own inner strength. You never recognize or credit the positive choices you make in your life, never see how you create changes—how you do, in fact, do many things right. I hear people say so often in Twelve Step meetings that "I didn't get sober; God did it for me." This kind of thinking fosters a total denial of self. I heard of a therapist who told a client, "My Higher Power does it; I'm just a channel," thus discounting years of training, hard work and study, and invalidating the discipline and talent it took to become a therapist. This is how you miss yourself and how you perpetuate the belief that you aren't good enough. Believing yourself a failure and inadequate, you can never see when and how you have used your own gifts healthily and creatively. Shame-based thinking robs you of power, self-respect, and dignity.

Magical thinking that God will fix you. This symptom is the natural offshoot of shame-based thinking. It takes you farther from reality and deeper into self-hatred and victimization, thus creating a fantasy relationship with God. Believing yourself inadequate and worthless, you sit and wait for God to do things for you. A young woman came to me, confused and angry, and said: "Father Leo, I went to church and suddenly got angry. I didn't know why I was angry, and I felt I shouldn't be angry in church. I prayed to God to take my anger, and He wouldn't. I prayed harder, and He still wouldn't and I was getting angrier that God didn't take my anger. I didn't want to be angry and God wouldn't take it away. I don't understand why God wouldn't help me." I suggested that possibly her anger had a purpose, that it indicated issues that needed to be addressed. Perhaps her energy would be better spent in therapy working on those issues rather than sitting in church childishly demanding that God take away her anger.

Months later, the same young lady came and thanked me. She had indeed sought a therapist, and in the process of working through her feelings of anger had discovered that her grandfather had been very religiously abusive. The resulting guilt and shame had created the anger she experienced in church.

Thus magical thinking unites with nonquestioning and black-and-white thinking to keep you farther from God and from yourself. My young friend never stopped to question why she was angry, or why she felt it was unacceptable to be angry in church. She felt not only rejected by God when her anger didn't go away on demand but also angry at both God and herself.

Magical thinking also permits religious addicts to accept abuse and to abuse others. Dr. Xavier notes that religious addicts have a distorted conscience and sense of guilt. Just having a sexual thought or impulse might send them into a frenzy of self-hate and fear of damnation, but, he says, "these same people often have no prick of conscience in being hateful to people with a different belief system."

Often it appears as if they believe that saying some magic words will absolve them from responsibility for their actions. Jimmy

Swaggart's televised confession is a good example of this: He carefully avoided acknowledging his behavior and focused instead on the magic words "washed in the blood of the lamb . . . never to be remembered against me." Magical thinking is also what allows people to feel perfectly justified in committing the most horrible acts as long as they are doing it for God. I have letters from several women who were sexually abused by ministers or priests who told them that their calling made such behavior all right.

The fantasy aspect of magical thinking sets you up to confuse the spectacular with genuine miracles. Oral Roberts threatened he would be called home if his coffers weren't filled and even claimed to have raised the dead. Jim Bakker offered what he called partnerships in paradise for major contributions. They created spectacles and called them miracles; eventually their followers could recognize miracles only as displays of spectacular events.

The miracle is not in the spectacle or the magic. The miracle lies in our response to the event. In the story of God parting the Red Sea so that Moses could lead the Jews out of bondage, the important message is that in finding the courage to walk through the parted waters, the Israelites walked through their doubt and fear into faith. This story still inspires people to take risks, to move out of the bondage of fear into positive action. So many religious people forget this important message and seek the supernatural fix. Wanting God to work the trick in our lives we often miss the sense of empowerment that comes with asking God to show us how to work our own magic—to create our own changes.

Scrupulosity: rigid, obsessive adherence to rules, codes of ethics, or guidelines. The fear of punishment and the resulting need to be perfect that come from shame-based thinking create an intense need to follow rules. Centuries ago, the Catholic Church noted how some priests gained an exaggerated sense of superiority and self-worth by rigidly adhering to rules, rituals, and doctrines. They were using these rules not to enrich or guide their lives, but as a means to avoid error and to gain authority and control. This became known as scrupulosity.

Such behavior is dysfunctional because the sense of right and wrong become totally lost in the obsession with minutely adhering to rules and rituals, which can render you incapable of questioning the validity of the rules or how they are applied. Instead, you use rules and rituals to give you self-esteem, authority, and control. Consequently, you often judge yourself and others mercilessly harsh based solely on adherence to rules and regulations. That intense focus on rules becomes a way to escape reality and an avoidance of choice and responsibility. Religious addicts do this out of overwhelming fear and a desperate need for safety. Rigidly clinging to rules and rituals offers a false sense of control, of safety; you can escape painful feelings by almost hypnotizing yourself with millions of little rituals: handwashing, prayers, mantras—all designed to serve as protection or absolution from supposed evil thoughts. This is one result of both magical thinking and black-and-white thinking: the idea that how well or how often you perform some ritual or saying will save you from punishment.

For years, the concept of scrupulosity has been treated as a minor problem within the Catholic Church or as a manifestation of the psychiatric illness known as obsessive-compulsive disorder. However, the more I work with religious addicts, the more I see this trait surface. No matter where they are, these are the people who immediately learn all the rules, observe them religiously, and treat those who aren't equally as rigid as inferior or slightly immoral.

People who have tried to escape religious addiction are often unaware of how they bring this addiction to rules with them to new belief systems or support groups. An example is the members of the support group who told the woman whose child was ill that she could cause her child to die by not totally embracing all the beliefs espoused in *A Course in Miracles.*

I see this symptom a great deal among people whose professions are bound by codes of ethics, standards, and guidelines: doctors, lawyers, therapists, social workers, and others. Whether they espouse a particular faith or not, they are easily recognizable as religious addicts when they literally make a religion out of the rules and ethics. Fearful and unsure of themselves, terrified of what punishment might result from not doing something right, they cling absolutely, dogmatically to rules. The black-and-white, unquestioning mind-set renders them incapable of evaluating situations on an individual basis, unable to see where certain conditions might demand flexibility or how such rigidity might cause harm. Equating mistakes with sins for which they will be punished, they want to avoid taking responsibility by saying they followed the rules.

I see such people come to Twelve Step meetings with the same absolutism, and judge harshly those who are not as scrupulously devoted to observing the traditions and customs, blind to the fact that the Twelve Steps are meant as suggested tools for recovery, emphatically *not* to be taken as gospel. Rigid adherence to rules gives a false sense of self-worth, based not on who you are, but what you do. This behavior reinforces the inability to see the difference between making a mistake and being a mistake.

The tragic result is that you end up bewildered and angry at God and yourself, when following the rules doesn't produce the expected rewards. "I did everything right. I followed all the rules. Why am I still so miserable?" you cry. Rigid adherence to rules and rituals, far from providing safety and self-respect, only serves to rob you of dignity and choices, leaving you feeling victimized, powerless, and out of control. Having done things right—said the prayers or chants, gone on crusades, burned the incense, cleansed the crystals, gone to meetings, done the Fourth Step—didn't help you like yourself any better, and you wonder why you feel so abandoned by God. Unable to recognize how you've made a god of your rules and rituals, you live isolated by your rigidity. You cannot see that, in giving away your power to the rules and rituals, you miss the chance to work as a co-creator with God.

Uncompromising judgmental attitudes. The need to control, to be perfect, and to feel superior often lead to religious addiction. Religion offers a new sense of identity and feelings of control and self-worth. Yet it is a false sense of self-worth based on putting down, humiliating, or even persecuting others who do not share your beliefs or follow rules as rigidly. In this symptom, the black-and-white and magical thinking, the inability to question, and the rigid rules merge to create increasingly destructive behavior and beliefs.

So much of religious addiction is built on fantasy—on beliefs that God will fix whatever is wrong or that being religious makes you a better person. By extension, Dr. Xavier says, religious addicts must create the fantasy that others are somehow bad, inferior, or evil in order to maintain a sense of superiority. So they fear anything that poses a threat to this fantasy-driven sense of self-respect. They preach bigotry and hatred based on race, religion, or political persuasion, unable to recognize the abusiveness and hypocrisy. Some even feel justified in killing people they consider evil. This is the rationale behind anti-Semitism and behind apartheid in South Africa; it gives birth to Nazism and the Ku Klux Klan. More recently, we have seen it in the Ayatollah Khomeini and Saddam Hussein as they used religious hatred to feed their holy wars against each other and against the United States and Israel.

As religious addiction progresses, the range of people whom you fear, who threaten your religious fantasies, grows wider—they may include your parents, siblings, spouse, or children. Projecting all of your self-hatred onto others, you judge them as harshly as you judge yourself—always pronouncing on others the same guilty verdict you secretly impose on yourself.

This extreme judgmentalness causes deep and lasting emotional scarring. I've heard people in Twelve Step meetings share how their religious addiction or abuse left them with an intense fear of being judged, which keeps them from taking risks and/or expressing their needs and feelings. When you have been judged mercilessly or have done it to others, you end up people-pleasing, avoiding responsibilities, or hearing shame and condemnation where it may not exist.

Compulsive praying, going to church or crusades, quoting scripture. These are the so-called using behaviors, the paraphernalia religious addicts use to get their fix. These behaviors do for religious addicts what snorting cocaine or swilling vodka do for substance abusers. When you hear religious addicts quoting scripture nonstop, imagine seeing heroin addicts shooting up. The praying, crusading, and witnessing are used to create a high. They also create a wall that separates religious addicts from other people, and from God.

These behaviors are also a means of control. With them come the elements of brainwashing and mind-control that often accompany religious addiction and abuse. They are the tools used by the unscrupulous to gain and maintain power. They utilize black-and-white thinking via simplistic dogmas and slogans, strengthened by injunctions against doubting and questioning, with a dash of charlatanism and magic to keep people hooked.

They also lead to avoidance of responsibility. Charles, whose story was told in Chapter 2, lost job after job because of chronic tardiness and absenteeism, and because of friction with co-workers created by his incessant proselytizing. Other symptoms include paying bills late or not at all, parents missing their childrens' school functions and other events, young people skipping school and failing to turn in assignments. The tragedy is that often these people are told that God will provide, take care of them, fix it. When God doesn't pay the rent, get the job, make the teacher accept the excuse, you either blame yourself for not being good enough or blame others for being sinful and so not heeding God's wishes. This distorted thinking is partly what drives religious addicts into insane acts of brutality or murder, just as it can fuel a kind of paranoid voice that tells them the Devil has possessed family members or others. These addicts perceive these people as standing between them and the so-called rewards of heaven.

There is nothing wrong with praying, going to church, missions, crusades, or talking about God, unless it is to the exclusion of all else. The key here is balance and choice. If you engage in these activities as a means to avoid responsibility, to avoid feeling discomfort, you ultimately lose all control, all balance. When you feel compelled to force your family and friends to follow your beliefs—and become angry and hostile when they choose not to accept them—you are not practicing healthy religion. You are being religiously abusive. When you resent anything that interferes with your religious practices, that is not healthy. When you flee from all other beliefs but your own, you shut yourself away from God.

Unrealistic financial contributions. This is the symptom that has been examined by the media in the scandals about Jim and Tammy Bakker, Oral Roberts, and other TV evangelists. In spite of the controversy when those outrages were first revealed, TV viewers continued to pour in money. Many disciples explained or excused their financial contributions by telling reporters that they were not sending money to the TV evangelist, but rather to the ministry, or to God's church, or to the work of the missions. However, God does not put the money in the bank or decide how much money to send to the missions, schools, or hospitals. The power politics involved in the making of these decisions reveals the seamiest, most sordid, and most abusive side of religious addiction.

Much of religious addiction is about control and power. Money equals power. As in any organization, from the smallest churches to the largest evangelical organizations, the big-money contributors are those with the most influence.

In today's materialistic society, so many people measure their self-worth by monetary standards: how much you earn and how many things you own mark your success. So it is natural that many people bring this attitude to religion. The way to feel appreciated, to feel worthwhile, is to give money. If you have a need to be in control, to feel powerful, there is no better way than to buy your way to the top. You become the biggest contributor, the best fund-raiser. In this pursuit of power and control, the whole purpose is lost: God becomes just another product. Congregations are seen not as people, but as donor-units. Any means justifies the end of raising huge sums of money. Both the abusers and the abused see nothing wrong, because they believe they are ensuring a place in heaven by getting and giving all this money in the name of God.

We can see what Erich Fromm meant when he said religion allows those in control to ease their consciences about their abusiveness. In fact, most are so deeply in denial that they cannot even see how they are abusive. In *Time* magazine, Jim Bakker was reported as saying: "Even if Jim and Tammy did everything we're accused of, does that give Jerry Falwell the right to steal my dream, my life, my home, my everything and my reputation from me?" Bakker's denial and victimized self-pity is similar to that of the alcoholic who blames the employer who fired him for being drunk. Like an alcoholic, Bakker still cannot accept that his disgrace is the consequence of his own actions.

For whatever reason, whichever guilt, shame, or fear button is pushed, many religious addicts give until there is nothing left. You might go bankrupt or abandon your family. Like alcoholics, drug addicts, and gamblers, some of you run your credit cards to the limit, write bad checks, sometimes even steal. The result, for yourself and your family, is guilt, shame, anger, despair, remorse.

Believing that sex is dirty—that our bodies and physical pleasures are evil. Listening to religious addicts' views of sex, we could easily get the impression that God created sex and then rather regretted it.

It all comes back to the dynamics of religion, morality, power, and control. Erich Fromm observes that the taboos against sex are a subtle way to break our will without our knowing it. He says that the system of "indoctrination, rewards, punishments and fitting ideology solves this task so well that most people believe they are following their own will and are unaware that their will itself is conditioned and manipulated."

So it is with sex. No other human impulse carries with it such intertwined power and surrender. I submit to you; you submit to me. I have power over you, or is it that you have power over me? Sex is scary. We become vulnerable, opening our physical selves to one another. Sex requires trust: I allow you to invade me; I place part of myself in you. There is so much mythology, mysticism, and fear bound up in the simple act of human coupling. It's easy to see how those who seek power can abuse it.

But the disadvantage of creating a taboo is that, once something is forbidden, it immediately becomes attractive. Bertrand Russell compares it to telling a boy not to like trains:

> *Suppose we told him that an interest in trains is wicked; suppose we kept his eyes bandaged whenever he was in a train or on a railway station; suppose we never allowed the word "train" to be mentioned in his presence and preserved an impenetrable mystery as to the means by which he is transported from one place to another. The result would not*

*be that he would cease to be interested in trains; on the
contrary, he would become more interested than ever but
would have a morbid sense of sin, because this interest had
been represented to him as improper. . . . This is precisely
what is done in the matter of sex, but, as sex is more
interesting than trains, the results are worse. Almost every
adult in a Christian community is more or less diseased
nervously as a result of the taboo on sex knowledge when he
or she was young. And the sense of sin which is thus
artificially implanted is one of the causes of cruelty, timidity
and stupidity in later life.*

Fromm also says that the creation of taboos immediately sets up a
rebellion—we want our freedom back. Rebelling doesn't give us our
freedom; it just creates more guilt. Moreover, he points out that taboos
actually create sexual obsessiveness and perversions.

Perhaps this explains why there is such a great correlation
between sexual abuse and religious addiction and abuse. Self-hatred
and black-and-white thinking, combined with the taboos against sex,
produce intense conflicts. I suspect that Jimmy Swaggart preached
some of his most scathing sermons against sex immediately following
his liaisons with prostitutes. Nor is this abuse limited to Christians. An
article in *Common Boundary* magazine chronicled rampant sexual
abuse by Vajra Regent Osel Tendzin, the second-in-command of the
largest group of Tibetan Buddhists in the United States. It described not
only Tendzin's alcoholism and sexual liaisons with both men and
women in his communes but also the extreme denial and codependency
displayed throughout the entire American Buddhist community.

This taboo against sex has caused incredible cruelty. Time after
time, I hear of religious addicts who brutalize their children or abuse
their spouses, all the while quoting scripture.

*It was the silence that was so maddening. Everybody
knew that the biblical texts were selected as an excuse for the
weekly punishments. I knew my father enjoyed giving us a
whipping but he read from the scriptures to make it okay. And*

my mother knew it. I think I am more angry at her because she knew he enjoyed it and yet she said nothing.

Tom, age forty-two

For no reason, he would hit the boys. He said they were arrogant and badly behaved. He accused them of sexual misconduct, indecency, and taking the Lord's name in vain. When they tried to answer back, he beat them—followed by a time of prayer! And I remained silent. For years I remained silent.

In the bedroom, he made me do things to him and then said it was sinful. What he said the boys were thinking, he did with me in bed. He transferred his feelings onto the boys and when he punished them, he was punishing himself. And I remained silent.

Mary, age sixty-two

The belief that sex is dirty has created religious sexual abuse. Religious addiction is built on the fear of any knowledge that challenges an addict's belief system; therefore, the withholding of knowledge is religious abuse. If your parents refused to tell you about sex because of their religious beliefs, and left you to learn about it on your own (presumably on your wedding night), that is religious sexual abuse. If you are excluded from ordination and active pastorhood because you are a woman, that is religious sexual abuse. If your religiously addicted husband is battering you and your infant child, and your pastor tells you to stay in the marriage because of the wedding vows, that is religious sexual abuse. Women are said to be given away in marriage; men are not. That is religious sexual abuse.

Many people with eating disorders overeat or starve because of their fear of sex, their belief that sex isn't supposed to be pleasurable. I have met numerous Catholic men and women in treatment centers who have serious sexual dysfunction as a result of the fear and shame instilled in them by nuns and priests from early childhood on. Marriages shatter, men and women stay mired in shame because of the dysfunctional messages received from religious teaching.

One very damaging aspect of religious sexual abuse is the pain it inflicts on homosexuals and their families—and on people struggling to cope with any sexual problems, especially sexual abuse. Many homosexuals struggle alone, terrified of rejection by family and church, unable to seek counseling. Many turn to drugs, food, alcohol, and sexually compulsive behavior to escape the feelings of guilt, fear, and loneliness.

Many men with sexual identity problems seek to hide in, or cure themselves with, religion. They may become almost violently homophobic—hating in others what they fear in themselves. Men who fear that the least bit of sensitivity in them might mean they are gay often become bullying macho men; homosexuals leading double lives are often the ones who speak out most loudly and visibly against homosexuality. They persecute homosexuals, abuse their wives, yet can be seen in the gay bars two cities away or secretly hiring male prostitutes.

The belief that sex is dirty creates intense shame about our very being. It fuels the belief that our bodies and any kind of physical pleasure are dirty; thus it fosters extreme self-hate and confusion about the sources of pleasure. It can lead to such abuses as anorexia, self-flagellation, or self-mutilation. Incest survivors in particular are vulnerable to these forms of self-abuse; this idea fuels their belief that they caused the abuse, so they take their shame out on their bodies, sometimes burning or cutting or trying to starve themselves.

This belief also provides justification for a great deal of the physical abuse some religious addicts heap on their families. One man wrote to me: "Mother would keep on beating me . . . literally trying to beat the Devil out of me, I guess. She'd scream scriptures at me all the time she was hitting me. I never understood how my own mother could think I was evil."

This particular symptom of religious abuse fuels the belief that we are mistakes, garbage, depraved. I believe that God created sex and made it pleasurable to us for a reason; not just to procreate, but as a means of physically expressing spiritual unity. To insist that it is dirty is an abuse of God's gift, and from that abuse springs more abuse: guilt, shame, humiliation, fear.

71

Lack of balance is the key to what makes this belief unhealthy. Ideally, balance is achieved not by rejecting our bodies, but by allowing God to continue to create through our minds and bodies. God created this world for us to enjoy. If we abuse the material things of this world, make ourselves miserable with them, that is not what God intended. But I do not believe we were intended to brand as evil the gifts that were given to us to enjoy.

Compulsive overeating or excessive fasting. Eating is a very sensual activity. I have heard compulsive overeaters describe certain foods as better than sex. As we discussed earlier, taboos against sex and against other external forms of pleasure, such as movies, rock music, and dance, leave few outlets for pleasure. I have observed time and again that religious addicts, especially women, are frequently overweight—and miserable.

So many religious addicts were brought up in a family system that was religiously restrictive. The rules were no smoking, no drinking, no dancing, no playing cards, and very limited relationships with the opposite sex until marriage. The one thing you were allowed to do, and were encouraged to do, was eat.

Much of church social life revolves around eating. Many women and men find their only source of self-esteem in the popularity of their cooking. There is almost an obligation to sample everything at pot-luck dinners in order not to hurt someone's feelings. The lonely and the insecure find approval by eating more and more, and before they know it, they've slipped into food addiction. Yet when they seek help, they are chastised for doing the very thing they were encouraged to do in the first place: eat.

Then there are those who have sought to cure their eating disorders with religion. Some actually do lose weight and even manage to keep it off, by switching food addiction for religious addiction. Like dry alcoholics and other addicts who have arrested a compulsive behavior, these people are often very angry and judgmental.

But usually, the compulsive overeater who seeks help via religion ends up feeling worse. It's hard to stay on a diet when your main support group is focused on food. Your guilt and shame at not being able to "give it to God" get worse. Your self-hatred increases. According to ever-rising statistics, most incest survivors end up with some form of eating disorder among other addictions. So on top of the initial abuse comes even greater abuse from pastors or fellow church members who reinforce your shame by saying you just aren't doing something right, or God would have removed your hunger.

This is a good example of how black-and white, magical thinking becomes harmful. God will not take away the hunger pains or the impulse to purge or starve. Remember, addictions are about escaping pain; therefore, recovery means facing and walking through pain. I hear people in Overeaters Anonymous describe how *choosing* not to eat compulsively, not to purge, not to starve gives them a sense of power that carries them through the pain of unwanted feelings. When they take responsibility—call their sponsors, go to a meeting, read a meditation—they emerge from the tough time feeling renewed and positive. This is how you empower yourself and become a co-creator with your Higher Power. To expect God to miraculously take your craving away without your doing anything is the way to keep yourself in victimization and shame.

The opposite spectrum of compulsive overeating is anorexia, which is compulsive starving. Anorexics are usually high achievers, extremely perfectionistic, with an intense need to control. They very often hate their bodies; frequently their disease comes from a deep fear of sex or of growing up and having to accept responsibility, so they want to keep their bodies looking childlike. Anorexics in particular live in fantasy; they have created a my-life-is-wonderful illusion, which is often difficult to break.

You can see how people with this dysfunction might be attracted to religion. It offers a way to control, to be perfect, to have order and structure. Like overeaters, some anorexics turn to religion in order to stop their disease. In many cases, religion becomes a good cover for the disease. If people notice you are not eating, you can explain it by saying you're on a spiritual fast. This gives anorexics a double dose of self-esteem and superiority, since anorexics get their feelings of self-respect by starving when others are gorging themselves. When you add religious piety to it, so much the better!

Again, it is lack of balance and the inability to stop that signals addiction. There is nothing wrong with enjoying the delightful variety of pot-luck dinners. Some people do find that they feel physically and emotionally better after a brief fast. But when you overeat to numb your feelings, when the only way you feel good about yourself is to fast, you have gone too far. No matter which type of eating disorder you have, the end result is increased shame, self-hatred, and isolation from others, yourself, and God.

Conflict with science, medicine, and education. Many religious addicts, because of narrow and restrictive beliefs, often have conflicts with medicine and education. These two disciplines challenge black-and-white thinking, the need for simplistic solutions, and the inability to think and question. Medicine and education both involve great changes, variety, and complexity. They require trust and choices, and you might not trust the right person, make the right choice. Better leave it to God. Then it's not your responsibility.

Frequently we read about parents who refuse to give permission for a doctor to perform an operation or administer a blood transfusion because of their belief in a certain faith. Some of these faiths manipulate scripture to justify their dogma. For instance, some cite Acts 15:29 as the basis for refusing transfusions: "That you abstain from what has been sacrificed to idols and from blood and from what is strangled, and from unchastity."

Those verses refer specifically to the Jewish rituals concerning preparation of meat, which is part of the Jewish Orthodox tradition called keeping kosher. Much of early Christian teaching was devoted to moving people away from Jewish tradition in order to distinguish Christianity as a separate religion rather than a sect of Judaism. Yet certain religions have twisted these verses to legitimize their stance against medicine or whatever it is they oppose.

So it is in other fields of study, especially science and the theory of evolution. Black-and-white thinking and the refusal to question or examine limit your worldview. By clinging to the word-for-word translation of Genesis I—"In the beginning God created the heavens and the earth . . ."—you lose the opportunity to see possibilities—that perhaps Darwin's theory confirms rather than opposes Genesis. Could God have set in motion the evolutionary chain? Are you allowed to notice that Darwin's order might parallel Genesis? For some people such thinking is absolutely forbidden and often considered sinful.

Could the miracles of medical technology represent God's miracles at work? God gave us brains and the ability to think. All the laws of physics, science, and nature are in place. What an astonishing miracle that we have discovered them and can use them! During his long battle with AIDs, young Ryan White held on to the hope of a miracle—not a fantasy that he would wake up and find himself well, but a belief that scientists and researchers would find a cure in time. His mother is donating much of the money contributed to him to AIDs research. This is faith. This is true partnership with God.

In contrast, some of you remove your children from schools in which they might be exposed to a different view. Seeking to protect your children from so-called "evil thinking," you unknowingly harm them by refusing to allow your children to use the greatest gift God has given them: the ability to use their minds. So your children grow up being taught to fear anything different, unable to evaluate for themselves, confused, isolated, and often in a rage against a world that constantly threatens their narrow view. This fearful attitude leads to censorship and to banning—even burning—books containing material that threatens your beliefs. In refusing to give yourself choices, you take freedom and choice away from others in the name of God.

We must not restrict God's activity to religion. God is at work in this world and speaks through artists, scientists, psychologists, and reason. Healthy spirituality allows you to see God at work in a flower, a prayer, a song, a work of art, or any of the technological wonders we take for granted today.

Psychosomatic illness: sleeplessness, back pain, headaches, hypertension. Healthy spirituality encompasses mental, emotional, and physical well-being. They all interact.

Many of the symptoms we have discussed so far carry with them physical, emotional, and mental stresses. As you get deeper into addiction, the fears, anxieties, and internal conflicts take their toll.

These discomforts, as well as anger, all can create high blood pressure, heart disease, ulcers and other intestinal disorders, and fatigue. Stress can also cause severe backaches, muscle and joint pain, headaches, and insomnia. Depression also has physical manifestations, including sleeping too much or not enough, memory loss and forgetfulness, chronic tiredness, and overall slowing down or just stopping all together. Many of you have been under medical care for these problems for years, perhaps trying to cure them with religion, not realizing these pains are caused by excessive religiousness.

Family members often suffer many of the same physical problems—but for different reasons. The symptoms can help them avoid the strain of arguments, put-downs, and conflict caused by religious abuse. Your spouse may have chronic headaches as a way to avoid watching religious TV with you. Your daughter may develop diarrhea so that she can't go to the church picnic. Only now are schoolteachers being taught to recognize that chronic stomachaches, headaches, and other complaints are often disguised cries for help from children who are enduring one or more forms of abuse—including religious abuse.

Progressive detachment from the real world, isolation, breakdown of relationships. At this stage, you are consumed by religion. Nothing else in the world seems to matter. Life revolves around the church or mission so that you become increasingly isolated and emotionally unable to be intimate with your loved ones. Eventually, you end up alone, without family or friends.

In this symptom, we see how all the other symptoms begin to snowball. The rigidity, judgmentalness, magical thinking, compulsive praying, and church involvement all distort your sense of reality. The increasing isolation and loss of interest in the world deepens the depression that attends addictions. It heightens the loss of reality. Sunk deeper into fantasy and delusion, you disengage from the world to the extent that, like other addicts, you neglect bills or even cease to work, thus creating hardships for your family. Your belief that sex is dirty may wreck your marriage or cause you to become sexually abusive to yourself or others. You might masturbate in secret, use prostitutes as did

Swaggart, or physically hurt yourself or your spouse during or after sex. The resulting guilt and shame only widens the gulf. Many religious addicts leave homes, families, and jobs under the delusion that they are freeing themselves to serve their faith. Again, discipleship and missionary work are commendable, but it is not healthy to simply abandon those who depend on you.

Like other addicts, you experience personality changes. Early on, you may feel genuinely happy, joyous, enthusiastic, and positive about your newfound beliefs. Singing hymns, discussing the scriptures, praying and fasting, telling the story of how you came to see the light and were reborn is exciting. It creates a natural high.

When you expect to stay in this heightened emotional state and it doesn't last, you get angry with yourself or with God. You didn't do it right. You might think your family and friends' less-than-enthusiastic reception of your conversion has caused you to feel bad. Anger, guilt, fear, and shame take over, causing you to withdraw and isolate yourself. You may grow so uncontrollably irritable and angry that you become what is called a rageaholic.

This change of personality concerns your family and friends. They see the increased withdrawal and isolation, the spells of depression or angry outbursts, the progressively strident preaching and proselytizing without regard for others' feelings. They see a changed person. Unlike the newfound church family who applauds such changes, your family of origin and old friends see very unhealthy behaviors. They don't like it at all, and they don't know what to do about it. They, too, may begin to exhibit some of the same dysfunctional behaviors.

Dysfunction begets dysfunction: The disease of religious addiction is a family disease, a relational disease. Religion often divides families in a way that other addictions do not. Children of religious addicts carry deep scars of guilt and shame, low self-esteem, inability to make decisions, fear of imperfection. Some become as abusive as their parents, perpetuating prejudice and hatred. Others abandon God or religion entirely, struggling to live with no spiritual nourishment and often becoming addicted to other substances as a result.

Manipulating scripture or texts, feeling chosen, claiming to receive special messages from God. This is a symptom of someone who is nearing the end stages of religious addiction and whose escape into fantasy is approaching insanity. Desperate efforts to control the uncontrollable have not succeeded: your family has not converted; God did not work the miracles you demanded; you feel frightened, ashamed, and despairing.

This is the symptom that William Martin, a sociologist at Rice University, was describing to *People* magazine when he noted that Jimmy Swaggart had gone from interpreting what he thought God's message meant, to announcing that God had given him direct orders. Swaggart's need to feel special, to justify his behavior and beliefs, took him away from reality, and from genuine humility.

Thus, the addict excuses bizarre behavior, unrealistic demands, and excessive judgments with such statements as: God told me to do this or to say this . . . to condemn those who are. . . . The spirit guided me in this decision . . . Christ came to me in a vision and said. . . . God is on my side.

These are the magic words that you think will give you credibility, absolve you from guilt, or keep you from having to accept responsibility for your behavior. "It's not my fault; I was just doing what God told me to do!" Your self-respect is so low that if you have a good idea, it must have come from God. You could not have thought it up all by yourself.

There is a difference between using scripture to support what you are saying and twisting it to justify irrational claims and behavior. People who are manipulating and twisting scripture will keep repeating the same things by rote, fixedly dogmatic. Healthy use of scripture or teachings to support ideas allows for discussion and differing interpretations—something religious addicts cannot do. So often when I try to suggest that it is possible to discover God's message in other religions or philosophies, I am confronted by religious addicts who keep repeating, "Jesus said, 'I am the way, the truth and the light'"no matter what I say. Often, I think they don't really even hear what I'm saying. I could ask if they beat their wives today and they'd still answer,

"I am the way, the truth and the light!'" They parrot these texts without really understanding what the words mean.

Nor is this limited to religions. I see the same symptom displayed in Twelve Step meetings by people who quote A.A.'s founder and the *Big Book* of Alcoholics Anonymous blindly, without any real sense of how the messages apply in their lives. The same goes for those who so rigidly adhere to rules, they forget that the Twelve Steps are meant as suggestions and, instead, make them absolutes. This distorts their thinking and the ability to reason, to see, and, more important, to use the truth in their lives.

I believe that God is involved in the world and is experienced through certain individuals as prophets, messengers who bring us new information and insights about God. This is quite different from those who claim that God is using them or sending them special messages. How do we know who to believe?

We don't. It is part of God's mystery that nobody knows for sure. Theological argument has held that one way to tell the difference is that God's messages are consistent with previous ones. If someone tells you that God said all red-haired people are to be killed, that is not consistent with the messages of love and forgiveness that have been revealed to us in the past.

There are certain spiritual values and characteristics that are usually present in genuine messages from God: truth, forgiveness, charity, understanding, acceptance, and diversity. Messengers from God will invite, encourage, even require us to question and examine. This is where our ability to doubt, think, and question becomes important, for in it lies the difference between on the one hand being led astray and victimized, and on the other embracing the word of God.

Ultimately, our relationship with God is built on faith, not certainty. God has given us the tools with which to discern truth. It is our choice to use them wisely, or not at all. In that choice, our faith grows.

Trancelike state or religious high, wearing a glazed happy face. If you are using religion or your belief system as a fix, then it follows that you are going to look stoned or spaced out. This is the religious addict's glazed happy face. It is the look of an addict actually high on a drug.

I have heard of a number of studies and theories about how our different emotions affect our body chemistry. Research is still being done on how our emotional reactions cause our bodies to create substances that can be called our own internal drugs—to which we literally can become addicted. This explains how people get high from exercise, gambling, relationships, shopping, or church, and how those activities become addictive. After a time, the body adjusts to these internal drugs, and we have to increase the emotional intensity in order to produce the good feelings.

This is the high produced by scripture quoting, praying, meditations, chanting, and crusades, which is why they are sometimes "using" behaviors. It explains the anxiety, irritability, and depression that result when you try to stop: You go through withdrawal just like other addicts. The glazed happy face is the same expression worn by drug addicts, alcoholics, and food addicts who are high as kites and feeling no pain.

The too-bright, falsely cheerful expression is also a mask. Underneath it seethe tension, anger, and rigid control. God's children are supposed to be happy; that's the fantasy, the illusion. Don't let anyone know that you're not happy, for admitting to not being happy in the Lord is to admit imperfection, failure, not doing it right. Such an admission courts disapproval, so you paste on your false smile.

Often the mask is meant to hide the fact that you aren't really there. In later stages, religious addicts seem oblivious to what is going on around them. This is similar to an alcoholic blackout, when the alcoholic is physically functioning and yet mentally and emotionally absent. Under extreme stress or trauma, our minds have the ability to dissociate, to "space out" in order to protect us from pain. It's an escape mechanism many of us use and don't know we do it; we just think we're daydreaming or absentminded. Religious addicts use it to create a sense of safety when they feel threatened by people who won't listen to them, or whom they think are unclean. If we see a religious person wearing this spaced look at home, at work, or in a situation where involvement is expected and/or necessary, then we are undoubtedly seeing someone in advanced stages of religious addiction.

Cries for help; mental, emotional, and physical breakdown; hospitalization. You have reached rock bottom. You hate yourself and may not even know why. Or, if you recognize that you are hopelessly addicted to your religion or belief system, you don't know where to turn for help. You can't stop the meditating, praying, incense-burning, crusades, and obsessive scripture quoting. Your family does not know what to do. You've tithed away your savings; maybe you are nearing bankruptcy. Certainly you are spiritually bankrupt—you can't sleep; your head aches; your stomach is in knots; you're so depressed you can barely function. You may have a nervous breakdown. Perhaps you may enter treatment for another addiction—thinking your eating disorder, alcoholism, or fits of rage are causing your problems.

When Jim Bakker broke down in his lawyer's office and was taken to a psychiatric hospital, he was diagnosed as having panic disorder. Probably the cause of that panic attack was his denial of his religious addiction and abuse—his sudden fear of facing the consequences of his behavior. This is how it can end: with you whimpering and sobbing, crouched in a corner, curled in a fetal position, broken, abandoned, and terrified.

But in this end can be a beginning. Proper therapy—with someone who can treat religious addiction—family counseling, and support groups can help you on the road to recovery. From the crisis, you can discover and create a new friendship with God as you understand God, and your willingness to take the steps toward change will move you into healthy spirituality.

WHO IS AT RISK?

I am often asked if some people are more vulnerable to religious addiction and abuse than others. Given our conditioning over the years to look to outside authorities to tell us what to do, I think we are all at risk. But there are some groups who are especially vulnerable.

Adult children of dysfunction. The most vulnerable, of course, are those who grew up in religiously addicted homes, because all the symptoms we have just discussed will have been ingrained in them. Other adult children from dysfunction, especially those who have suffered physical or sexual abuse, are also vulnerable to religious addiction.

When you have been abused, the need to escape and be safe is overpowering. Sexual abuse survivors in particular try to cleanse their sense of feeling used and dirty with religion. The belief that sex and our bodies are dirty becomes an explanation for the abuse. The magical thinking and fantasy aspects of religion, the twin lures of escape and fix, are powerfully attractive to those who have been sexually or physically abused.

The same applies to people who are suffering from sexual identity problems: homosexuals, asexuals, or people with severe body-image problems. People with sexual dysfunction or sexual-identity problems frequently try to cure themselves by turning to religion. I suggest that Jimmy Swaggart is an excellent example of a sexual addict who sought to cure his sexual addiction with religion. Many homosexuals, fearful of rejection by families and society, struggle to hide their sexual orientation in religion. Sadly, the guilt and shaming messages most religions dispense about homosexuality only serve to increase the guilt, shame, and torment. Often they are unable to seek help from a therapist; some commit suicide as a direct result of their attempts to cure themselves with religion.

Adult children of dysfunction have a great need to escape and to control their surroundings. They have grown up in homes that were ruled by the don't talk/don't trust/don't feel credo—now recognized as a hallmark of dysfunctional families. Thus not questioning, black-and-white thinking, and even magical thinking are already second nature to them. They may fall prey to the escape/control mechanisms of scrupulosity and may already have learned how to put on a happy face to hide their family's dysfunction. So they are primarily at risk.

The sick and the elderly. You can see how the idea of being rewarded, the need to atone, and the magical belief in a fixer make this group at risk for religious addiction. These are the prime targets of the TV evangelists, who coldheartedly and calculatedly push every guilt, shame, and fear button imaginable in order to get money from these people.

Because the elderly are so frequently abandoned by their families and left to fend for themselves, their loneliness and isolation often drive them to religious TV for comfort. They are made to feel like part of a family again—like they matter. In their loneliness, the idea of being able to be with loved ones in the hereafter becomes compelling, as does the need to make doubly sure this happens. Thus they are the main target for those demanding unrealistic financial contributions, and they are especially likely to engage in compulsive praying, crusading, and proselytizing.

People write and call me all the time about a parent, grandparent, or other elderly loved one who is squandering Medicare money, retirement funds—all the savings—on a church, mission, or evangelist.

They tell me: "I don't know what to do, Father Leo. My mother's sent everything she's got to her church. Now she's sick. I don't make enough money to help care for her . . . we've spent the kids' college money on her doctor bills."

The tragedy is that religious addiction victimizes not only senior citizens, but their families and friends as well. Sometimes, the strains cause divorce, bankruptcy, or permanent rifts in families torn apart by someone's addiction to a TV evangelist. Yet these same evangelists claim to be pro-family.

This also applies to the sick, particularly those with congenital birth defects, terminal illnesses, or degenerative diseases, such as multiple sclerosis. When God is presented as the universal fixer, it is easy to understand why a sick person could become a religious addict. I met a young woman who, as her son slowly died of leukemia, became religiously addicted in her desperation for him not to die. She sent so much money to churches and televangelists that she had no money left for her son's burial. She adopted a literal understanding of all the messages she heard about how Jesus heals; as her addiction progressed, she truly believed that if she sent enough money, attended enough services, and prayed hard enough, her child would be healed. His death left her bitter and angry at God, at the preachers, and, most of all, at herself.

Minorities and the young. If you are shamed, put down, oppressed, alienated, or discriminated against because of your age, gender, sexual orientation, or ethnic background, you are likely to be attracted to the messages of escape and redemption many religions teach. If you feel powerless and victimized, hearing that God punishes sinners gives you hope that your oppressors will get theirs, if only in the next life.

Minority groups and the young are especially attracted to the fantasy, the magical thinking, and feelings of control offered by religious addiction. Young people, in particular, are vulnerable because of the sense of identity and belonging provided by religious involvement. The need for validation and the struggle for identity and acceptance that are a necessary part of growing up make young people very vulnerable to religious abuse and addiction.

Sometimes it is loneliness and low self-esteem that drive them into religion; other times, it is rebellion: an I'll-show-you rejection of parental values. They seek attention and respect any way they can get it. This also applies to many minority groups.

The sense of mission, the feelings of power and control and of being included that come with belonging to a church or cult is very attractive to both minorities and young people. Adolescents have one foot in childhood and the other in adulthood. They still have a child's black-and-white thinking and need for structure, with an adult need for choice. Religion gives them the chance to choose their structure yet allows them to continue to think in terms of black or white. The dogmatic rightness of religion validates them and gives them a feeling of power and control that they may not feel at home or school.

People with other addictions. Anyone who is looking for a fix is at risk of becoming religiously addicted, especially those who are trying to stop or cure another addiction. I hear from many addicts who switched to religion in order to stop drinking, stop starving or overeating, stop raging out of control or overspending. Some of them simply abandon a fundamentalist religion for a New Age belief system and take their addictive baggage with them.

Most addicts are very compulsive people, though many compulsive people do not become addicted to specific substances or behaviors. People with compulsive personalities have certain traits that make them susceptible to religious addiction.

In *The Boy Who Couldn't Stop Washing,* Dr. Judith Rapoport described someone with a compulsive personality as

> . . . *a restricted, undemonstrative person, one who is perfectionistic to a degree that demands that others submit to his or her way of doing things. A compulsive personality is often indecisive, and excessively devoted to work to the exclusion of pleasure. When pleasure is considered, it is something to be postponed and sometimes never even enjoyed. . . . People with compulsive personalities tend to be excessively moralistic, and judgmental of themselves and others.*

You can see how this kind of person would be vulnerable to religious addiction, especially to the scrupulosity, black-and-white thinking, and judgmentalness. This particular kind of person is very drawn to the rules and rituals—again, from that need to be safe, to do it right. Religion offers the ultimate safety and assurance that they'll be perfect.

No matter what the cause, the symptoms of religious addiction are the tangible signs of a deep-seated shame, a terrible sense of worthlessness, and a desperate need to escape or fix that sense of having been born a blotch on existence. In the next chapters, we will consider how, as Matthew Fox observed, these symptoms cause you to believe that your life is "broken" and that you have no power to fix it.

Chapter 4

Religious Addiction:
A Family Disease

I don't know where to turn. My wife left me
and took three of our children. They're just kids,
for God's sake, but they write me letters telling
me I'm evil and unclean and they can't come
around me until I've repented and been saved.
My younger son came with me. His brothers and
sisters won't speak to him except to try to
convert him, and he's so confused and hurt. My
wife has her whole church behind her, and
there's no one here who understands about
religious addiction. I don't know what to do.
She's gone insane with this stuff, and people tell
me *I'm* nuts!

David, age forty-two

RELIGIOUS ADDICTION CANNOT exist in a vacuum;
nearly every religious addict abuses someone. Like David, quoted
above, family members often find themselves accused of being nuts
when they try to talk about the abuse they endure or try to seek help. Just
as there are symptoms that make it easy to recognize religious addicts,

so there are certain patterns in the ways religiously abused families manifest their dysfunction.

A religious addict's need to control, judge, and proselytize make abuse a virtual imperative. The all-or-nothing mindset, the belief that sex is dirty, and the other symptoms unite to build a wall of shame and fear around the spouses and children of religious addicts. When a religious addict's rage is couched in scripture, when it literally appears to be the wrath of God, the guilt and shame imbedded in the family go straight to the core. In this way, religious addiction destroys families as much as do other addictions.

In order to examine the patterns and characteristics of religiously abused families, we will look closely at two types of families: blue-collar religious addicts and country-club Christians. The profiles described here are generalizations, but they illustrate the symptoms and life-styles that will undoubtedly be recognized by survivors of religious addiction and abuse.

BLUE-COLLAR RELIGIOUS ADDICTS

You may know this family as the loud family. They always seem to shout and yell at the top of their lungs. They appear very explosive and are likely to be constantly quarreling, even in public. This family is usually low to middle income, and the members are often described as hardworking, well-meaning folks.

Blue-collar religious addicts tend to be poorly educated or even illiterate. They may have finished high school or trade school; a few may have attended junior or community colleges. Generally, their lack of higher education makes them vulnerable to misinformation, rigid dogma, and simplistic thinking. Since they may lack some of the resources and training that enable people to question and examine what they are told, they tend toward being dependent on preachers, experts, and leaders.

In the blue-collar family, the father is clearly dominant. He brings his family to church because his upbringing has taught him he's supposed to do that. He is often rigid and authoritarian; quite frequently he is tyrannical and regularly has fits of rage. He may be an active alcoholic or a dry alcoholic who feels he has been saved by the Lord and has therefore quit drinking—but has simply traded in his booze for the Bible. He was probably physically and emotionally abused as a child. He may batter his wife. He may sexually abuse his children or possibly have a sexual addiction. He uses the Bible and scripture to hide his excesses and to justify his bigotry and rage.

He is caught between conflicting messages and beliefs that leave him feeling inadequate and angry at himself and the world. He cannot reconcile the harsh reality of his economic status with the promises of rewards he hears from preachers and evangelists. He has probably been taught that sex is dirty and that only whores enjoy sex. Yet he enjoys sex, and more confusing, at times his wife seems to like it, too. These conflicting messages create enormous shame and guilt, which make him feel weak. Being physically or sexually abusive restores his sense of power and control. He selectively uses verses from the Bible to legitimize his abuses and to salve his conscience.

The blue-collar mother is often passive, beaten down physically and emotionally—often sexually abused. She is typical of both the battered wife and the religiously abused wife. She feels too powerless to challenge her husband's authority. More than likely, she is aware of her husband's physical or sexual abuses of her children. She is likely to bury her guilt and shame in compulsive overeating or secret drinking.

She may or may not share her husband's religious beliefs. She might have been initially attracted to him because he was a good church-going boy. As so many of these wives have expressed to me, however, such religiosity can grow progressively frightening. One woman said, "He's gone crazy with it, and I'm scared for my kids."

As fearful as she is, she cannot break out of the abusive marriage. All of her religious upbringing has told her she must stay for better or for worse. Her pastor will usually reinforce this, even when there is clear evidence that her spouse is physically abusive to her and her children. She does not want him abusing the children; she hates the religious indoctrination being forced on them. Yet she is trapped in a tangled web of guilt and shame. Half the time, she believes her husband is the one who is sick, and like other codependents, she frantically searches for something that will fix or change him. However she's not entirely sure that something isn't wrong with her, and the confusion keeps her on the edge of emotional breakdown.

The father tries to offset his abusiveness at home by acting in public as the jovial, swell old boy. People say that he is basically a nice guy if you don't make him mad, so family and co-workers tend to walk on eggshells around him. He has no close friends but gathers a circle of drinking buddies, sports cronies, or church members around him, which feeds the illusion that he's okay.

When the wife in a blue-collar family is the religious addict, she too will be full of rage. She may also be an alcoholic; more likely, she is a compulsive overeater. She will undoubtedly be a survivor of childhood physical and/or sexual abuse. As an addict, she is rigid, controlling, and authoritarian—clearly the dominant spouse and parent. Her inner rage is generally manifested in extremely harsh judgmentalness and condemnation, which usually leave her isolated and friendless.

You've undoubtedly seen her: tight-lipped, face set in a stern scowl, arms folded across her chest. She always seems tense, as if perpetually ready to do battle, for she is forever at war with herself and the world, struggling to rise above the many evils she believes are out to get her. She is compulsively perfectionistic, for she equates perfection with salvation. Thus she is extremely critical; nothing is ever done to her liking. She may elbow others aside at a church function to make sure dishes are washed correctly or food prepared her way.

Other female blue-collar religious addicts will adopt a rather out-of-date, little-girl look. No matter what clothing style is in vogue, she always seems to dress ten or fifteen years behind the times. I can recognize her instantly: dressed in dowdy clothing, usually with the puffy short sleeves and wide frilly collars that were stylish in the 1940s and 1950s or in the gaudy pantsuits that were the rage in the late 1960s and early 1970s. It is as if she uses clothing to separate herself from the world as it is today. Sometimes she uses this childlike effect as an outward sign of submissiveness to her husband, while secretly using it to control him, especially sexually.

One type of female blue-collar religious addict is sexually repressed or perhaps frigid. She may use sex as a means of control over her husband. Her inner conflicts about her sexuality make her vulnerable to sexual abuse by a minister or church leader, for she can be manipulated into believing it's not a sin to have sex with a so-called man of God. This is particularly true of women who resort to the childlike look; there is generally an element of seeking a nurturing daddy in their religious addiction.

A large number of male incest survivors whom I have counseled had mothers who were religious addicts, frequently also alcoholic. They describe similar patterns of drunken beatings and sexual abuse, accompanied or followed by a frenzy of prayer, scripture quoting, and religiosity.

These women are outwardly disapproving of sex, yet can frequently be heard discussing very personal sexual information. They will often focus on something sexual when gossiping about someone—always making sure to tie in some judging scriptural or religious context to conceal the fact that they are actually gossiping.

This kind of family is apt to exhibit nearly all of the symptoms of religious addiction: black-and-white thinking, obsessive praying, quoting scripture, avoiding family reunions, belief that sex and material pleasures are evil, uncompromising judgmental attitudes, and rejection of developments in science, medicine, and education. No one in the family is allowed to think independently or to question authority. Just as their thinking is black-and-white, so are their behaviors: violent rages and abuse along with prayers before every meal plus church on Sunday. "God Is Love" is embroidered on a wall hanging, but they treat their neighbors with condemnation and distrust.

These families stay in chaos and conflict, each member confused and angry. Family members don't talk to one another except on the most superficial level. They are too busy trying to survive and stay out of the addict's way.

Except for church activities, some blue-collar religious families rarely do things together. One child is likely to stay home into adulthood as the caretaker or dutiful child; another child may grow into adulthood as the one the family depends on as the emotional and financial fixer; the other children get away as quickly as they can.

Other blue-collar families may become clannishly enmeshed, dependent solely on one another, shunning outside influences. They might all be involved in a family business or forever working on such projects as remodeling one anothers' houses. While outwardly close and supportive, the individual members often secretly resent this togetherness and try to escape via other addictions. A few become the family black sheep and leave the fold.

We can see some of these patterns and their effects at work in the story of Jim and Helen Davis. The Davis family is a composite of several people I have encountered; their emotional issues and behaviors have been placed in different contexts to preserve their anonymity.

JIM AND HELEN DAVIS'S STORY

Jim, fifty-three, owns a successful plumbing business. Born in Kentucky, he is the eldest boy of five children. His father, Frank, was a coal miner—an abusive alcoholic who went on payday rampages, violently beating his wife and children and brawling with anyone foolish enough to fight with him. Jim's mother, Pauline, was a strict Southern Baptist: obese, rigid, furiously angry with her lot in life. She did everything she was raised to do yet was somehow punished with this alcoholic husband. Her religious beliefs made divorce absolutely unthinkable; instead, all her energies were poured into reforming him. Unsuccessful, she took her rage out on her children and anyone within earshot who might lend a sympathetic ear about what she called the cross she had to bear.

When Frank was disabled with black-lung disease, Jim quit school to help support the family. He eventually went to trade school to learn the plumbing business. Jim had despised both his father's drinking and his mother's strict religiosity and vowed never to be like them. Yet the pressures of trying to support his mother and siblings proved too great; he began to drink heavily. One day he exploded at work and nearly beat a co-worker to death. Shocked and frightened, he vowed never to drink again. Believing that his family was causing his drinking, he moved to Ohio, where he met Helen.

Helen's father, Roy, was a passive, quiet alcoholic, thoroughly cowed by his wife Marjorie, who was rigid, controlling, and anorexic. Marjorie did not remember her own sexual abuse and hid her fear of and disgust with sex behind strict Catholicism. Helen was an only child and very lonely. Her mother was lost in her staunch Catholicism. Marjorie's religion was hers alone; she seemed not to care, indeed, not even want her husband or daughter to share it with her. Bereft of his wife's companionship, Roy turned to Helen for emotional and sexual support. Helen despised him for his weakness, hated him for the sexual abuse, yet he was her only source of nurturing. She fantasized about the husband she would one day meet: strong yet gentle, able to take care of her and stand up for her against the world.

Having been raised with the rules and regulations of her mother's Catholicism, Helen gravitated toward a Pentecostal church, which gave her the same structure and met her needs for a sense of family and belonging. There she met Jim, who had been brought by a friend he met at work. At first, Jim was turned off by the church; it reminded him too much of his mother's stern Baptist ways. But he wanted to continue to see Helen, so he joined the church in order to please her, giving it lip service and a wary skepticism that he kept to himself. Although not drinking, he struggled with violent temper outbursts and a constant craving for liquor.

Jim and Helen married a few months after they met. Early in Helen's pregnancy with their second child, he got drunk following a quarrel at work. He was still drunk and in a rage when he picked Helen up from her job. He refused to let her drive and got into an automobile accident that nearly caused her to lose the baby. Frightened and repentant, he believed the preacher who told him that only God would take away his terrible desire to drink, and only if he gave himself to Jesus might God allow Helen and their child to live.

Jim threw himself into his work and into the church. Gradually, the rest of his family moved to Ohio to be with him, and eventually he found himself giving financial and emotional support to not one, but five families. He continued to suffer periodic cravings to drink, as well as outbursts of rage, which he interpreted as signs he wasn't being good enough for God. As time went on, he grew increasingly more volatile and bitter, which he tried to cover with scripture quoting and church activities. The angrier and more bitter he grew, the more Helen withdrew from him. He began to seek sex with prostitutes as a release and to create a tangible reason for the badness in him that he felt prevented God from curing both his craving for alcohol and his temper. Outwardly, he was regarded as a man anyone could count on in a pinch—the kind of man who would repair an elderly couple's plumbing at no cost rather than see them go without water. His family, children, and neighbors saw him as a wonderful person, as long as they didn't get on his wrong side.

When she first met Jim, Helen thought he was her dream come true: a strong, quiet man who appeared to share her faith in God. Like her mother, Helen kept her religious views to herself; she loved the structure and guidance the church gave her and the sense of belonging. From her mother, she also learned the very simplistic belief that if she followed a set of rules to the letter, God would grant all her needs and secret wishes. This certainly seemed to be true when she met Jim. As the years went by, however, things seemed to go wrong. Jim withdrew from her emotionally; the nurturing and love she had gained from him, so like that she had received from her father, disappeared. She began to take refuge in food and began a long battle with obesity.

When not comforting herself with food, she took refuge in their four children. Throughout their childhood, she often sided with Jim in his rigid judgmentalness until he became physically abusive. Then she would comfort them by pouring out her fears and grief to them as her father had done. Although she was never physically sexual with any of her children, her dependence on them became emotionally incestuous. Fearful as they were of their father's rages and religiosity, they could at least predict what would trigger his outbursts and so learned to stay out of Jim's way. But Helen's inconsistency confused them; they never knew when she would side with Jim and abet his abuse or try to protect them from his anger. She behaved similarly with her in-laws, alternately siding with Jim in his tirades or running to them for comfort or to try to make up for his abuse. Consequently, no one in the family trusts her, yet they all depend on her to smooth things over after one of Jim's rages.

In Jim and Helen, we see how growing up in religiously restrictive homes sent them into religious addiction. Both of them were seeking a fixer: Jim wanted to cure his alcoholism and violent temper; Helen wanted the nurturing she had missed as a child. We can see how the black-and-white and magical thinking, rigidity, and judgmentalness only created further dysfunction and led both into other addictions. The blue-collar religious family is generally characterized by rage, since the economic rewards they believe have been promised are forever out of reach. Frustrated and furious, they can be manipulated into taking their rage out on any group or belief system depicted as being the cause of their problems. This is the source of the righteous anger they often exude; they feel perfectly justified in their bigotry and don't care who knows it.

GOD, MONEY, AND APPLE PIE: COUNTRY-CLUB CHRISTIANS

Country-club Christians, unlike their blue-collar counterparts, care deeply about how they appear. The quintessentially perfect all-American family, they present a squeaky-clean, apple-pie face to the world. This type of family is ruled by external validation. Their rule of thumb is: If it looks good, it is good. And if it's good, it must mean that God approves.

The father in this family is typically a perfectionistic workaholic. He probably grew up as the overachieving fixer in a dysfunctional home, possibly a religiously addicted one. He may have grown up in poverty or was raised in a home in which money equaled success. He is basically insecure and seeks to validate himself with money and prestige. Whereas the father in the blue-collar family might send money to crusades, this father pours his money and energy into his local church and community. He craves the gratification of being recognized as a major contributor. He gets his high, his sense of power and control, from being visible in his church and community.

He is likely to have a weight problem, which he controls with crash diets and excessive exercise. Because of the need to keep up outward appearances, his addictions will be hidden: workaholism, sexual addiction, prescription drug abuse, general obsessive/compulsiveness about any project he undertakes.

The mother is probably also the product of a dysfunctional family. She too believes that material possessions are a sign of success. She undoubtedly views marrying a successful husband as a measure of her own self-worth. She is hooked into the idea that looking good is good, so appearances are everything to her.

Nonetheless, she generally wages a chronic battle with weight. She has been addicted to diet pills and prescription drugs for years and doesn't know it. She is in such denial of her feelings that she cannot recognize that her endless dieting, overexercising, occasional bouts with bulimia via vomiting or laxatives are all symptoms of inner pain.

This kind of woman lives through her husband. Although she sees herself as his partner, the role she actually plays is a secondary, supportive one. She is a religious and social appendage. She is extremely perfectionistic and critical, but her criticisms are sugarcoated. She will never directly say to her children: "I'm disappointed in you." Instead, she rules by implication: "You can do better. . . . Don't upset your father. . . . Don't let the family down." The implication is always that by not doing better, by upsetting Dad, by letting the family down, they are letting God down.

When the wife in the country-club Christian family is the religious addict, instead of living through her husband, she lives through her church and civic activities. She is often involved with such groups as the Junior League and on the boards of directors of museums, ballets, and symphonies. Quite often she will have her own career. On the surface, it will appear that she has a genuine marital partnership with her husband. In truth, she controls and manipulates him; like her blue-collar counterpart, she may use sex to maintain her power—frequently by withholding it.

Quite often her religiosity appears low-key; she does not proselytize or quote scripture as openly as do her addicted spouse or the blue-collar addicts. After all, she is invested in image and looking good, and it isn't quite socially acceptable to be obnoxious about her religion. However, her value system is set-in-stone rigid; she is every bit as judgmental as her fellow addicts. She will not openly condemn drinking or smoking, but she will comment archly that she prefers not to associate with people who engage in those activities. She is apt to be very visible in the Right-to-Life movement, more likely in the administrative part than actually out on the front lines.

She will give her daughters rudimentary information about sex, always couched in terms of the sanctity of waiting for marriage. She may send her sons to their father for sexual education. She, too, may sexually abuse her sons, often by emotional incest—constantly talking to them about sex and how it feels to a young woman to have what she may call "those pressures" applied by boys. Or, she may rely on them emotionally to fill the emotional void not filled by her spouse. With her daughters, she will not address the issue of birth control, relying instead on their fear of losing her approval as a means of keeping them sexually inactive. Because women in this type of family rule by implied threat of disapproval, rejection, and abandonment, her children live in terror of letting her down.

This kind of family is horribly enmeshed. They work together, play together, and worship together, which makes it look to the outside world like they are a close, loving family. They are close. Too close. In this family, it's hard to tell where one person stops and another begins. The children are required to reflect their parents' values as a sign of their love. It's almost as if they exist to prove their parents are good in the sight of God.

In reality, love in this family is measured with money and material possessions, and no one in it even remotely knows how to express love by sharing feelings. So they are generally lacking in true Christian compassion. If love equals money, then the way to show they love God is to give Him money. God's love for them is reflected in their material success.

Although country-club Christians make a great show of contributing to Christian charities, they often have little sense of true Christian charity: that Christlike compassion for all people regardless of circumstances. Deep inside, they view those less financially fortunate as somehow not worthy in the sight of God. The blue-collar family might treat those they perceive as unsaved with outright contempt; country-club Christians merely detach. Those who do not share their financial status and religious denomination merely have no place in their lives.

Like the Davis family, the McBride family described here is a composite of several people, all of whom have attitudes and behaviors that typify the country-club Christian family.

DOUG AND KAREN MCBRIDE'S STORY

As a child, Doug McBride was regarded by his teachers as an endearing troublemaker—one who could get away with almost any infraction or outrageous behavior because he was so polite and well-mannered. His role models as a child were Robin Hood and the sophisticated gentlemen thieves sometimes portrayed by Cary Grant in the movies. His father, Bill, was a low-level diplomat whose travels hid a double life as an adulterer and embezzler. From Bill, Doug learned the art of legal stealing and of living two very different lives. Doug's mother, Amelia, turned a blind eye to Bill's adultery and financial misdeeds, adopting his government service as a cover for the frequent moves they made in order to escape being caught padding his expense accounts. Amelia's mental and emotional energies were spent protecting her three children from knowledge of their father's secrets. The children, emotionally abandoned by both parents, became extremely enmeshed and emotionally incestuous. Doug knew his sister was sexually abused by his father but did not know that his mother had sexually abused him prior to his younger sister's birth. Early on, Doug learned how to manipulate, minimize, or deny his own behavior so that he never had to be morally responsible for it, always skating on the edge of breaking rules outright.

Doug planned to be an architect, a career that would afford him the prestige and style he had longed for as a child. His father's relatively low status and frequent moves kept the family out of the social and financial class to which Doug had yearned to belong. Openly contemptuous of his father once he learned the truth, Doug secretly plotted to do it better—show him up at his own game. Always overweight as a child, he had never been athletic and grew up amid taunts and jeers about being a wimp and a queer. Indeed, Doug began having secret homosexual affairs and attachments as early as grade school. While in his mid-twenties, Doug met his mentor, Mike, who would have a profound influence on him. Mike, an entrepreneur, was an architect with a reputation for landing all the city's building and design contracts. He adopted Doug as his protégé, bringing Doug into his circle of business contacts and introducing him to the world of high-level wheeling and dealing. Mike was also a religious addict and made it clear that Doug's acceptance into his world must include embracing his religion. Being both ambitious and a people pleaser, Doug went along with Mike's requirements.

At last, he found what he'd been looking for. Mike's fellow church members were businessmen, upper management, and corporate presidents whose prayer breakfasts served double duty as business networking. It was like one big, happy family—a rich, powerful big happy family. Image was paramount: People would trust you if you were clean-cut, Christian, and a family man. The church became a focus for Doug's con games and a cover for his homosexual drives. He could associate with the men of the church and continue hero-worshiping to fill his emotional needs for male bonding. His visibility in the church made it unlikely that anyone would suspect that he occasionally hired male prostitutes.

He met Karen shortly after his thirtieth birthday. Mike had quietly mentioned that it was time Doug exchanged his eligible bachelor standing for family-man status. Doug set about shopping for a wife who would be an appropriate appendage. Karen was the granddaughter of a Methodist minister; she had grown up in a comfortable middle-class home that reflected the strict values with which her mother, Sarah, had been raised: no smoking; wine or champagne only on very special occasions; no sex before marriage; and active church membership as an integral part of a good, Christian life. Karen had a degree in business administration and was managing a small insurance office when she met Doug. Outwardly sociable and pleasant, Karen was inwardly rigid, perfectionistic, and critical. Although she made no secret of her church involvement, she never openly proselytized to her co-workers. Instead, she invited those who appeared interested to come to church with her. While her fellow workers appreciated her not preaching to them, they often noticed a judgmentalness and condemning attitude about her that made them uncomfortable. Some privately called her two-faced. Others observed that she had a tendency to give more business referrals to those in the office who were also Christian, and that she often wrote more extensive policies at lower rates for clients who were Christian, especially her church members. Like Doug, she was waiting for the potential mate who would provide the proper image for her as an upstanding, successful Christian.

They dated a year before marrying, both making sure the other passed muster with their families and friends. Karen joined Doug's church and began to take classes to learn more about his business so that she could retain a career yet be as supportive as a model wife should be. Doug lavished gifts and clothes on her, ingratiating himself to her family with his attentiveness. He gave her brother a job in his office and used his influence to help Sarah buy a new condo. At church, they became known as the dynamic duo, always available to help out with high-level fund-raising and entertaining. Doug quickly became known as the man to see if someone needed help getting a loan or a job. To him, this was simply showing Christian caring and charity; he was unaware that he was addicted to the sense of power and self-esteem he gained from being so helpful.

Both of them battled weight. Doug dieted incessantly; unknown to him, Karen became bulimic following the birth of their second child. By the time their fourth child was born, she was secretly addicted to prescription drugs. Meanwhile, the marriage and their careers faced difficult times. When their preacher's right-hand assistant broke away from their church to form his own congregation, they went along. Doug arranged for the new church to be built on a lavish scale and invested heavily in the property, which he then leased to the church. Always one to find and use any legal loopholes, Doug began to use less scrupulous methods so that his reputation as the church's benefactor remained intact. He had become hooked on the glory heaped on him—the praise and admiration. His hero was now Stan Collins, the new preacher who was on his way to become one of the next generation of popular televangelists. Their role model was televangelist Robert Schuller, whose emphasis on positive business salesmanship and Christian family values makes him attractive to the upper-middle-class, country-club Christians. Stan wanted to rival Schuller; Doug wanted to become known as the architect of the next Crystal Cathedral. They thought they made a good partnership; yet each was secretly planning to oust the other as soon as their fortunes were made.

Karen sat passively by, watching her husband become more and more a user, enduring his increasing criticisms and put-downs. As his business deals began to unravel, he grew more irritable and controlling. Nothing she did pleased him. He had encouraged her to get involved in the PTA and had seemed proud of her presidency of the Church Women's Guild. Now he complained endlessly about her involvement in these activities—she was gone too much. Secretly jealous of her popularity, he accused her of having affairs, of neglecting the children and him. Stan and the church didn't appreciate him; maybe things would be better if they changed churches. He began to look around for another church—one that would appreciate his service. When he found one, a great rift in the family occurred: Karen's brother liked Stan's church and didn't want to go to the new one. The children resented having to give up their friends in the former church and buried their anger at having their feelings ignored.

Karen and the children never got as involved in the new church, which caused Doug to double his efforts at building his power base in the church. Desperate to win praise, Doug volunteered to help build a new sanctuary. His habit of cutting corners turned into outright illegalities; building inspectors slapped him with fines, which eventually cost him his license. The church was never finished. Ashamed, Doug moved the family to a new state to start a new career. The family attends a local Presbyterian church but with minimal involvement. They think that changing churches shows that their religious days are behind them, yet all of them bear the scars.

In the McBride family, we see the effects that feeling inadequate and trying to cure that inadequacy with religion can have. Country-club Christians in some ways exemplify what Erich Fromm says about religion being used to salve the consciences of those who are abusive of their power. To a certain extent, country-club Christians represent all that the blue-collar addicts want to attain and can't. Blue-collar addicts try to gain a sense of power from bigotry, prejudice, and anger. Country-club Christians gain their sense of power from their use of money and the ability to hide their abuses behind a religious cloak. In both types of families, this dysfunctional use of religion fails to bring the sense of self-esteem and closeness to God they seek. Instead, it leads to ever-increasing pain.

Of course, not all religiously addicted families fall strictly into these categories. The patterns and characteristics I described, however, are representative of behaviors and attitudes found in most, if not all, religiously addicted families. Like many survivors of physical or emotional abuse (including sexual abuse), children of religious addicts often grow up to be perpetrators themselves—religious abusers.

WOMEN AND RELIGIOUS ADDICTION

Both men and women suffer from religious addiction and abuse. In most cultures, however, women are particularly vulnerable to these behaviors because of the secondary roles into which they are cast. For women with a Christian background, religion has given a definite message concerning their conduct:

> . . . *women should adorn themselves modestly and sensibly in seemly apparel, not with braided hair or gold or pearls or costly attire but by good deeds, as befits women who profess religion. Let a woman learn in silence with all submissiveness. I permit no woman to teach or have authority over men; she is to keep silent. For Adam was formed first, then Eve; and Adam was not deceived, but the woman was deceived and became a transgressor. Yet women will be saved through bearing children, if she continues in faith and love and holiness, with modesty.*
>
> *(1 Timothy 2:9–15)*

> *Wives, be subject to your husbands, as to the Lord. For the husband is the head of the wife as Christ is the head of the church, his body, and is himself its Saviour. As the church is subject to Christ, so let wives also be subject in everything to their husbands.*
>
> *(Ephesians 5:22–25)*

These verses have been the basis for the religious sexual abuse of the female population. They help make women susceptible to becoming both addicted and abused. When religion is used as an external means of identity, of finding self-respect, these verses can become the standard against which women measure themselves. The woman who has been abused, who is seeking to purify herself or attain perfection, has only to adhere to this code to assure herself of salvation. This is how women use religion as a fantasy means to compensate for their secondary status—by becoming exemplary models of that role.

At the same time, these texts set up a rebelliousness, an internal conflict that causes some female religious addicts to become abusive and sexually conflicted. The most telling example of this is Anita Bryant. Ken Kelley, touring with Bryant to interview her for *Playboy* magazine at the time of her anti-gay crusade, wrote a fascinating exposé of the stormy relationship between Bryant and her manager-husband, Bob Green. Kelley describes Green as "the moving target for the slings and arrows of Anita's abuse," which he bears stoically knowing that Anita will eventually realize that "the Lord is pissed at her for being pissed at [Green]."

> *For, as Anita knows, her greatest sin against the Lord is her innate reluctance to "submit" to her man, as the Lord says a good wife must. Furthermore, Satan's shadow is always lurking about and his black angels continually egg her on to kick Bob's ass when Bob does something dumb. But the Lord's forces—and those she must please, if she is to sip from the divine chalice in the hereafter—command her to be meek, humble and, above all, submissive. She is to obey Bob, no matter what he tells her to do. The Bible tells her so.*

Kelley seems surprised by Bryant's conflicting personalities, describing her as both "independent spirit and cowering wife . . . a demonstrably intelligent woman who stays steadfastly ignorant. . . ." Yet his description illustrates many of the conflicts women suffer as a result of the contradictory messages given by religion. Feeling caught between natural desire and conflicting messages about what to do with those feelings, religiously addicted and abused women often lash out at their spouses, children, neighbors, or at a social issue, such as abortion or homosexuality on which they can vent their rage.

Just as often, the same verses that might offer comfort to women are used to justify sexual abusiveness. The idea of women as examples of submissive purity and sanctity sets up powerful conflicts in men, which have contributed to sexual double standards and abuse. Even today, the myth persists that there are sexual acts that men should not perform with wives, but rather with mistresses. Another myth holds that women should remain sexually inexperienced, but that men should know what they're doing. Hence, many men were actually sent or taken to brothels—often by their fathers—for their first sexual experiences. The conflicts produced by such mixed messages no doubt add to the rage and sense of guilt felt by many religious addicts. One brutalized religious codependent wife told me:

> *I truly believe that my husband was attracted to this extreme fundamentalist church because of what it said about women and the place of women in the home. I was constantly told I was inferior or secondary. I was to obey him. Physical abuse was excused by scriptural texts. And for years I believed I was a bad person!*

Whether a woman is the addict or the codependent, dysfunctional use of religion keeps her victimized and limited, keeps her from using her full creative potential. The scriptural role of women as caretakers entrenches—even sometimes actually creates—codependency and makes it much harder for women to break free of religious abuse. For this reason, I may refer more to wives than to husbands in our discussion of religious codependency. This in no way should discount or mitigate the suffering of men who are religious codependents. Religious abuse is devastating, no matter what your class, race, or gender.

RELIGIOUS CODEPENDENCY

Why can't he just do his own thing and leave us out of it?

Joanne, age thirty-eight

As we have seen, religious addicts always involve their families in the addiction. Even when their families are not required to participate, which is rare, the addictive behaviors affect the family. All addictions signal a dysfunctional relationship with oneself; when our relationship with ourselves is unhealthy, we cannot have healthy relationships with anyone else: spouse, children, friends, co-workers. We most particularly cannot have a healthy relationship with God.

In our descriptions of religiously addicted families, we have seen certain common denominators: rage, judgmentalness, rigidity, perfectionism, sexual dysfunction, control, manipulation, and at the core of it all, a pervasive sense of inadequacy and lack of self-worth. In the context of religious beliefs that are supposed to create a happy, loving family, these behaviors produce double messages, which create extreme conflicts in spouses and children. As addicts sink deeper into guilt and shame while the disease progresses, as they go farther into addiction, they intensify their behaviors in the struggle to make it work. This, of course, only makes life worse for their families.

Thus, wishing a religious addict would just do his own thing is rather like throwing a stone into a pond and expecting it not to make ripples. In this expectation lie the seeds of the family's dysfunction. Family members keep asking the stone not to make ripples. They frantically go about trying to slip the stone into the water without disturbing the pond's surface. Those frantic behaviors are the family's disease—the co-addiction that is now commonly referred to as codependency.

Codependency is its own disease. When spouses, family members, and friends become so entangled in and focused on someone else's behavior and attitude that they lose themselves, they are suffering from codependency. It explains how children from dysfunctional families carry their childhood experiences into adulthood and repeat the dysfunctional patterns. There are several ways to define codependency.

Robert Subby, in his book *Co-dependency: An Emerging Issue,* describes co-dependency as

> *an emotional, psychological, and behavioral condition that develops as a result of an individual's prolonged exposure to, and practice of, a set of oppressive rules—rules which prevent the open expression of feeling as well as the direct discussion of personal and interpersonal problems.*

In *Wives of Alcoholics: From Co-Dependency to Recovery,* Marie Schutt says that codependency is a "protective stance adopted by the spouse that keeps the husband from facing the consequences of his drinking."

Religious addicts live by many dogmatic rules; this is how they try to control the uncontrollable. Unfortunately, their families get trapped in the restrictive rules and beliefs. Religious codependency is the result of trying to coexist with these rules. In doing so, spouses and families allow, even enable, addicts to avoid responsibility for their behavior—and at the same time, avoid taking responsibility for their own codependent behavior.

Religious addicts manipulate with guilt. Who dares to argue with the Bible? Who dares not side with God? How can anyone object to a godly life-style? How can wanting your family to reap the rewards of heaven be abusive?

When there is no balance, when religious addicts give their families no choice, when there is no room for differing opinions and beliefs, it becomes abuse. When they restrict their families' lives, continually trying to force them into a belief system under threat of rejection, punishment, or abandonment, it becomes abuse.

As addicts move deeper into speaking for God, almost as if they are God, religious codependents also lose sight of the difference. When God is used as a weapon, people often see God as the abuser, rather than the addict. Religious codependents cannot recognize the distinction. This is how so many religiously abused people end up hating and fearing God. They cannot see that the addict's dysfunctional beliefs are causing the abusive behavior, so caught up are they in trying to cope with the behavior.

In religious codependency, the family members either take on the belief system that the addicts bring into the home or resign themselves to putting up with it, living in martyred victimhood. They may also rebel.

When the family members take on the addict's belief system, they rarely do so out of their own inner convictions. Children who are raised in this kind of religious environment seldom have an opportunity to question those beliefs, especially if they are raised in a home in which doubting and questioning are punishable sins. Because of religious teachings about women being submissive to men, wives usually follow their husband's lead. Either they are not aware of their own needs and beliefs, or they set them aside to follow those of the addict. They become as judgmental, dogmatic, rigid, intolerant, and perfectionistic as their addicted spouse or parents.

As a result, they have their own struggles with issues of control, guilt, shame, inadequacy, and fear. Religious codependents are extremely out of touch with their emotions; they have been conditioned not to think for themselves. They live very narrow, restrictive lives, avoiding people who do not meet their strict standards.

The families who resign themselves to living with religious addicts are walking pressure-cookers ready to explode. Resentment, fear, rage, and anxiety seethe beneath the surface, because putting up with the status quo set by the addict entails not rocking the boat. They may attend the same church, swallowing feelings of hypocrisy and anger. Some try to adopt an approach that says do what you want, but leave me out of it—coexisting in stoic martyrdom.

Spouses and children may suffer from addictions, such as alcoholism and eating disorders. In these codependents we are likely to see an array of physical ailments associated with stress: asthma, chronic headaches, backaches, hypertension, insomnia, and chronic fatigue.

In resigning themselves to the addict's behavior, they become victims, feeling helpless, powerless, confused, and frustrated. They may alter between arguing with the religious addict or tuning out by avoiding or ignoring the addict's behavior. The passive-aggressiveness that comes with being a victim may manifest itself in the form of extramarital affairs, hiding or hoarding money so the addict can't tithe it away, or belittling the religious addict to family and friends.

The families who rebel often have the hardest time. Spouses frequently find themselves pitted against a powerfully united church front. The dissenting spouse is portrayed as sinful and ungodly. Worse, when children are involved, they are often caught in a good parent/evil parent situation, creating great guilt and confusion.

A friend of mine knew a family in which the father, in an effort to find his identity, embraced his Jewish heritage by deciding to adhere to

Kosher dietary restrictions. His wife was a nonpracticing Christian who initially had no problems with his finding his roots in this way. However, he was very inconsistent about it; friends who invited him to dinner never knew whether or not to serve him special foods. The worst effect was on his son, who was in constant conflict over what he was allowed to eat, what religious holidays were acceptable, and whether he was Jewish, Christian, or neither. The child went from being very outgoing to being withdrawn and anxious; my friend recalled seeing him stare at a plate of food in terror, fearful of whether it was safe to eat. The little boy became very overweight, since the only safe foods on either side were candy and desserts.

Besides overeating, other forms of rebellion include alcoholism, drug addiction, sexual acting out, and compulsive spending. Sometimes family members may change religious denominations or faiths. Others reject organized religion in favor of independent spiritual or metaphysical groups.

The worst effect is that many religious codependents rebel by abandoning God altogether. They have been so abused in God's name that, after a while, they have no use for God at all. Often they refuse to give their children any kind of religious exposure or training. I have a friend who feels extremely inadequate and ashamed because she knows nothing about the Bible or religion at all; her father was so turned off by his religiously abusive parents that he refused to allow his wife and children to go to church.

These religious codependents are spiritually adrift, angry, bitter, searching for something to give their lives meaning. They frequently have difficulty grasping the spiritual part of Twelve Step programs, for often the God of their understanding is vicious, judgmental, and unloving. It is hard for them to imagine turning their will and lives over to the care of such a God. These are the people who cry, "Father Leo, I want to love God, but I hate God!"

THE RELIGIOUS CODEPENDENT SPOUSE

Dysfunction begets dysfunction. The addict's behavior triggers certain behaviors in the spouse. The collective parental dysfunction creates greater dysfunction in the children, which in turn triggers more unhealthy reactions from the parents in a never-ending cycle.

Stories like those of David, Helen Davis, and Karen McBride are common among religious codependents. They illustrate the loss of self and spiritual degradation experienced by many spouses of religious addicts—the walking on eggshells described by Marie Schutt in *Wives of Alcoholics*. Schutt notes the desperate attempts wives of alcoholics make to force their spouses to stop drinking, believing that if they just make life perfect enough—with the children well-behaved and academically successful—the drinking will stop. Since neither she nor her children have caused the drinking, however, all her struggles for perfection fail, and she ends up frustrated and angry, perpetually compliant to avoid creating more conflict.

In the stories of the Davis and McBride families, we can see how some of the rules of caretaking described by Marie Schutt apply to religious codependents:

Peace at any price.

Maintain the conspiracy of silence.

Never quit.

Never discuss feelings.

Try to appear normal.

Peace at any price. Your spouse is angry, irritable, judgmental, and shaming. Scriptural dogma rules your home. Any infraction of the rules by you and the children is likely to produce an outpouring of prayer sessions, scripture quoting, and possibly physical abuse. Perhaps, like Helen Davis, you see yourself as the only buffer between your spouse and your children.

So you give in. You set aside your own religious beliefs and preferences and give up hobbies and interests that conflict with the dogmatic rules. You allow your clothing, appearance, and behavior to be dictated by your spouse. You constantly nag the children not to break the rules. Both Helen Davis and Karen McBride did this with their children, leaving the children even more confused and angry.

All your energy is focused on keeping your spouse appeased, which includes telling family and friends how to behave. So you become controlling and manipulative. Helen Davis spent a great deal of time explaining to her children, in-laws, and friends exactly how they should behave in order to keep Jim from losing his temper.

Peace at any price is sometimes rooted in basic codependency. It never occurred to Karen McBride to ask Doug to attend her church. Later, when he wanted to change churches, though the rest of the family members were happy where they were, she did not dare resist.

But the price is loss of awareness of your own feelings. You lose yourself, grow isolated and alienated as gradually you are consumed by your spouse's religious life-style. The whole quality of your life is measured on someone else's very unhealthy terms. You cease to exist. You crumble under the sustained abuse of the religious addict. You no longer have the resources to challenge the black-and-white thinking and perpetual scriptural judgments or to reject the constant criticism. Your increasing isolation denies you access to intelligent criticism or affirming support. The only way to survive is simply to shut down and try not to rock the boat: peace at any price.

Maintain the conspiracy of silence. The religiously addicted family suffers in the lie of silence. Because the concept of religious addiction and abuse is still so new, spouses and family members fear they will not be believed, as indeed they often are not, when they try to describe what living with their spouse is like. When David first called my office, he was astounded that my staff immediately understood his situation, because he was so accustomed to being put down for talking about his wife's addiction. He had his pastor call me so that I could explain the disease of religious addiction to him.

To some, it still seems crazy to call an excessively religious person an addict, and so you remain silent, afraid to speak. You put up a stoic front pretending nothing's wrong, which covers your fears about the finances, the deteriorating relationships between your spouse and children, and the progressively distorted thinking.

Most often, the silence covers abuse: physical, sexual, emotional:

I think my mother knew my father sexually abused me. I was fourteen years old, and he was still watching me shower and bathe—insisting that he dry me with the towel. That is not normal! Always the touching. Always the caressing. And nothing said. Everything done in silence. Yet my father always read the Bible aloud, and always made sure everyone knew we went to church each Sunday. I think he had to shout about his religion so loudly so it would cover up what he did in silence.

Barbara, age twenty-six

If I did not go to Mass I could not eat that day. The family sat around the table and I was alone in the corner. If I missed confession, I could not eat with the family. Nobody spoke to me. Nobody was allowed to comfort me. All this was done in the name of God! It was the silence that hurt; it is the silence that I remember.

Paul, age twenty-eight

In order to cope, you minimize or even deny the truth of what goes on, trying to cure your unease with magical thinking. Helen Davis rationalized the behavior of both her father and her husband; Karen McBride knew her husband was illegally cutting corners yet tried to tell herself it was for a worthy cause, and thus excusable. You are mired in shame, confused and fearful that no one will understand how such an apparently fine Christian could be so very sick.

Never quit. Magical thinking is contagious. Usually codependents contract this symptom in the form of denial. Your spouse's behavior and beliefs aren't wrong—*you* are. You just haven't been good enough, prayed enough, raised the children properly enough. When the whole family outlook is focused on a universal fixer who is going to make everything better, you start believing it. If the fixer doesn't make it better, it's because you did something wrong. So you frantically try to do it right.

Sometimes you lose the distinction between God and your spouse's addictive behavior. You blame God for your family's misery. Believing that God has caused your pain, you pray that God will do something to relieve it. Addiction is partly an avoidance of responsibility, and codependents assist that avoidance by blaming themselves or God for the unhappiness.

Resigned to your victim role, you believe you have no choice but to keep shouldering that cross and going on. You wait for God to work a miracle; you wait to get good enough for God to fix your life. You cannot see that in never quitting, you have given up. To never quit can be the same as suicide.

Never discuss feelings. The judgmentalness, black-and-white thinking, conflicts with science and medicine, and never-quit attitude conspire to keep religious codependents from ever knowing, much less expressing, their feelings. If you are to keep the peace, remain silent, and never quit then it is not safe to let your feelings show. Your fear of your spouse's anger and judgmentalness, of what will happen to the children, of what the neighbors will think is too great. Helen Davis expressed her feelings about what was happening to everyone but Jim. Karen McBride swallowed her feelings and then literally vomited them up with her bulimia.

Like other codependents, religiously abused spouses must bury their feelings—minimize and dismiss as irrelevant problems that their religion cannot solve. The fantasy of religious addiction is that they are supposed to be happy in the Lord, or happy, joyous, and free in Twelve Step recovery. To admit otherwise seems to be admitting to failure—to not being good enough. Feelings are considered a sign of weakness, especially feelings of abuse.

Religious addiction is a disease of contradictory messages: God is love but also wrathful and judging; sex is dirty but sanctified in marriage; love your neighbors but destroy the ungodly. The effort to reconcile and rationalize these contradictory messages creates conflicting feelings that are frequently numbed with alcohol, prescription drugs, cigarettes, food, or sex.

Try to appear normal. This is the ultimate goal of religious codependents, for the family of God should not have problems. Indeed, it is the stress and strain of trying to appear perfectly normal that produces the need for the other symptoms of codependency: keeping peace at any price, maintaining silence, never quitting, and never discussing feelings.

The religious fantasy is that all family members love one another and are always happy. The children get good grades. The house is clean all the time. No one has any hazardous health habits (that is, drinking, smoking, or staying out late); the wife is nurturing and affectionate; the husband takes care and takes charge; the children's friends come from so-called good families. Alcoholism and drug addiction and physical, sexual, or emotional abuse are unthinkable in such a family. This is why silence is so paramount: You mustn't let anyone know things are not normal.

As we have seen in our two family profiles, the reality is often quite the opposite. Yet for the religiously addicted family, any failure, imperfection, or scandal is seen as a disgrace to God, the church, the ministry, or the preacher. The taboos against expression of feelings and the urgent need to look normal make the religiously enmeshed family a breeding ground for the secret addictions: anorexia, bulimia, sexual addiction, compulsive spending, gambling, workaholism. With these come the need for silence, never giving up, never discussing feelings, and above all, peace at any price.

Chapter 5

Suffer the Children:
The Consequences of Religious Addiction and Abuse

RELIGIOUS ABUSE IS a hidden disease; it is often difficult to see from the outside. When you grow up in an alcoholic home, or one in which the abuse is obvious, like physical abuse, it is much easier to pinpoint the source of your own dysfunctions: Mom's drinking or Dad's rages created the chaos that bred your problems.

In contrast, people who grew up in homes that appeared to be stable and in which material comforts hid emotional neglect have great difficulty identifying their families as dysfunctional, much less abusive. They frequently reach adulthood with a deeply entrenched belief that something is wrong with them, rather than with their family. When you grow up believing that God has judged you and found you rotten to the core, the damage is even more profoundly devastating.

The patterns of religious addicts and their codependents create a blueprint of dysfunction for the children growing up in such a home. Claudia Black, one of the pioneers of the Adult Children of Alcoholics movement, coined the slogan "don't talk, don't trust, don't feel" as the credo by which children of dysfunction are raised. For children of religious addicts, the rule is similar: Don't think, don't doubt, don't question.

As with other children of dysfunctional homes, children of religious addicts take on one or more roles within the family. In her book *Another Chance,* Sharon Wegscheider-Cruse defined these roles as the Hero, Scapegoat, Lost Child, and Family Mascot.

The Hero is the one who takes charge and keeps things going in the midst of chaos. Often appearing to be personally and professionally together—successful and stable—family Heroes inwardly suffer from low self-esteem and constant self-doubt.

The Scapegoat feels rejected and unloved by the family and bottles up those feelings until they explode in some kind of misbehavior. What is initially merely mischievous attention seeking slowly grows into deeply rooted self-hate, which becomes evident as increasingly antisocial behavior.

The Lost Child also feels rejected and has no self-esteem, but the low self-worth comes from years of feeling ignored and unseen. While Scapegoats angrily rebel against being rejected, Lost Children accept rejection, believing they deserve to be excluded and ignored.

Like the Hero, the Mascot seeks positive attention but by entertaining rather than achieving. Mascots help the family forget its woes. In doing so, they get control of the family, gain attention, and temporarily distract focus from the addict and the deeper family troubles.

Children of religious addicts manifest these roles differently in blue-collar and country-club Christian families.

BLUE-COLLAR CHILDREN

The heroes. Joyce Davis Bolles is often described as a bull in a china shop. She doesn't live her life, she explodes into it, commanding attention by her take-charge attitudes and behaviors. The eldest daughter of Jim and Helen Davis, who were described earlier in the fictional profiles, she is extremely obese, dangerously codependent, rigid, perfectionistic, enmeshed both with her family of origin and with her husband and daughter. Her husband, Mike, works for Jim in the plumbing business. Although he claims to be supportive of Joyce's catering company, he is secretly jealous and fearful that she is more successful than he is. Joyce lives entirely through him; her only means of relating to others is by gauging how Mike would respond, especially to other women.

When she is not trying to live through Mike, she is forever struggling to live by the rules. Entering a new group or organization, Joyce jumps right in, eager to be accepted, to do it right, always wanting to rescue or fix. Her role as family hero has conditioned her to always have the right solution to any problem; for her, the answer comes in learning the rules. She is regarded as opinionated and insensitive; it never occurs to her when she automatically quotes scripture or offers Bible readings that others might not have the same beliefs. Her hurt response to rejection or criticism is that she was only trying to help. Just tell me what the rules are, she says, so I can do it right.

Joyce is typical of many blue-collar heroes. She is the one to whom the family looks to keep everyone in line. Earlier, we saw how the inability to doubt or question causes many religious addicts to place people on pedestals. Joyce has placed her husband on a pedestal; her religious training taught her that she must be secondary to him. Yet the reality is that she is brighter and has better business acumen. She covers this up by worshiping him. She never talks about her own feelings; she views everything in terms of Mike or the church.

Heroes in both kinds of religiously addicted families—blue-collar and country-club—manifest this trait of hero worship by finding someone to place on a pedestal and at the same time wanting to be admired and revered. Blue-collar heroes will often pursue a white-collar profession. The men may enter either the ministry or the military as a means for gaining the necessary education and training. Women generally work their way through the ranks either as teachers, secretaries, or in the retail business. These heroes are always looking for role models—someone to emulate who can show them the way to succeed.

However, their role models tend to be those who also have narrow, rigid beliefs—especially the preachers. Those who escape into the ministry tend to pattern themselves after the preachers they knew when they were growing up. One former preacher wrote to me that his first heroes were preachers. High up in their pulpits, he said, they seemed far removed from life's troubles. His whole childhood was spent being formed in their image.

Like Joyce, the female blue-collar hero may put herself through school (after her husband), and she often surpasses him in education, training, and earning power. Like Joyce, her religious upbringing causes her always to place herself second. At the first sign of family trouble, she gives up her job to take care of children or an ailing parent. She expends her creative energy on volunteer work, usually at church. She's the one everybody counts on to get things done in a pinch. She stays almost frantically busy to avoid letting herself know how dissatisfied she is with her life.

No matter what their gender or profession, blue-collar heroes take with them the rigid, black-and-white thinking and dogmatism of their family of origin. These superachievers are often the scrupulous by-the-book types who adhere strictly to guidelines and rules; they are unable to bend. They stay obsessed with doing it right, whether it's work, religion, or a Twelve Step program, and they beat themselves up emotionally when they think they've failed.

They mask their painful feelings behind workaholism and perfectionism. Their tendency to put people on pedestals causes them to place unrealistically high expectations on themselves and others; they thus become rigid, critical, and intolerant of themselves and those around them. They are stern and impatient with their children, given to verbal abuse or neglect. They think that because they do not beat their wives and children and do not force church on their families, they have risen above their parents and thereby broken the cycle.

The scapegoats. One of the most painful aspects of being a scapegoat is that, from birth, you always feel unjustly accused of having done something wrong. Although he never consciously thought it, Jim Davis always blamed his son, George, for the drunken automobile accident. In addictive fashion, Jim's subconscious reasoning was that George's conception caused him to have to work extra jobs, which caused him to be in the fight, which caused him to get drunk and have a wreck. George was always the visible reminder of Jim's humiliation and thus could never do anything right in his father's eyes.

George bore the brunt of his father's rage; he was beaten and verbally abused far more than the other children. Jim's methods were puritanically harsh: The children were often made to sit or kneel in submissive positions, sometimes for long hours at a stretch, quoting every Bible verse they could think of that remotely pertained to whatever infraction Jim thought they committed. Although less than two years older, Joyce often tried to protect George and comfort him, yet she was angry that he always seemed to make Daddy mad so that the rest of them suffered. Fearing Jim's reprisals, even Helen was harder on George; where she would take the other children aside and try to explain what they did to make Daddy angry, with George all she could manage was exasperation, saying things like, "Why do you do that when you know it makes Daddy mad?"

Like other scapegoats, George grew up feeling worthless, inadequate, and doomed to failure before he even tried. He learned early that the family's expectation of him was that he would always get into trouble no matter how hard he tried not to, so he quickly gave up and began to fulfill his role as family troublemaker. The sad thing about scapegoats is that their siblings and playmates quickly learn who to blame for their own misconduct. George Davis could count on everyone pointing to him when squabbles arose: The magic escape from Dad's punishing hand was simply to say, It's George's fault.

Thus, in any conflict, scapegoats are never believed. A woman wrote telling me that she had been molested by her Sunday school teacher for many months. When she finally sought help from her minister, she found to her horror that, though only fourteen, *she* was the one accused of being the seducer and was ostracized from the church. Later, she married a religious addict who beat her in her children's presence. As a family scapegoat, she was accustomed to being blamed for everything and thus believed that even these abuses somehow were her fault.

Blue-collar scapegoats don't want to believe they are as worthless as they are told, and they are angry about it. Frequently, they rebel by using drugs or alcohol, especially in very fundamentalist families; many fail in school or drop out. In blue-collar families, it is often the scapegoats who totally turn away from religion and God, or see God as a monster that is out to get them.

In *The Road Less Traveled,* M. Scott Peck describes the case of Stewart, who, though he professed to be an atheist, held a deep-seated view of a vicious, cutthroat God and a dog-eat-dog world. Stewart's father was a rigid fundamentalist preacher; his mother was just as dogmatic and rigid. As Dr. Peck explored Stewart's life, gradually an explanation of Stewart's negative worldview took shape: His parents preached about a God of love, professing that Jesus is love incessantly, yet they beat him with brooms, sticks, and belts. Their philosophy was that a beating a day made a good Christian of him, he said. He grew up believing the world was a vicious place and that he needed to be able to hold his own in it. Thus he became a user—self-serving and critical.

Feeling unjustly accused, scapegoats adopt the attitude that somebody's out to get them. Thus they are never able to take responsibility for their own actions. Blue-collar scapegoats, in particular, are most vulnerable to extreme fundamentalism or right-wing support groups; perhaps they may even join such extremist groups as the Ku Klux Klan. Their long-standing rage at their victimization boils over, and they take it out on those whom they are told are inferior, or who pose some alleged threat. They balance their sense of feeling wrong or shameful by doing something that makes them feel "right." To spite his Pentecostal family, George Davis became a Jehovah's Witness. This gives him a sense of superiority and control, for he knows he's always a topic of conversation at family gatherings as a result of his defection.

Scapegoats often try to cure themselves with religion. Like Jim Davis, they are likely to have conversion experiences in order to arrest chemical dependency. They seem to get saved and quit drinking, but the rest of the problem is still there: the inner rage and victimization. They are also most vulnerable to sexual addiction and gambling or to any secret vice with which they constantly test their worthiness/unworthiness in God's eyes.

The lost children. Although everyone was aware of George Davis's anger and pain, no one had a clue that his brother Tom was suffering his own private agony. So Tom's suicide at age twenty-five left the family stunned. Only Joyce knew that Tom had been an alcoholic for years. However, not even she knew that Tom was gay. He lived his role as lost child so well that most of the family did not even know that he drank at all. So invisible was he that when he openly grieved the death of his so-called best friend from pneumonia, they had no idea that the man was his lover or that the cause of his death was AIDS.

Having seen too late how abusive Jim was to George, Helen Davis determined that her second son would not suffer the same fate. From the cradle on, she imparted to him that the best way to avoid Jim's rage was to be quiet and to stay out of the way.

Tom was the most deeply affected by Helen's inconsistency. Being quiet and undemanding kept him safe from his father's religious wrath, but it also deprived him of Helen's attention. Because he was the least trouble to care for, the least childlike, Helen often poured her troubles out to him as her father had to her. Although she was never physically sexual with him, her emotional dependence on him was incestuous; increasingly, he became her nurturer. As a boy, Tom yearned for a loving, kind father who would be sensitive and gentle. He began having crushes on male teachers while still in grade school.

Jim's attitude toward homosexuals was loudly, intolerantly clear: They did not deserve to live. Tom struggled and struggled with his own sexual identity for years. In junior high school, he dreamed briefly of becoming a monk or a priest; then he thought about becoming a preacher. But the loud, angry preaching he heard on Sundays repulsed him; he did not want to be like that.

He went through a brief phase in college of being extremely religious, trying somehow to exorcise the demon he believed lived in him. By this time, he had had several homosexual experiences; he knew this was his sexual preference. He began drinking to numb his guilt and fear. To escape his father's pious wrath, he moved to another town, ostensibly to take a new job. The family was so focused on coping in the midst of its chronic chaos, they barely missed him. Although he continued having gay relationships, he did so with great shame and fear.

Despite the care and support he lavished on his dying lover, he secretly believed AIDS was God's punishment for homosexuality. When he himself was diagnosed with the disease, he knew he would not be able to keep his secret for long. Believing himself already doomed to hell because of his sexuality, he chose to take his own life rather than endure his father's wrath. He had grown up watching George being whipped, abused, and humiliated. Although an adult, Tom believed his father had the power to create the same kind of hellish punishment for him: Banished and ostracized, he would die a long, slow death alone, friendless, forsaken by family, friends, and, above all, by God.

Amid the angry chaos that is the dominant characteristic in most blue-collar religiously addicted homes, the lost children are just that—lost in the chaos. Their overwhelming motivation is a need for quiet safety—whatever it takes to not rock the boat. These children learn early to sacrifice themselves in order to stay safe.

Like Tom, they believe they deserve to be ignored and not seen, that they deserve whatever life hands them. Blue-collar lost children are most likely to stay home into adulthood, taking care of their parents and still being ignored and unappreciated. I find that many women who were molested far into adulthood are lost children from blue-collar religiously addictive families. The never-quit mentality learned from their codependent parent(s) keeps them perpetually hoping that something will change and that they will at last be seen. Or, even more sadly, they feel that the abuse they still endure is better than being totally ignored—bad attention is better than none at all.

These lost children respond to the family's religious dysfunction either by totally rejecting God or by creating a fantasy in which only God or Jesus can be trusted. Those who reject God and become bitter atheists or agnostics see the family's neglect as evidence of God's neglect or that there really isn't a God at all.

Although the scapegoats rebel against the message that they are born depraved and will never amount to anything, the lost children believe it and live with a pervasive sense of hopelessness and despair, feeling that they can never change. Their black-and-white thinking is turned on themselves, believing, as Wegscheider-Cruse says, that they truly deserve to be neglected and abandoned: by themselves, by their families, and by God. This was Tom's belief when he took his own life.

Blue-collar lost children become proficient at escaping as they search for a safe place. Although the scapegoats always seem to seek change, lost children want only to feel safe, secure, and loved. That's why many become food addicts, because food is safe and is not forbidden, as are drugs or alcohol. Some seek safety in God alone, bypassing human relationships. They frequently become nuns, priests, or missionaries. Those who do not specifically take religious vows often live sterile, monastic lives.

The mascots. Peggy Davis was treated more like a pet than a sibling by her older sisters and brothers. Seven years younger than Joyce, Peggy became her live baby doll. Helen, worn down by years of coping with Jim's religiosity, had little emotional energy left to invest in her last child. Peggy's siblings taught her tricks; she learned quickly that performing got her attention. In her family, the best way to win approval was to sing hymns for Daddy or to recite verses from the Bible. When Daddy got mad and started screaming or throwing things, Peggy could distract him by bursting into a chorus of "Jesus Loves Me." Like many blue-collar mascots, Peggy grew up to be a choir leader, Sunday school scripture reader, and head of her youth-group social committees. While their hero-type siblings gain attention by assuming superresponsible roles at home, school, and church, mascots will do anything that puts them in front of an audience; Peggy was no exception.

The religiously addicted family depends on the mascot's humor and joviality to further the illusion that everything is fine. Perhaps the best example of such a mascot is Tammy Faye Bakker, who literally paints on a clown's face to mask the pain of her family's dysfunction. The garish makeup, outlandish clothes, and copious tears alongside the fixed Gospel Grin have made her the focus of media jokes.

In making herself into a joke, she creates an effective smokescreen not only for her own addictions, but for her husband's as well. Tammy Faye epitomizes the religious codependent's denial, black-and-white thinking, unquestioning loyalty, and refusal to doubt or to question authority. When her husband collapsed, and later, when he was found guilty, she put on a great show of singing, crying, and hand-wringing. But where were her real feelings? Where was honest emotion: grief, loss, anger, pain? Buried beneath her mascot's mask.

More important than trying to boost the family's self-esteem, mascots are seeking to create a family of God that will provide the healthy nurturing so lacking in their family of origin. In her role as entertaining peacemaker, Peggy Davis depends on their collective magical thinking to make her jovial clownishness effective. Although she has long since abandoned any real religious belief or affiliation, she is still able to use it to tease her father back into good humor by summoning up stories about people or events in their past and making Jim look like the good guy—something that she recognized early on would get him out of his foul moods. So she tells tales of Deacon So-and-So's misadventure at the church picnic or the time the choir director fell asleep and snored loudly during the sermon.

She carries this pattern over into her career as well. An emergency room nurse, Peggy is much loved at work. Her sense of humor helps break the tension surrounding so much death and disaster. Yet she secretly believes herself a hypocrite and liar. Fearful of becoming obese like Joyce, she has been bulimic for years, totally unaware of her mother's bulimia. Since Tom's death, her tricks have increasingly failed to lighten the family's moods. Despairing, she is turning more and more to tranquilizers, which she steals from the emergency room supply cabinet in order to blot her pain.

Like all mascots, she appears outwardly to be consistently the same cheerful Peggy. Inside she is seething with rage at her father's rigid religiosity; at Tom for dying under circumstances that afford her no opportunity to laugh; at her mother and/or Joyce for not knowing what was wrong with Tom—at God for making such a mess of her family that she cannot heal it.

COUNTRY-CLUB CHILDREN

In the blue-collar family, the children struggle to reconcile the family's chaos and abusiveness with messages of a loving God. But in country-club Christian families, the abuse often takes the form of emotional neglect. The sense of doubt and worthlessness that assail the children is more insidious because, in a home in which creature comforts are abundant, they feel that they are living in a barren desert.

The heroes. Mark McBride, whose family profile was described earlier, is eighteen, captain of the varsity basketball team, class president, and a past president of the youth group at church before his father insisted they change churches. He is determined to graduate at the top of his class so that his parents and church will be proud of him. On the surface, he is the quintessential all-American kid: clean-cut, polite, respectful of his father, devoted to his mother, and mindful of his siblings. Underneath, however, he is secretly terrified of failure and of not being good enough.

He appears to have many friends, yet none are really close, intimate confidants. Mark's friends are a coterie of hangers-on, both at school and at church—people who want to bask in the reflected glory of his popularity. Mark is likable enough but rigid and walled off from his feelings. His perfectionism and drive for success put people off. His teammates regard him with grudging respect: He plays well, and as captain of the team, his perfectionism has paid off in a winning season. Off the court, they shun him. Mark doesn't engage in any of the locker-room shenanigans; his religious upbringing has made him prudish and judgmental. He is desperately lonely and doesn't understand why. He's done everything right, according to what he's been taught. Why does he hate himself so much?

Like Mark, heroes in the country-club Christian family are always superachievers and honors students, club presidents, varsity captains: all-American kids. They might choose a Bible college or university. Mark McBride is thinking of applying to such religious colleges, feeling he might fit in better there.

If female, the hero will almost certainly be anorexic. The family rules about appearance and the emphasis on the godly life leave her feeling chronically not good enough. The guilt and shame these feelings produce make her vulnerable to anorexia. In fact, it is not uncommon for daughters of these kinds of families to be anorexic or bulimic. A woman who called my office recently described her family, which could have been the model for our country-club Christians: She holds a doctorate in chemical engineering; her sister is a lawyer; both suffer from anorexia as well as other effects of religious abuse.

What drives the heroes in this household is an overwhelming denial of the lack of feelings and true intimacy in the family. The enmeshment—an outward closeness and togetherness—creates extreme inner conflict. It looks so good on the outside, but it feels very bad inside; often, nobody really knows why. Like Mark McBride, heroes assume something is wrong with *them.* Their superachieving is a desperate attempt to fix the bad feelings in order to further the illusion that this is a wonderfully loving family.

The scapegoats. Although only fourteen, Amy McBride has just had an abortion. She told her mother she needed the money for a Christian walk-a-thon in which she had finished first, but friends who pledged funds had reneged. She wanted to win the prize she had earned, she said. Amy knows how to manipulate her parents, especially her mother.

Amy has grown up deeply resentful of the emotional barrenness in her home. At a very early age, Amy sensed the strain between her parents. She has known about her mother's bulimia since she was five or six years old and caught her vomiting after a chocolate binge. She accidentally saw strange notations in her father's appointment book and suspects that he might be having an affair. She finds his men friends gross and sees something vaguely disturbing in his constant hero worshiping.

From the time she was a small child, she was aware of the inconsistencies and hypocrisies in her family. It became a game for her to search out clues, keeping a scorecard of her parents' attitudes and behaviors that belied their supposed Christianity. Her quest for points kept her forever in trouble, for she was always sneaking about, getting into trouble, daring, challenging. She has become contemptuous and hostile toward her parents. Her siblings are a little afraid of her, for they don't understand her constant sarcastic remarks and misbehavior.

Unlike heroes, scapegoats like Amy are bitterly aware of the hypocrisy and double standards in the family. They know this enmeshment is not real love, and like other scapegoats, they are constantly being punished for wanting to tell the truth. While the heroes don't want to know that all is not well in this picture-perfect family, the scapegoats know it all too well. Some, like Amy, use this knowledge to blackmail the family by constantly getting into trouble, chipping away at the family image. Boys may have a string of drunk-driving arrests; girls may run with the wrong crowd, may even jeopardize their mother's position in the Right-to-Life Movement by getting pregnant and having a secret abortion as did Amy. They frequently leave the church or change affiliations.

For these scapegoats, rebellion is not necessarily against the belief that they are inherently bad—which is the belief that so scars the blue-collar scapegoats. The country-club Christian scapegoats see very clearly the hypocrisy and dysfunction in their families but lack the emotional resources to detach in a healthy way. Amy sees her parents' dysfunction yet cannot separate herself from them. If they are wrong, then she is wrong. This is the result of the family's enmeshment: Amy cannot see where her parents end and she begins. But she doesn't want to be like them, and the only way she can separate herself is to misbehave.

The lost children. If the lost children in the blue-collar family are lost in angry chaos, lost children in the country-club Christian family are outshone by the rest of the family's attention seeking. Carol McBride is such a child. At sixteen, she is dangerously anorexic, quiet, and studious. She is not aware that she is genuinely well-liked, although her friends have been puzzled by her increasing withdrawal in the last year. Unlike her siblings, she was happy to change churches; Pastor Collins had been molesting her for two years. She is so quiet and unassuming that no one in her family really notices how thin she is or how withdrawn she has become.

The family's lack of balance affects these children deeply. Usually, they are as bright as their superachieving siblings; frequently they are the most talented, but they never call attention to themselves. If they do, it is by being chronically ill or anorexic, as a silent plea for caretaking. Carol McBride has a near-genius I.Q. and maintains a solid 4.0 average—a fact somehow lost on the rest of the family, which is focused on Mark's more outgoing, superachieving exploits.

These children frequently take refuge in church doctrine and dogma, exchanging the richness of true intimacy for the safety of structure and rituals. Such a need led Carol McBride to seek out Stan Collins for counseling. At fourteen, she had been a lovely, blossoming young girl on her way to becoming a very beautiful woman. Her religious-based fears of boys and dating made her want to hide behind church rituals. Collins had a more direct method for curing her fears: She needed a man, not a boy. When she found she could not turn to church ritual, she began to ritually starve herself. Lately, she has begun to mutilate herself, trying to make her body ugly so Stan won't want her. Carol is trapped between messages that tell her to honor her parents, obey her elders, serve God and, in contrast, the increasing shame and guilt that following these beliefs has produced. Her inability to question authority prevents her from stopping the abuse. Deep down, she believes she must have done something to deserve this.

Often these country-club Christian lost children, shamed and disgusted by the hypocrisy and double standards they witnessed as children, simply reject God altogether. They are truly lost, having no spiritual guide or awareness of their spirituality. These are the people like Tom Davis, who stun family and friends by committing suicide. No one knows them or has a clue that they are in pain. While the scapegoats and mascots might frequently threaten or attempt suicide as an attention-seeking cry for help, these lost children truly believe there is no one who will help—no one who cares—so they never reach out. Carol McBride's only way out of her sexual abuse is to simply wither away, which is a less obvious version of Tom's suicide.

The mascots. In the country-club Christian family, the mascots are, as always, the ones whose function is to make the family feel better about itself. Although Mark McBride wins honor after honor, there is something unsettling about his intense competitiveness. The real star of the family is twelve-year-old Jason, who displayed an astonishing gift for tennis at a very early age. Slowly, Jason's tennis game has come to rival the church as the consuming focus in the household. Doug counts Jason as one of the assets he brings to a church: a shining light for the Fellowship of Christian Athletes. Gifted children like Jason are able to use their family's money and prestige to further their ambitions, and their families use them as examples of the rewards of living a good Christian life.

While the heroes work very hard to get attention, the mascots come by it naturally, with very little effort. Mark McBride works very hard at his sports and schoolwork. He tries to be proud of Jason and feels guilty and ashamed that deep down inside he is extremely jealous of his little brother. His jealousy frightens him; it smacks of Cain and Abel and feels sinful. He alternately encourages Jason and then constantly criticizes his game, which confuses the boy, who genuinely worships and adores his big brother. He doesn't understand what he's done wrong.

Jason is already a seasoned people-pleaser. He knows he is valuable only as long as he keeps winning. He lives in terror of losing or of some accident that would rob him of his ability to play tennis. He truly believes his family and God would abandon and reject him if he were to start losing. So he works hard at ingratiating himself to people, trying to create a back-up career as a little comedian—something to fall back on should he suddenly become unable to play tennis.

Mascots often become super-salesmen, the jovial high-pressure pitchmen who always win the salesman of the year awards. Heroes may become good salesmen on the way up the corporate ladder, but their goal is in being seen as successes. Mascots sell for the applause; they are so desperate for approval that they would literally sell their souls to feel accepted. Is it any wonder that the smiling brothers assisting the televangelists' fund-raising all look and sound like stereotypical used-car salesmen?

Such families definitely exist. In *Starving for Attention,* her moving account of her battle with anorexia, Cherry Boone O'Neill describes virtually all the symptoms and characteristics discussed here. Hers was the classic all-American family; her father, Pat Boone, worked hard at maintaining his apple-pie image even in hedonistic Hollywood. In order to do that, O'Neill writes, her parents early on imposed an endless string of rules, which she found oppressive but rarely questioned or challenged. She began dieting with the aid of prescription pills stolen from her mother's medicine cabinet. She never felt good enough, even for God. She was the family hero, always rushing in to make peace and smooth things over. As she chronicles the progression of her anorexia, she also, unknowingly, documents the emotional shattering that occurs when religion ceases to provide a spiritually nurturing structure and balance and becomes instead a prison.

ADULT CHILDREN OF RELIGIOUS DYSFUNCTION

We have seen how children of religious addicts fit into the roles adopted by other children of dysfunction. The following profile of Mary illustrates how children of religious addicts also exhibit characteristics found in adult children of alcoholics.

MARY'S STORY

Mary's first words as a child were Jesus and God—not Mommy and Daddy. Prayer, the Bible, heaven—and the fear of hell—ruled her childhood. Religion was a fact of life, like the air she breathed.

She grew up in Akron, Ohio, the only child of extreme fundamentalists who belonged to the Church of God. That was exactly how they saw themselves: they were THE Church of God. From childhood, she was told that her church was the only church: the faithful, the remnant, the people of Jehovah. Thus she was not permitted to make close friends with children who belonged to different Christian denominations or other religions; they were considered heathens. Hers was a religion of what not to do: Don't dance; don't play on Sundays; don't go to the movies; don't listen to the Beatles; don't wear sinful clothes; don't smoke; don't drink; don't curse; don't complain; don't answer back; don't question; don't. . . .

She was a very lonely child. She would watch other children playing, but because she was not allowed to play with them she felt different. She was told they were evil, but often in her isolation wondered if she wasn't the one who was bad.

Evil seemed to include everything everybody else did that looked like fun. She decided that God's children weren't supposed to have fun. Life was strict, rigid, and serious; rarely did anyone laugh in her home, as if laughing were a sin. Hugging wasn't allowed; she was permitted a light kiss on her mother's cheek before she went to bed, and never did her parents kiss her.

She was expected to pray before every meal. Pray before she went to bed. Her mother and father prayed extemporaneously; they felt they were led by the spirit, often speaking in tongues that she could never understand. As she grew older she was expected to pray in the same manner. She was to confess any sins that she had committed or imagined during the day—first in her prayers, then to her parents. Her parents meted out harsh punishments for her sins, always with the dire warning that God would also punish her later. She gave up trying to understand God; He was merely to be fearfully obeyed.

She was given no sex education. When she began to menstruate she spent hours frantically searching for the cut, confused as to what she might have done to cause it and terrified and ashamed to tell her mother. All her mother did was to wordlessly hand her a sanitary napkin with the terse instruction to put it over the bleeding and a vague reference to "this" now happening every month, whatever "this" was. What had she done wrong? Why did she get the feeling something very shameful was happening? Her fear and shame were only intensified when she was told to ask the preacher if she wanted to know more.

The one source of anything remotely pleasurable permitted in her home was food. Her mother cooked huge meals, heavily laced with thick gravies and fat, and she always served Mary adult portions. Yet the child was expected to clean her plate; if she got full before she finished it all, she was told to think of the starving children. It was as if she was supposed to eat for them. Thus she was fat from infancy on. Today she still finds it hard to leave food on her plate; she agonizes over wasting food.

I met Mary at an eating disorders unit. She was twenty-six years old, about five-foot six inches, and weighed 250 pounds. She still lived with her mother. Her father had died when she was twenty. She looked and dressed like a frightened and lonely old woman. To her, God was a judge who would punish her mercilessly for associating with the wrong people, so she was afraid of everyone. Most of all, she was afraid of God.

In one of my lectures on spirituality and recovery, I discussed how anger, fear, and isolation feed addictions. Interestingly, Mary did not connect these feelings with her eating disorder, but she did connect them to her religion. She told me that she was angry at her life, angry at her parents, angry about what she had missed. Much of what she had been told in her religion she no longer believed—but all her life she had acted as though she did believe; she never wanted to upset her parents. Mary said that all through her teenage years she hated going to church. It was a small church, with less than one hundred members. For most of her life she had been the youngest member. She was angry at her people-pleasing tendencies.

She hated the isolation that had made her feel different. Because she did not play or socialize with other children, she did not know how to talk with them at school. She hid behind books. She became an A student. But she was always lonely. She had no friends her own age; she talked like an adult rather than a child. She cleaned, ironed, washed, knitted, and read the Bible. Food was her only friend.

She said that she always loved her father but was afraid of him. Once, when she was about eight, he caught her jumping rope on Sunday. He made her kneel on the jump-rope for an hour holding the Bible straight out in front of her. She never forgot that incident or the punishment. Mary spent the rest of her life trying to please her father, and stuffing down her feelings of anger, frustration, abandonment, guilt, shame, and fear with food.

Hearing my lectures on food and alcohol addiction, Mary immediately recognized the same symptoms in her father's use of religion. She began to understand that her father was not a bad man, but a religious addict. His parents had practiced the same strict faith; so he too was an adult child of religious addicts. He was obsessed with his evangelical religion. He was at church every day, three times on Sunday. Religion, worship, meetings, Bible study, and services of witness took priority over everything else in his life; he even missed Mary's high school graduation to attend a Christian convention! Yet he never appeared happy. Now Mary also understands that her mother was religiously abused by her father's scriptural understanding of women; she was viewed as man's help-mate. Her mother was expected to obey, like Mary.

Today, Mary is working on her Overeaters Anonymous (O.A.) program and going to meetings of Adult Children of Alcoholics (A.C.O.A.). She is beginning to love herself. After her father died, she stopped going to church. She could no longer bury her anger at the messages of hate and intolerance. She had never believed them and was, as she said, "angry at God for being so hateful." In her last letter to me, she said that she is discovering a God that she can understand, a God who is loving and accepting. Today, her God is a friend.

Mary's story illustrates my belief that not only do children of religious dysfunction share traits common to all adult children of dysfunction, but they also manifest them in ways that directly display the symptoms of religious addiction. Janet Woititz' descriptions in her book, *Adult Children of Alcoholics,* provide a framework of characteristics that we can use to examine the effects of growing up with religious addicts.

Adult children of religious addicts guess at what normal is. Because of the oppressive rules, black-and-white thinking, and taboos against thinking or questioning that religious addicts set for their families, their children have no sense of what a normal life is. This is the effect of a lack of social and intellectual balance. You have learned to think in terms of extremes: People are either good or evil; feelings are good or bad; nothing is allowed to be questioned. This creates a constant turmoil of fear, guilt, and shame, because you do not know how to evaluate people, situations, or your own spirituality.

Adult children of religious addicts have trouble following a project through to the end. As a child, nothing you did was ever good enough. You were always trying to be perfect, trying to be what God, the preacher, the church, father, or mother wanted from you, but it was never enough. When and if you were praised, it was often followed by admonitions to do even better next time or to not get too proud because it is really God, not you, doing the good job.

If you were told from the cradle on that you were born depraved or would never amount to anything, you probably grew up acting like a failure, since you learned early in childhood that you had failed before you started. You go to job interviews convinced you aren't good enough. You don't pursue relationships with people who attract you because you are sure the other person won't like you. Your attitude is, why bother or what's the use?

This negativity further entrenches you in emotional isolation and fear of intimacy, increasing your overwhelming fears. The vicious cycle of failure breeding self-hatred is always the most difficult to overcome. But for you who have been taught from birth that you are worthless in the sight of God, gaining self-respect and true spirituality becomes an almost impossible task.

Adult children of religious addicts lie when it would be just as easy to tell the truth. Religious addicts, like other addicts, are temperamental, moody, and often unpredictable. In order to survive in that dysfunctional environment, you had to learn to lie, manipulate, pretend, and deny. Fear of criticism and being judged led to dishonesty—with others and with yourself. The black-and-white thinking, indoctrinations about the evils of the flesh, and inability to question and assess situations or authorities set up a powerful conflict. To avoid guilt and shame, you became such a skillful liar, so good at denial, that often you truly do not know when you have lied.

Adult children of religious addicts judge themselves without mercy. You grow up knowing that nothing you do is ever good enough. You were given role models impossible to emulate: Jesus, the Virgin Mary, the prophets, the holy men and women, the guru, the leader.

Often, you were raised with the clear message that you were so bad that only God could love you! But is God's love safe? To young children, the many Bible stories about sacrifices and the wrath of God being visited on the sinful can be very frightening. Children are very literal-minded. They cannot distinguish between fable and reality. You are told that God is watching you, that God will get you, and you are not sure just what God will do to you when He gets you. This is a very real fear—the literal fear of God—which can take root so early that it remains locked in the subconscious, festering. So the desire to be good, to not be judged, carries with it a subliminal terror, which is frequently masked with rage and anger.

You do not want to be found lacking in the eyes of God and you are angry over the fear that you will never be good enough. James M. Wall, in an editorial on Jimmy Swaggart in *Christian Century,* explored possible sources of Swaggart's obvious anger. "It is a simple psychological fact that we tend to preach hardest against the things which threaten us personally," he writes. Later he says,

> . . . *so much of Jimmy Swaggart's angry preaching has been directed at those who fail to live up to the high moral standards of . . . "the model, Jesus Christ."*
>
> *But surely Jimmy Swaggart has been preaching to himself, too, all these years. And if so, maybe there is room to mourn. For the man has had to perform before audiences of millions knowing that, as he would probably describe it, he was living a life far short of the sanctification he sought.*

Adult children of religious addicts have difficulty having fun. In the religiously addicted home, kissing, wrestling, football, dancing, music, magazines, theater, or the circus could be considered sinful. Even Halloween, that magically scary night of tricks and treats, is taboo for some children. One child of religious addicts told me that for years as an adult she'd become deeply depressed at Halloween. As a child, she'd sit quietly alone, feeling different and left out, while classmates chattered excitedly about their costumes and adventures. Each year she struggled with guilt and shame about those feelings. She was always told that she was one of the chosen and the other children were the outcasts. "But I never understood why it didn't make me feel good to be 'chosen,'" she said. "I just wanted to belong and see what it felt like to have fun."

The fun, joy, and comfort of a meaningful sexuality is lost to you because of the messages about the evils of sex and physical pleasure you received in childhood. Adult children of religious addicts find it difficult to even talk about sex, let alone enjoy it. You body is sinful, therefore sex is sinful. Fun and sex are incompatible. Again, black-and-white thinking and the resulting fear of anything in between set up a powerful struggle. As James M. Wall observed, in talking about Jimmy Swaggart,

> *. . . the excessive emphasis on outward behavior is a heavy burden for anyone to bear, and it becomes especially difficult for young people who hear more about holiness than they do about love and forgiveness. While we cannot fully comprehend Jimmy Swaggart's psychological makeup, we have to admit that there is considerable anger in the manner in which he preaches about sin. And that much anger suggests something about his inner life.*

Perhaps, inside Jimmy Swaggart, there lives a confused, terrified little boy who is in a rage at the loss of the innocent joys of childhood and who wants, just for a time, to put down his cross and go out and play.

Adult children of religious addicts take themselves very seriously. This goes along with not having fun. One reason it is difficult to have fun is because, growing up, everything was so serious—and frightening. The constant injunctions to beware of the sinful—and the confusion that arose out of those so-called sinful things being fun—take the simple pleasures out of life. Living in the moment is difficult for all children of dysfunction, but it is especially difficult for the children of religious addicts.

After all, from infancy, you are preparing for the next life. At the same time, you are being told that this life is booby-trapped, that Satan is out there trying to trick and tempt you; you must be ever watchful lest you fall into the snare. Pat, a woman I met who is recovering from religious addiction, told me that she still feels guilty and awkward when she is in a room where people are laughing or being silly. Pat is in her fifties and has never experienced a belly laugh or cried with laughter.

Adult children of religious addicts have difficulty with intimate relationships. When you are told from childhood that people are sinful, fallen, depraved, or evil; when the focus of spirituality is outside your body, your person, your humanness, it becomes difficult to share or allow another person into your life. When touching, holding hands, hugging, kissing, or even expressing feelings were absent or forbidden in your lives, then intimate relationships become not only difficult but also scary. Yet you want them!

This conflict often produces the dual diseases of religious addiction and sexual addiction. The dogma about the evils of the flesh—teachings that only whores enjoy sex and that love is not nurturing but angry and condemning—conflicts with the human desire for closeness. James Wall, concluding his article on Swaggert, noted: "I have read that interest in pornography stems from an intense loneliness. A longing for intimacy is basic to us all. Most of us don't turn to pornography to meet that need, but we all have our ways." Wall has correctly identified some of these core issues of religious addiction: the loneliness, anger, and shame, and the resulting distance from others and from God.

Adult children of religious addicts overreact to changes over which they have no control. Much of religious addiction and abuse revolves around control. Things and concepts are kept orderly, with everything in its place. There are no questions or doubts, no confusion. It's a carefully constructed system, a mind-set designed to create safety by trying to eliminate any source of fear or error.

The safety of black-and-white thinking is that it eliminates the hazards of making a wrong choice, of making mistakes, and of not being perfect. You cling to rules and become rigidly scrupulous in order to feel safe. Thus you resist change, because with changes come new rules. You fear questions or conflicting information, because everything you have been brought up to believe is right might be proven wrong. Hence your fearful anger when a text or belief is questioned or criticized.

You socialize only with people who have a similar mindset and are completely unable to sustain relationships with those people whose religious beliefs might be the slightest bit different. Cherry Boone O'Neill writes of the sadness of terminating a long-standing relationship with her boyfriend, Warren, because she could not accept his religious beliefs. Her rigid religious upbringing and need for control did not permit a marriage to someone whose beliefs did not absolutely match her own.

Adult children of religious addicts constantly seek approval and affirmation. You have probably received these kinds of mixed messages since birth: God loves you, you are chosen, you are specially blessed in baptism—and yet you are sinful, in need of redemption, and stained by the worldliness of original sin. Therefore, your self-esteem and confidence are rooted in acceptance and approval by God, the church, and other people. You are codependent on religion.

You are unable to create or discover God in your life. You are unable to discover God in the beauty of your physical body and relationships. You have forgotten that these are part of the image of God in which you were made. You have lost sight of the image of God within yourself and constantly look for God outside—in large congregations and the impressive ritual and pomp of the church. You find self-worth in becoming one of those numbers by whatever means it takes: making excessive financial contributions, giving up jobs, friends, even family members. The need for approval—to belong and to feel valued—is stronger than all other ties.

Adult children of religious addicts usually feel different from other people. Of course you feel different. All your life you were told you were different. You were the chosen, the sanctified, the blessed, the people of God—and the people who existed outside your sect were the ungodly children of Satan.

As a child, you lived differently. Often you did not dress like your contemporaries, avoiding bright colors or current styles; you had food laws and regulations. You were forbidden to go to dances, theater, and other worldly entertainment. You were only allowed to hear music deemed acceptable by your particular denomination. Someone told me about going into a Christian music store to buy a copy of Handel's *Messiah;* the clerk scornfully told her that they only sold *Christian* music in that store.

Growing up, you did not socialize with people outside of your group or religion, but developed a language, culture, and worship that emphasized your difference from other people. You not only felt different but also told people that you were different in order to validate yourself. Being different made you feel special.

Yet being different only increases your emotional isolation and fear of intimacy. Being different feeds into the good-or-evil thinking, which in turn makes you vulnerable to such hidden addictions as anorexia, bulimia, sexual addiction, or gambling. These fuel your guilt and shame; instead of feeling better than others, you secretly feel that you are worthless and damned. Thus the vicious cycle continues.

Adult children of religious addicts are super-responsible or super-irresponsible. The contradictory messages that children from religiously addicted homes receive make them ambivalent about responsibility. On the one hand, you feel your implied chosenness gives you a message for the world. You feel superresponsible for family, friends, co-workers, and members of your congregation. You want everybody to share in the fruits of righteousness, and you will go to any lengths to convert people to your belief system.

This sense of mission makes you highly insensitive to others' beliefs and feelings and ultimately creates irresponsible behaviors. Those people who knock on our doors to proselytize rarely seem to consider that they may be disturbing someone who is sick, works a late shift, or is spiritually happy in a different religion.

This double standard is a common characteristic of religious abuse. You literally become incapable of recognizing when you're being destructive. A friend of mine worked in a bookstore in a town where several fundamentalist churches commonly instructed their members to put religious tracts in the local bookstores' sex education sections and other areas deemed sinful by the churches. These religious addicts were unable to recognize that they were, in fact, vandalizing the stores. They had been led to believe they were helping people to get saved. It did not matter that the store employees had to work late to stay and clean up the litter, or that the sales clerks were frequently cursed at by customers who found the pamphlets offensive.

These experiences have left my friend bitter and untrusting of any Christians. "When people tell me they've been saved," she says, "I want to get away from them before they do something bad to me."

In this irresponsible behavior we see the effects of brainwashing and manipulation of scripture, refusal to question, and uncompromising judgmentalness. Adult children who have grown up with religious addicts or have become religious addicts as a result of other dysfunction have no sense of right or wrong; they lack the ability to evaluate except by very structured standards. When they seek to convert others and don't succeed, their response is one of increasing anger and hostility. If they don't win converts, their church will disapprove—even more terrifying, God will disapprove—and withhold or rescind their salvation. They react with violent fury when others jeopardize their salvation by refusing to convert.

Because of messages like these and the dysfunctional upbringing they experienced, people from religiously addictive homes often reject God, religion, and the church in adulthood. Having been the hero, scapegoat, lost child, or mascot in a religiously abusive family was so painful that in adulthood they react with anger, cynicism, and irresponsible behavior.

Adult children of religious addicts are extremely loyal, even in the face of evidence that the loyalty is undeserved. One of the messages that children of religiously addicted parents learn is the need to be loyal. This message also enables the cycle of control to continue. Since being disloyal is seen as a sin, harmful incidents that happen in the family or church are kept secret within the family system.

Connected with the characteristic of loyalty is the manipulated use of forgiveness. If your parents did something harmful—physical violence, sexual abuse, or emotional abuse such as sarcasm or shaming—they would appeal to the Christian principle of forgiveness: Don't say anything to anybody, don't do anything to cause scandal for the family or church. Again, the loyalty strings get pulled, along with those that admonish the victim not to talk or question.

The Jim and Tammy Bakker scandal is an example of this dynamic. The members who contributed financially remained loyal in the face of mounting evidence of fiscal extravagances and corruption in church leadership. They invented excuses or mitigating circumstances to maintain their loyalty. *Time* quoted one viewer, who contributed nearly $10,000 annually to televangelists and was irritated by all the criticism of the Bakkers:

> *"These people have done a lot of good in their lives," he says. . . . an Idaho freight salesman is not bothered by the lavish lifestyle that the Roberts and the Bakkers are said to enjoy. To him, their rewards should be great, because they've done great things for the Lord.*

Adult children of religious addicts tend to lock themselves into a course of action without giving serious consideration to alternative behavior or possible consequences. This trait is the end result of black-and-white thinking. In these behaviors we see that the disease has progressed from a refusal to think, doubt, or question to a virtual inability to do so. Adult children of religious addicts, whether themselves religiously addicted or not, exhibit the same loss of control and powerlessness as do end-stage addicts. All choice is gone; life is increasingly unmanageable. They feel powerless and out of control, grabbing impulsively at anything to fix their pain.

Adult children of religious addicts are often torn between two worlds: the rigid, restricted religious world, and the world as it really is—with all its spiritual delights and earthly temptations. For adult children of addicts who have themselves become religious addicts, living in this world is a torment. Many flee by working for a church, religious group, or religious company; they watch only religious television, read only religious literature, and desperately try to keep their families away from any and all temptation. Others are at war constantly between their very human desires and the rigid dogma of faith. Not knowing how to blend these two worlds, they struggle with feeling that they must choose one or the other.

No matter what the source of the dysfunction—alcohol, drugs, food, or religion—growing up amid the chaos of such homes leaves you emotionally wounded and crippled, unable to enjoy the riches life can offer. It diminishes the ability to discover your positive creativity.

Recovery from such devastating wounds requires recognizing your own dysfunction, and the willingness to take whatever steps are necessary through therapy and support groups for adult children of religious addicts or any other addiction. It is not an easy process, but it brings with it the joys of a kind of spirituality you may never have dreamed was possible.

Chapter 6

Recovery:
The Twelve Steps to Healing Your Wounds

IT ONLY TAKES a moment. A moment of sanity. Clarity. A moment in which you know, deep inside yourself, that you've had enough. You've lived in pain too long. It's time to change.

My moment came following my car crash as I sat on a curb: drunk, ashamed, my bloodied head buried in my hands. I was faintly aware of the scandalized buzzing of the gathering crowd. "It's Father Leo," they said. "Drunk again." It came to me that no one was very surprised to have seen my car and me go sailing through the air. ". . . only Father Leo . . . drunk as usual. . . ." Just a fact of life in my parish: birth, death, and Father Leo, falling-down drunk.

Suddenly, I didn't want it to be a fact of life any more—my life or anyone else's. I knew then that I was, irrevocably, undeniably an alcoholic. I didn't know how I would change or what it would take to change. I only knew, in that moment, that I wanted to change more than anything in the world, no matter how impossible the odds seemed at the time. I'd had enough pain. I wanted out.

That moment was what I call a natural intervention, a time when life sat me down and said, "See here, Leo: look what you've done to yourself." I believe far more people enter recovery as a result of natural interventions—those moments when the pain finally gets so great they must move out of it or die—than as a result of the more formal kind of intervention done by family and friends.

Natural interventions take many forms. Mine came as a result of my car crash. A friend of mine who was immensely obese had her moment when her lover said to her: "I'm ashamed to be seen with you." The pain of that brutal honesty sent her back to Overeaters Anonymous for one last try—and she's been abstinent from compulsive overeating ever since. A rageaholic told me his moment came when he reached out to hug his son and the child drew back in terror, expecting to be beaten.

Sometimes our moments come in stages. In a treatment center where I am a spiritual consultant, someone said: "Father Leo, I came here for my food addiction. But I found out my problem is really religious addiction and abuse!" Others have their moments in the quietness of their rooms when, alone, wracked with emotional or physical pain, they reach the point of surrender and say to themselves: Enough, no more.

We who are in recovery also have experienced many times when we could have stopped, could have stepped off the elevator before it hit the bottom floor; but we didn't. We were in pain all right, and may have genuinely wanted to quit our addiction. But we had not reached a point at which we were ready to choose to get out of the pain. I had such moments: baptizing a baby boy with a girl's name; falling into the open grave at a funeral service I'd conducted; or waking up in a wet bed. These were embarrassing, even shameful moments, but not painful enough to make me want to quit. I still was not ready to see that I was an alcoholic, much less that change was possible.

The disease of addiction tells us we have no choices; we believe we can't stop and can't change, that there's nothing wrong with us; others are causing the problem. A successful intervention, whether natural or deliberate, shows us the pain we are in and allows us to see the possibility of change. In those brief moments of clarity we see that we have choices after all. We become open to hearing and seeing what others may have been telling or showing us.

I said earlier that the scandals involving TV evangelists created a national intervention by bringing religious addiction and abuse too close to home to be ignored. Those scandals spurred people to act and to call for change. When awareness inspires action, that moment becomes an intervention.

Sometimes, our moments come when we see others mirroring our own attitudes and behaviors. I saw this illustrated clearly when I appeared on a radio call-in show with an extreme religious addict. During the commercial breaks, he kept frantically searching through a huge notebook for material to use against me. In the end, there could be no dialogue with this man. He literally did not breathe as he quoted one scripture after another, manipulating and twisting both the Bible and my words.

The more he ranted and raved, the more clearly he illustrated how religious addiction looks and sounds. Initially the calls to the station were more supportive of him than me. As he lost control of himself, however, the calls changed. People began telling the interviewer that they hadn't believed religious addiction really existed, but that this gentleman's behavior changed their minds. That demonstration became an intervention: not for the addict but for the people listening to the interview who heard him clearly exhibiting disease and dysfunction. I still hear from listeners who heard themselves mirrored in that interview and, as a result, resolved to change. In this case, one addict provided the moment of intervention for others.

Taking Advantage of the Moment: The Steps to Change

Your moment has come. You have resolved to change. Where do you begin? At this point, most people seek out a support group. As of this writing, there is no national Twelve Step program for religious addiction and abuse. I have heard from several groups attempting to form such a program and have encouraged them to work together. In the meantime, I recommend that you seek out local Adult Children of Alcoholics or Codependents Anonymous groups.

Religious addiction and abuse is deeply rooted in codependency—in looking to something outside of yourself to give you self-respect or happiness. As a religious addict, you hand over responsibility for your own welfare to a religious figure or to a belief system, then you passively wait to be miraculously fixed. When you attend support group meetings and describe your codependency in terms of how you have behaved around religion, you will discover that you are not alone. When you begin to talk about your religious codependency, you are likely to help others identify similar behavior. Before you know it, you will have built a support group of people who share your experience with religion.

I also encourage people to seek therapy, either individually or in groups. I've observed that those with the most lasting recovery are those who combine therapy and as many Twelve Step programs as apply to their lives. Walking through the pain of confronting our addictive behaviors as well as addressing childhood abuses often requires the skilled guidance of a trained therapist. This is much different than the guidance of your peers in Twelve Step groups. Both provide valuable, necessary tools for recovery.

I also encourage entering a treatment center if possible. Often, you need to remove yourself physically from your surroundings, especially if you are codependently entangled with a spouse or parents. Treatment centers offer safe, full-time protection from outside influences and distractions. This can be important if you are to begin to confront any kind of extreme abuse, whether emotional, physical, or sexual. As religious abuse often includes all of these, treatment centers provide appropriate settings for beginning your recovery.

Recovering religious addicts have shared with me that by simply revising the Twelve Steps of Alcoholics Anonymous they are able to address their religious addiction and abuse within the context of other Twelve Step programs. Using some of their suggestions, I have adapted the Twelve Steps to apply to religious addiction and abuse. As we explore the steps, we will discuss why it is necessary to change some of the time-honored wording of A.A.'s Twelve Steps in order to better address the disease of religious addiction.

The spiritual insights of the A.A. steps remain the same; we can change the words yet retain the message. With these steps and the principles of the Twelve Step fellowship as a guide, you can create the changes in your life that will ensure ongoing recovery.

▲ ▼ ▲

THE TWELVE STEPS FOR RELIGIOUS ADDICTS

1. We admitted we were powerless over our dysfunctional religion or beliefs—that our lives had become unmanageable.

2. Came to believe that a Spiritual Power within ourselves could guide us to sanity.

3. Made a decision to turn our will and our lives over to the care of a Spiritual Power as we understood this Spiritual Power.

4. Made a searching and fearless inventory of our dysfunctional religious beliefs and behaviors.

5. Admitted to our Spiritual Power, to ourselves, and to another human being the exact nature of those behaviors.

6. Were entirely ready to work with our Spiritual Power in replacing all these old behaviors.

7. Worked with our Spiritual Power to help replace our dysfunctional patterns.

8. Made a list of all persons we had harmed, and became willing to make amends to them all.

9. Made direct amends to such people whenever possible, except when to do so would injure them or others.

10. Continued to take personal inventory and when we made mistakes, promptly admitted it.

11. Sought through prayer and meditation to improve our conscious contact with our Spiritual Power, as we understood Spiritual Power, praying only for knowledge of that Power's guidance and the willingness to carry that out.

12. Having had a spiritual awakening as a result of these steps, we tried to carry this message to others, and to practice these principles in all our affairs.

STAGES OF RECOVERY FROM RELIGIOUS ADDICTION AND ABUSE

Recovery happens in stages. It's an ongoing process as your awareness of your addictive patterns changes and grows. There are six stages to recovery: perception, stabilization, early stage, midstage, last stage, and ongoing recovery. As we examine each stage, we will look at the corresponding Twelve Steps that help you move through these stages. Each step has exercises that you can do on your own. You might want to have a journal handy as you do them.

Perception: Steps One and Two

The first stage is often the hardest to work through. Your disease is indeed cunning, baffling, and powerful; it will fight back. You need to know that there are certain feelings at different phases of this stage, and that they are natural. You will grieve. You will resist. You will go through withdrawal. But you will survive.

Many people who experience these feelings after their moment of intervention think that having such feelings is a sign of failure, or that they can't recover. Because recovery is an ongoing process, you will cycle through the feelings and phases many, many times. Learning to comfort and encourage yourself with the awareness and acceptance that you are in a natural phase of an ongoing process is one of the keys to staying in recovery—no matter what stage you are in.

Early on, coping with those feelings is difficult and scary; you've been numbing your emotions and running from them a long time, so they'll be intense at first. After you've experienced them a few times and survived, however, you will greet them as familiar signals that you have once again entered a certain cycle or phase of your recovery. You might even welcome them.

In the beginning of recovery, as in the beginning of the disease, it is natural to experience a great deal of denial. You know you have a problem; you want to change but don't see how you can change. The feelings that emerge when you think of changing may be so overwhelming that you want to convince yourself that you don't have a problem, or that it's not as bad as it felt during your moment of intervention.

You may feel helpless and victimized, like food addicts who moan that they have an eating disorder but can do nothing about it since they have to eat to live. Your black-and-white thinking makes you believe that you must give up God totally, which of course feels unacceptable. You do not yet see that your dysfunctional beliefs about God are what must be abandoned.

In this stage, you may find yourself struggling with the tendency to minimize the seriousness of your addiction or abuse. You may compare yourself with others, seeking to prove to yourself that it isn't that bad and thinking to yourself, I didn't go bankrupt . . . I wasn't raised by religious addicts who preached damnation to me all the time . . . I wasn't beaten and humiliated by the nuns. . . .

In this stage of trying to minimize the problem, addicts often submit rather than surrender—following rules about not drinking or overeating, or trying to curb their religious activities. You may have gone to a treatment center or may be working on these issues with a therapist, but you have not yet surrendered—not truly taken Step One and admitted powerlessness and unmanageability.

So you continue to binge, continue your high-risk activities. You may relapse into watching religious TV or send a huge contribution to your church. You might comfort yourself by burning incense and chanting mantras or compulsively reading meditation books.

In this phase it's easy to slip into euphoric recall: romanticizing your disease, glorifying the good times and shutting out memories of the guilt, pain, and shame. You still have the need to control, to somehow make it work, like alcoholics who try to control their drinking by having beer only on weekends. You think you can just cut back on the number of church services you attend. Maybe you'll bargain with yourself and tell yourself that if you're really good you can go to that one special crusade you were saving up for. You want help, but you aren't ready to see that you really are powerless.

You may experience a tremendous craving for something to fill your life along with a great fear of the emotional hunger, sense of emptiness, and loss that may overwhelm you if you give up your self-destructive behaviors. Earlier, I discussed how activities like crusades, witnessing, and compulsive prayer actually generate your body's internal drugs. You will experience withdrawal not only from those internal drugs but also from the activities as well. Smokers experience this; their addiction is as much to the habit of having the cigarette in hand as it is to the nicotine. So the feelings of agitation, isolation, and fear may indeed become overwhelming. This is the stage at which many addicts relapse. The emerging feelings may seem so intolerable that the pain of your dysfunctional behavior appears preferable to the pain of experiencing certain feelings for the first time in a long time.

This is the point at which all addicts need as much support and understanding from families and friends as can be given. It is also the time when the families need their own support. All addicts in withdrawal experience wide mood swings: anger, irritability, blaming, and tearfulness are often present. You frequently lack control over these emotions, especially if you are attempting to remain abstinent. You aren't using the old fixes and have not yet acquired healthy coping skills. Don't give up! Using your sponsors, therapists, and support groups, both you and your family can survive the early emotional upheavals and so come out into the next phase. The greatest help, though, can come from working and re-working Step One.

Step One. We admitted we were powerless over our dysfunctional religion or beliefs—that our lives had become unmanageable.

When you find yourself wanting to deny your disease, the First Step is always a reminder that your life is every bit as powerless and unmanageable as it felt during your moment.

Just as the Steps themselves fall into an orderly sequence, the individual Steps divide into logical parts. I find that those who have difficulty working the Steps are often trying to work the last part before they've done the first. Step One requires first an admission of powerlessness, which leads to an awareness of unmanageability.

▲ ▼ ▲

Exercise: A good way to begin Step One is by starting a journal. First, record a thorough history of your religious obsession, starting with the earliest messages or experiences you are able to recall. Then list incidents and activities over which you were powerless. Pay careful attention, particularly when writing of childhood messages and experiences, to how you felt at the time.

Next, write about how those messages, incidents, and activities made your life unmanageable. Again, try to include how you felt. If you gave money excessively, examine your emotional motives: Were you trying to feel superior and powerful, or simply trying to gain self-respect by giving so much? What feelings did you actually feel? You may also want to write about how you feel now, as you review your old behavior.

The key here is unmanageability, getting yourself to recognize that the abusive, obsessive use of religion has not made life better, has not brought you close to God, but instead has created distance from God, from your family and friends, and from yourself. If you seem to have trouble getting specific, you might want to calculate the amount of time spent on religious activity and on searching for and/or memorizing scripture quotations, or add up the amounts of money tithed or donated.

Some addicts find it helpful to create a chart in which obsessive behaviors are listed in one column, the feelings they were meant to fix in another, and the actual feelings or results of those behaviors in a third column. When you chart them this way, you can see more clearly how your dysfunctional religious beliefs made your life unmanageable. Following is an example.

OBSESSIVE BEHAVIOR	FEELINGS TO BE FIXED	ACTUAL RESULTS
Scripture quoting	Not being good enough, need to control, fear, inadequacy, people pleasing	Anger, invalidation, isolation, feeling rejected, not good enough
Constant attendance at missions, crusades, revivals	Loneliness, inferiority, need for approval, sinfulness	Increased isolation, anger, disapproval of employers and family, exhaustion
Excessive financial contributions	Need to control, feeling not good enough, fear, people pleasing	Financial strain or bankruptcy, family arguments, resentments, guilt, shame, rejection by family/friends
Being angry, self-righteous, judgmental, critical	Fear, perfectionism, in-feriority, sexual confusion, guilt, shame	Isolation, increased anger, rejection by family/friends, loneliness, self-loathing, fear, shame

Using these kinds of writing exercises and charts will help you see that your pain, discomfort, loneliness, low self-esteem, guilt, shame, isolation, and family problems are the result of your powerlessness over dysfunctional religion; it will reveal the resulting unmanageability. Once you admit you have a problem and truly see that you are powerless, then you can begin to experience the power and manageability that come with self-confrontation. This is the true meaning of Step One, for in the knowledge of how we are powerless comes power—the power of surrender. With surrender comes not only the desire but also the willingness to change. You are ready to move on to Step Two.

Step Two. Came to believe that a Spiritual Power within ourselves could guide us to sanity.

The words "came to" often indicate a return to consciousness or awareness, like an awakening out of a long sleep. Sometimes that reawakening is sudden; sometimes it is gradual. But whether sudden or gradual, coming to is a process. You need to see clearly how you victimize yourself over and over again by trying to control people, places, substances, and God.

You may find it helpful to list incidents and behavior that illustrate your religious insanity. This kind of writing evokes the feelings you've wanted to avoid; with those feelings can come recognition of how truly insane your thinking and behaviors have become. When you can focus on the insanity of your attitudes and behaviors, you can increase your desire to be restored to sanity.

For most religious addicts, the most difficult part of recovery is the issue of God. Because many religious addicts have shared with me that the concept of a Higher Power greater than themselves reinforces their belief in their sinfulness, I suggest substituting the phrase "Spiritual Power within ourselves." Similarly, I have replaced "restore us to sanity" with "guide. . . ." The idea of something restoring me indicates that I have no role or responsibility in this restoration and perpetuates the magical belief in a fixer.

▲ ▼ ▲

Exercise: Make a list of all the ways your dysfunctional use of religion keeps you from taking action and responsibility in your life. In what ways do your beliefs tell you that you are inadequate, inherently bad, or have no choices? Do your beliefs tell you that only an outside source will make you better? How?

▲ ▼ ▲

The process of coming to believe involves developing a new relationship with a Spiritual Power, which permits the concept of ourselves as co-creator with our Spiritual Power, rather than the traditional and inherently abusive master/servant roles. We consult this Power as a guide and navigator rather than waiting for God to do something for us. Seeing ourselves as co-creators opens the door to choice and to re-empowerment. It allows each of us to find our inner positive creativity.

As you come to this step, you may want to use affirmations such as:

- I now permit the Spiritual Power within me to guide me to sanity.
- I am a positive and creative person.
- I am the key to my sanity.

STABILIZATION: STEP THREE

The most important aspect of the stabilization phase is the movement from a mere desire to change to taking actions that create change. You have taken a hard look at the crises your religious addiction has created in your life, and you have experienced renewed unmanageability either through withdrawal or relapse; you have seen the insanity in your life. Not only do you want to change, but you are beginning to believe that you can. Now, when you are told that religious addiction can be arrested, you listen. When you ask how you can change, you no longer say it with a helpless, victimized tone. Like those who have decided to take the necessary steps, you are saying, Show me the way. You have arrived at the next stage.

Step Three. Made the decision to turn our will and our lives over to the care of a Spiritual Power as we understood this Spiritual Power.

In this step, the important phrases are "made the decision to turn..." and "Spiritual Power as we understood this Spiritual Power." We cannot change until we have truly decided that we want to—until we *make the decision* to change

▲ ▼ ▲

Exercise: Write about what making a decision means to you. Have you ever attempted to change something that you really didn't want to change—hadn't genuinely decided you wanted to change? Did it work? Or was it a halfhearted effort? How many times did you try to change your religious obsession? What did you do? Why do you think it didn't work?

▲ ▼ ▲

What are we changing when we try to recover from religious addiction? I have observed that many people struggle with the idea of "turning it over," because it fosters the notion that they are putting something or someone else in charge of their lives—handing over responsibility. The key word here is *turn*. What do we do when we turn? We change direction. Turning it over is not a passive act of surrender, but a conscious choice to take a different path. Step Three is about making a decision to change directions, to change our course of action. It speaks of asking for guidance and choosing to accept that guidance to do things differently and to move in the direction of recovery.

In Step Three, the concept of Spiritual Power *as we understand* Spiritual Power frees all of us, especially the religiously addicted and abused. It allows us to discover an inner guide whom we can trust to take us in a healthier direction. Coming to a new understanding of God or Spiritual Power will take time. For many, that new understanding grows with our physical, mental, and emotional recovery.

Spirituality encompasses our physical, mental, and emotional well-being. The spiritual self is the total self. To understand God, we must first understand ourselves. In the book *Twelve Steps and Twelve Traditions* of Alcoholics Anonymous we find the statement: "We can have faith, yet keep God out of our lives." It is hard to understand or allow into our lives any kind of Spiritual Power, which I call God, if we are abusing our bodies, if we are deeply depressed and entangled in addictive behaviors. We will find it difficult to love anyone, including God, if we are actively hating ourselves. Nor can we fully accept God's love for us—or anyone else's love, for that matter.

The first power we must come to believe in is the power of self-love. When we can find and accept ourselves, we can come to a new understanding of a Spiritual Power, one we can allow into our lives and trust to care for us.

You begin this process by re-examining your beliefs about yourself mentally, physically, and emotionally. If you suspend the belief that you were born utterly depraved and a blotch on existence, and practice replacing it with the idea that you are a positive, creative human being, then you can start looking at yourself differently.

There are some practical exercises that you can do to help you begin to turn your image of yourself from negative and shaming to positive and encouraging. If you have not done these kind of exercises before, you may find the concept a little strange. Give them a chance. I have seen time and again the therapeutic and healing value of writing to a part of yourself: your body, mind, or a belief or attitude. Most people find it an effective way to begin to be gentle and loving with themselves, to acknowledge self-destructiveness without emotionally beating themselves up for it.

Part one—physical: God is alive in our bodies. Therefore, God exists in sexuality, intimacy, childbirth, hugs, exercise, nutrition, how we look, and how we act. All are aspects of spirituality.

▲ ▼ ▲

Exercise: Write a letter to your body. Make amends to it for the ways in which you might have abused it: substance abuse, eating disorders, over- and under-exercising, believing it is dirty, abusing it with sexual addiction.

Next, find things to praise about your body: What qualities are attractive? Has your physical health remained fairly good despite any abuses? Thank your body for being your earthly temple. Make a contract with your body to treat it with love and nurturance.

Part two—mental: God is alive in our minds. Therefore, doubting, asking questions, and changing attitudes and beliefs are part of spiritual growth.

Exercise: Look at the ways you have abused your mind with your dysfunctional beliefs. Do you avoid using your mental faculties because you won't think, doubt, or question? Do you limit what your mind can do by reading only religious-related material? Do you negate your own talents and efforts by telling yourself that God or your Higher Power is responsible for getting you where you are? Do you avoid your creative abilities because you believe material pleasures, which include art and music, are evil?

Write a letter to your mind making amends for the ways in which you have abused it. Find three to five qualities about your mind that you can appreciate.

▲ ▼ ▲

Part three—emotions and feelings: God is alive in our emotions. Spiritual growth includes talking about feeling abused, discounted, abandoned, judged, sinful, inferior, angry, or lonely. It also allows us to feel joy, happiness, freedom, and hope. Spirituality is knowing that God made all our feelings and therefore loves and accepts them all.

Exercise: Write a letter to your feelings. Tell them you know now how you have hurt them by believing they were bad or by ignoring, discounting, or minimizing them.

Then tell each feeling something positive about it. If you have done this kind of work before and feel comfortable with it, you might also want to describe a healthy way you've learned to express each feeling. For instance, you may have been taught not to bring people down by telling them you're feeling sad; your dysfunctional pattern was therefore to put up a front or just to isolate. You may have now learned to acknowledge your sadness and ask for a hug as a healthy expression of feelings.

Doing these exercises will help you begin to come to a new understanding of yourself and, ultimately, of your Spiritual Power and the role it can play in your life. The physical, emotional, and mental aspects of our lives unite to create a spiritually whole self. Dr. Martin Israel, in his book, *Precious Living,* explains it this way:

> *The very distinction between spiritual and material or sacred and secular is ultimately invalid, for the spiritual mode finds its place in all actions, whether physical or psychical, that leads us to a fuller knowledge of God. Whatever leads us to a knowledge of God is spiritually based; it also leads us away from preoccupation with ourselves to a fuller participation in the world's affairs and the concerns of other people. . . .*
>
> *The beauty of nature, the marvelous rhythm of the cosmic flow, and the processes of our own healthy bodies are all fundamentally physical in scale, and yet are also deeply spiritual in content, for they lead the beholder to rejoice in God the creator and sustainer of the universe. Great art,*

again sensual and physical in its outer manifestation, is humanity's finest spiritual creation, for it leads the weary soul to its Creator who is the end of all beauty. Likewise the scientist dedicated to the pursuit of truth is God-centered and spiritually based, for in God is all truth. Those whose lives are devoted to service and care for others are equally spiritual in orientation, for they tread the path of self-giving in love, and God is above all else in love. From this we can deduce that physical communication has strong spiritual overtones when it is inspired by the highest values we know—beauty, truth, and goodness (or love).

As my understanding and acceptance of myself grows, so does my understanding and acceptance of my Spiritual Power. The God of my understanding today is different from the God I knew early in recovery, because the Leo I know and love today is different. My love and appreciation of my Higher Power has deepened with my love and appreciation of myself.

Yet to get to that self-love has required patience, practice, and the continual working of the Twelve Steps. In the early days of recovery, my belief in my insanity and powerlessness was strong; my new understanding of God was but an embryonic hope. Remaining in recovery, continuing to create and work my program, has nurtured that embryonic hope into a mature, secure belief and faith.

EARLY STAGE RECOVERY: STEPS FOUR, FIVE, AND SIX

Once you have made the decision to change and have begun to discover within yourself the tools that will create change, you are into the early stage of recovery. You recognize your religious addiction and religious abuse. You see the dysfunction in the messages you received about God and start seeking healthy spiritual values with which to replace those old messages. You begin to recognize your behavior patterns and see when you are wanting to use religion as a fix. You are learning to live in reality, in the present moment.

At this stage, you begin to feel your pain and are sometimes able to connect your attitudes and behaviors to your feelings. If you are irritable, critical, and judging, you may see that you are feeling not good enough or are fearing rejection. Often this insight comes after the behavior, such as angry words to a family member or friend. You have greater willingness, however, to recognize this and make amends for your behaviors, and an increased desire for change.

Step Four: Made a searching and fearless inventory of our dysfunctional religious beliefs and behaviors.

Step Four helps you clarify your patterns and behaviors and prepares you to begin clearing them away. You might want to look at the list of symptoms of religious addiction and examine how they apply to yourself.

THE SYMPTOMS OF RELIGIOUS ADDICTION

Inability to think, doubt, or question information and authority

Black-and-white, simplistic thinking

Shame-based belief that you aren't good enough or you aren't doing it right

Magical thinking that God will fix you

Scrupulosity: rigid obsessive adherence to rules, codes of ethics, or guidelines

Uncompromising judgmental attitudes

Compulsive praying, going to church or crusades, quoting scripture

Unrealistic financial contributions

Believing that sex is dirty; believing our bodies or physical pleasures are evil

Compulsive overeating and/or excessive fasting

Conflict with science, medicine, and education

Progressive detachment from the real world, isolation, breakdown of relationships

Psychosomatic illness: back pains, sleeplessness, headaches, hypertension

Manipulating scripture or texts, feeling chosen, claiming to receive special messages from God

Trancelike state or religious high, wearing a glazed happy face

Cries for help; mental, physical, and emotional breakdown; hospitalization

Exercise: Write about each symptom, listing at least five ways in which you manifested it. Then list at least three ways in which you harmed yourself and others. You might also want to begin listing people you harmed.

Next, list ways in which you have begun to change this belief or behavior. Noting changes is always a way to reinforce the steps you've taken—a clear illustration that not only can you change, you already have changed. This worksheet will help you prepare for your Fourth and Fifth Steps and will be valuable when you are ready to take the next Steps.

▲ ▼ ▲

These steps mark the beginnings of a healthy spirituality as you begin to discard your old behaviors and to uncover your true self. Family and friends start noticing changes as self-esteem begins to creep in. Slowly, gently, you are coming to a healthier understanding of God and are beginning to reflect that power and creativity in your life.

SYMPTOM: Refusing to think, doubt, or question

MY BEHAVIORS	HOW I HURT MYSELF AND OTHERS	HOW I'VE CHANGED
1. Believed only our church had right way	1. Gave my family no choices; deprived my children of friends	1. Try to keep open mind
2. Not listening to others with different beliefs	2. Was rude to co-workers, especially Jane and Bill	2. Let the family choose their friends and where they want to go to church
3. Reading only approved scripture	4. Didn't examine Joe Doe's financial record; now I'm ashamed to say I voted for a state treasurer who embezzles money	3. Reading other books about spirituality
4. Voting only for church approved candidates		
5. Picking my children's friends to keep them safe from evil ways		

SYMPTOM: Belief that sex is dirty

MY BEHAVIORS	HOW I HURT MYSELF AND OTHERS	HOW I'VE CHANGED
1. Not initiating sex with spouse	1. Felt extreme guilt, shame; hurt my spouse	1. Working with therapist on developing healthy sex life
2. Picketed adult bookstores; left religious tracts in sex education sections of mall bookstores	2. Humiliated bookstore customers during picketing; caused inconvenience to other store's sales staff	2. Apologized to bookstore personnel; refused to join anti-porn group
3. Condemned homosexuals to hell; refused to visit cousin dying of AIDS	3. Abused dying cousin; hurt his family; denied my children a chance to say good-bye to a favorite relative	3. Took a letter to my cousin's grave making amends for my bigotry; trying to learn about homosexuality
		4. Started looking at my own sexual abuse issues

For all addicts, the Fifth Step is a powerful turn toward self-forgiveness and self-respect.

Step Five. Admitted to our Spiritual Power, to ourselves, and to another human being the exact nature of those behaviors. This is a step toward restoring balance, for taking it usually reveals that we were neither the worst nor the best.

Notice again the change in wording. Some religious addicts have shared with me that when this step is read in other Twelve Step meetings, they subconsciously hear the word "sins" instead of wrong behavior. Focusing on behavior, which is always changeable, helps avoid the old belief in inherent sinfulness and depravity, which is always a pitfall for religious addicts.

For religious addicts especially, Step Five can be frightening; there is an aspect of confession, which could trigger old feelings of guilt and shame. It is particularly important to choose someone whom you trust not to judge you—or allow you to judge yourself. This is another reason that including changes you have already made in your Step Four chart can be beneficial. It allows you to give yourself credit—something religious addicts have a difficult time doing.

▲ ▼ ▲

Exercise: As you prepare for your Fifth Step, list the changes in behavior and attitude you have made, as noted on your chart for Step Four. Congratulate yourself for those changes. You might want to make affirmations with them: for example, I congratulate myself for being more flexible with rules.

After you complete your Fifth Step, write your feelings about what you shared. How do you feel about yourself? Can you see how your actions and attitudes came from great pain? Patrick Carnes, in A Gentle Path through the Twelve Steps, suggests having the person who hears your Fifth Step also write his or her feelings on hearing your Step. You may want to include this if both of you feel comfortable with it.

▲ ▼ ▲

The purpose of Step Five is to lay the foundations of self-acceptance and self-forgiveness, which are so necessary to loving yourself. It is one of the most difficult tasks all addicts face: the process of learning to love ourselves wholly, including those parts of ourselves we think are bad or unacceptable. This is especially difficult for religious addicts who are told you are born bad and can't change that inherent badness.

Step Six. Were entirely ready to work with our Spiritual Power in replacing all these old behaviors.

Many religious addicts have shared with me their difficulties with the concept of a Higher Power taking away their defects of character. Based on their input, I suggest using the idea of working alongside your Spiritual Power to replace dysfunctional behaviors with healthy ones. Remember, healthy spirituality includes taking responsibility for our lives. So many dysfunctional religious messages, whether Christian, Muslim, or New Age, promote the idea that you are not in charge of your life.

The focus of Step Six is the willingness to let go of disease and the recognition that it cannot be done alone by you or God! In the past you might have waited for the fixer to wave a magic wand and make you perfect; now you understand that your Spiritual Power is a guide and a navigator, but you must do the footwork. You participate in your life rather than wait for something to come out of the sky (or out of a past life) and hand you information. You are moving closer to finding a Spiritual Power who is a friend and partner, not an abusively angry parent or judge. You begin to reflect this new understanding of God in the way in which you treat yourself and others.

▲ ▼ ▲

Exercise: First, write about how the concept of replacing old behaviors with healthy ones gives you choices and allows you to take responsibility for your life. When viewed in this context, do you find that the idea of changing behaviors becomes easier and thus increases your readiness to replace them? Why or why not?

MID-STAGE RECOVERY: STEPS SEVEN, EIGHT, AND NINE

Now you are getting the big picture. Not only do you see how truly unmanageable your life was but also you are able to see how widespread that unmanageability was. Steps Four and Five allowed you to see how it affected all your relationships: at home, at work, at church. More important, you see how it affected your relationship with yourself. You are coming to understand how you missed yourself—disowned or discredited your own strengths, capabilities, and power of choice. You gain greater understanding of how your addiction or abuse connects to your other issues, especially if you were active in other addictions.

This is the stage at which many will surrender to acceptance of other addictions and begin to work additional Twelve Step programs. You may begin to attend A.A. or begin to address an eating disorder after several years of sobriety. Those who have been in Al-Anon, Adult Children of Alcoholics, or Codependents Anonymous groups may now identify a sex and love addiction and begin to address those issues. Taking Steps Four through Six gives you greater willingness to look at those issues and at how you have behaved in terms of them. You work harder in therapy or begin therapy for the first time.

Step Seven. Worked with our Spiritual Power to help replace our dysfunctional patterns.

The changes begun in the earlier stages are cementing as you grow more comfortable with your recovering self. Steps Seven through Nine allow you to clear away the wreckage of the past, as it states in the *Big Book* of Alcoholics Anonymous. You are replacing that wreckage with new values and beliefs. Rather than humbly kneeling before that magical fixer who is going to mystically take away your old patterns, you work with your Spiritual Power. The God of your understanding is becoming less and less the old boss who ordered you around at whim, but a partner and a friend alongside of whom you work as a co-creator of your recovery.

▲ ▼ ▲

Exercise: Using the same format as in previous exercises make a
list of dysfunctional beliefs and behaviors you wish to replace.
Then list the actions you can take to help you replace those
beliefs or behaviors. How do these actions demonstrate
healthy partnership with your Spiritual Power?

▲ ▼ ▲

The changes you are making are beginning to enhance your
relationships with others. With your family and friends, you make a
greater effort to restore healthy communications, and you increase your
sensitivity to others' needs, beliefs, and values. You are beginning to
develop new friendships based on the honest, open sharing of feelings.
You are ready to work the next step.

Step Eight. Made a list of all persons we have harmed and
became willing to make amends to them all.

It is important that you approach this step and the one following it
with the attitude of clearing away wreckage, of restoring and/or
replacing healthiness. I have seen many people in Twelve Step
programs spiritually and emotionally bludgeon themselves with these
steps because they take them in guilt and shame. You do not take these
steps to show what a sinner you are, how bad you were. You take them
as a means to rebuild open, honest relationships.

Step Nine. Made direct amends to such people wherever possible,
except when to do so would injure them or others.

One way in which many recovering people ensure that they do not
shame themselves with these steps is that they include themselves in the

list of those they have harmed and to whom they make amends. Often the person you have harmed most consistently is yourself.

▲ ▼ ▲

Exercise: Before you make your list, reflect on your concept of harm. Do you think it implies conscious intention to hurt? Do you recognize that you may not have intended harm? What feelings does the recognition that you may have unintentionally harmed someone bring up? Do you think making amends will magically erase those feelings? Be honest! If you are trying to ease your shame, you may not be ready to begin amends.

Next, write an amends letter to yourself. Include not only the things you have done in the past to harm yourself but also a list of the things you are doing to create your recovery. Your letter of amends to yourself can serve as a model for the amends you might make with others. As a practice exercise, you may want to write to one person to whom you feel you might have difficulty making amends. I have found it is powerfully beneficial to read such a letter to a sponsor, friend, or other mentor and then to burn it. It is amazing how freeing the act of burning it can be and how much easier it is then to move on to making amends to others.

▲ ▼ ▲

These are the relationship steps that pave the way to richer, more rewarding relationships with others, with yourself, and with God. Remember that making amends does not always mean sitting down with someone, confessing, and apologizing for mistreating that person. Sometimes that's not possible; people die or move away. Here again, writing a letter and burning it makes an effective tool. Often the changes brought by recovery are the best amends we can make, simply by ceasing to engage in old behaviors and beliefs.

Working through these steps brings you to a deeper awareness and understanding of how the dysfunction in your childhood has continued to operate in your life. In this stage, it is not uncommon to hear people saying that they are going through it all again and had thought they were through with those issues. You have been peeling away the layers and have come to the core issues of guilt and shame. You may experience anew the anger and rage you never permitted yourself to feel as a child.

The emotional intensity may be even more painful than the first withdrawal, but in this stage, the pain is welcomed, embraced. No longer do you wish to escape it, to run and hide. Less and less do you victimize yourself with your pain but, through it, find power and strength. Although you are feeling extremely painful emotions, you are more in control, unlike the early days of withdrawal. You see how you victimized yourself, and how you, as a religious addict, have been abusive. Where possible, you make amends. Family and friends now find you easier to talk to and confide in. Suddenly, you find that making friends has become easier and more rewarding as you are able to share yourself healthily.

LAST STAGE RECOVERY: STEPS TEN AND ELEVEN

The intensity of the work begun in mid-stage recovery begins to really show in healthy personality changes. From rigid, angry intolerance you move to becoming open and accepting. You no longer need to control others; you no longer feel threatened by beliefs that are different from your own. Your new self-acceptance is reflected in the way you treat others. This is the benefit of the next step.

Step Ten. Continued to take personal inventory and when we made mistakes, promptly admitted it.

This is a vital step for religious addicts, as it helps you address your perfectionism and judgmentalness. I have replaced the phrase "when we were wrong..." as used by A.A. with "made mistakes..." to help make the distinction between making a mistake and being a mistake. Saying that you were wrong carries strong overtones of the black-and-white, right/wrong thinking, and it can subliminally reinforce the idea of inherent sinfulness or wrongness. Thus it is healthier for religious addicts to begin to think in terms of having made a mistake rather than being bad.

This allows you to be imperfect; that is, to be human. When you can let yourself be human, it is easier to allow others to be human, too. Thus it opens you to richer and more rewarding experiences and relationships. You become healthier as you move away from your stifling religious isolation. Your life is becoming more balanced and whole. Greater attention is paid to physical health and nutrition. Because you now permit variety in your life, your horizons broaden; you become part of the world and are up to date on world events. You rejoin society, allowing yourself to enjoy movies, TV, and other recreation. You experience the richness of human diversity and can rejoice in the varieties of human experience. You begin to find, as I wrote in *Meditations for Compulsive People,* "God in the Odd" and discover God in the simple, ordinary things of life. You have arrived at the next step.

Step Eleven. Sought through prayer and meditation to improve our conscious contact with our Spiritual Power, as we understood Spiritual Power, asking only for knowledge of that Power's guidance and the willingness to carry that out.

We do not get spirituality; it has already been given. Recovery from religious addiction is about uncovering our true spirituality, which has been hidden beneath our diseased and dysfunctional beliefs about ourselves and God.

I often hear the slogan, "Praying is asking. Meditating is listening." In your dysfunction, you asked for the fixer to tell you what to do, believing you did not have the right answers within you. In recovery, as you work through the earlier steps, you are discovering that you do have the answers. The letters you wrote in Step Three to your body, mind, and feelings were forms of meditation and conscious contact—of looking inside and finding that you have the tools after all. Your Spiritual Power is a guide who offers suggestions about what tools to use. Step Eleven is a healthy way of seeking assistance, which allows for choice and self-responsibility.

▲ ▼ ▲

Exercise: Writing in your journal, reflect on the value of taking a daily inventory as a means for taking responsibility for your actions or attitudes. Pay attention to your feelings as you take your daily inventory, especially to any feelings of shame and judgment that may arise.

Next, write about the concept that the more you are able to make choices and take responsibility, the more you look to your Spiritual Power as a guide to making healthy choices rather than as a fixer. List some examples of how this may be working in your life.

▲ ▼ ▲

ONGOING RECOVERY: STEP TWELVE

At last, you truly find yourself. No longer are you a passive victim, waiting for God or something else to fix you. You find your own power and control by taking responsibility for your life. In your religious addiction, you left things to God. In recovery, you take action: You work with your therapists, use your sponsors, deepen your involvement in Twelve Step groups. In your religious addiction, you saw yourself as innately bad—a sinner. In recovery, you see yourself as a positive, creative human who sometimes makes mistakes. You have a program and you work it daily, to the best of your ability, at peace with the knowledge that you may not always work it perfectly. You are now able to take the final step.

Step Twelve. Having had a spiritual awakening as a result of these steps, we tried to carry this message to others and to practice these principles in all our affairs.

No more do you experience God "out there." You have filled the void—not from the outside in, with substances and other things and not like a religious robe you wore to protect yourself. You have filled it from the inside out. It is like the healing process that takes place when one has had a puncture wound, or has had a cyst removed. The wound isn't just covered, which is what addiction does. It fills in, rejoins, from the bottom up. This is true spirituality—looking in the mirror and seeing God in yourself, in your positive creativity. You have choice. You have power. You have broken the chains and are free.

Your freedom is clearly reflected in your life. You will mirror qualities others want for themselves, and when they ask you how they can get what you have, you are able to share your experience, strength, and hope: not by proselytizing or preaching as you once did, but by simply sharing your experience. You can relate what you were like, what happened, and what you are like now.

Recovery is an ongoing process, constantly cycling and recycling, full of painful periods of growth followed by ever-lengthening periods of serenity. We are constantly evolving, changing, refining and redefining ourselves. Out of our one big moment will come many smaller moments—times when we will recognize that we are ready to change another old pattern that is limiting or diminishing our lives. Within this process lies the miracle of the discovery of that Spiritual Power within us who, if we can but reach out our hands, will lead us charging headlong into our shouted Yes! to life.

Chapter 7

Toward a Healthy Spirituality

> Before ever a Yes to God can be made, the
> creature must come alive to the moment and the
> circumstances and the implications that have to
> be faced.... Spirituality is not simply a widening
> of the consciousness as some enthusiasts for
> drug-cultures have suggested, or an increasing
> of the sensitiveness of human beings, but the
> employment of all that we have of sensitive
> awareness and rich consciousness in acts of
> faithful living. The prayer that we make is the
> focusing of that effort. [What we need] ... is to be
> more adequately prepared in the persons we are
> for that engagement of ourselves with God.
>
> Alan Ecclestone

YOU HAVE COME alive to the moment. You have examined the circumstances and implications of your religious addiction and abuse. Your work on the issues that contributed to your dysfunctional belief system is preparing you for a healthy engagement with God—not the old God of your diseased thinking, but a new God to whom you can shout a wholehearted, Yes!

Becoming more adequately prepared for this requires clearing away the negative, shaming messages and beliefs of the past and replacing them with messages and beliefs that nurture and express our positive creativity. It requires letting go of the dysfunctional qualities we once attributed to God and replacing them with healthy ones.

I have said often that we reflect the God of our understanding. If the belief system we embrace is judging and condemning, we will judge and condemn. If we believe in a compassionate, forgiving God, we will be compassionate and forgiving. We behave according to our beliefs. In *To Have or To Be?*, Erich Fromm noted:

> *Thus, our religious attitude may be considered an aspect of our character structure, for we are what we are devoted to, and what we are devoted to is what motivates our conduct. Often, however, individuals are not even aware of the real objects of their personal devotion and mistake their "official" beliefs for their real, though secret religion. If, for instance, a man worships power while professing a religion of love, the religion of power is his secret religion, while his so-called official religion, for example Christianity, is only an ideology.*

In making the distinction between our secret religion and our official ideology, Fromm has hit upon the source of much of the hypocrisy that marks addiction to any religion, belief system, or code of ethics. I often hear the complaint that religious addicts clearly do not practice what they preach. As Fromm explains it, this is because what they believe and what they preach are not the same. They may not be practicing what they preach, but they are definitely practicing what they believe. This is probably why religious addicts do not see the hypocrisy in preaching about a loving, forgiving God and being judgmental and intolerant: They do not believe in a loving God. Deep down, they truly believe God is angry, wrathful, and judging. Or perhaps, they secretly worship power and control. Religion is the means they use to get it.

Thus, recovery from religious addiction and abuse requires us to examine our deepest beliefs and motives with utmost honesty to see where our behaviors and our ideologies do not match. Then we must take the steps to bring them into alignment so that our insides match our outsides.

This means abandoning our old dysfunctional beliefs about what God is like and replacing them with healthy ones. Here the use of affirmations becomes especially effective. They serve as the replacing tool that you can use to exchange unhealthy beliefs and behaviors for new ones. I often hear those old beliefs referred to as old tapes. Consistent use of affirmations erases the old message and records a healthier one in its place. You should take care, however, that you don't use affirmations unhealthily or compulsively. Affirmations should always enhance some positive quality about yourself, as well as affirming your own choice and responsibility. I often hear people say, "There are no mistakes" as an affirmation. Statements like this actually reinforce a lack of responsibility along with some magical thinking. The statement, "I am a positive, creative human who is allowed to make mistakes" is a more effective affirmation. We will be using affirmations and other exercises in this chapter as we explore ways to create a healthy spirituality.

GOD'S VALUES AND QUALITIES

It has been said that the qualities we exhibit in our lives often reflect the qualities we attribute to God; likewise, we may examine many of the qualities usually attributed to God to see how we might apply them to our lives. There are four such qualities that increasingly reflect healthy spirituality the more we develop them in our lives. They are truth, energy, love, and acceptance.

Truth

The concept. The spiritual pursuit of truth is fundamental to our creating a meaningful relationship with God because it conveys our desire to be honest. Truth conveys our desire to be honest. Truth reflects our desire to integrate our thoughts with our feelings, the matching of parts of ourselves that allows us to be real, to have integrity. It allows us to reveal our true selves while confronting those hypocritical aspects of our personalities. The search for God necessitates that we get in touch with our true feelings and allow ourselves to be vulnerable.

Practical application. When you share your true feelings with others, you become real. You discover that, contrary to your initial beliefs, when you are real with people, they are able to love you more.

In your religious addiction, you learned to hide your feelings behind rituals and rules, magical thinking and fantasies, control and perfectionism. Sharing your real feelings first requires learning to identify them, then learning to risk sharing them. It's a process which takes time, one in which, ever so slowly, you *become.*

Affirmations.

I am powerful when I am honest.

I discover God when I express my true feelings.

I rejoice in sharing my true beliefs.

Energy

The concept. I agree with Teilhard de Chardin, that we as humans are energy moving toward Source, that God is pure energy, and we are channels of the same energy.

God is often revealed most powerfully and gloriously through creative energy. The sheer artistry found in the caprices and complexities of the way in which our world is put together manifests an imaginative and creative God. If such imaginativeness and creativity exist in God, I suggest that they must also exist in us.

Religious addiction is, in many ways, an avoidance of energy, a self-abnegation, especially of the creative self. The passive waiting and denial of personal power that mark the religious addict is a refusal to acknowledge, much less use, one's own energy. Remember, miracles exist not so much in God's acts as in our response to them. God gives us talent and creativity, and we grow closer to God when we choose to use our talents and thus appreciate that creativity. That is partnership with God.

Practical application. Recovery permits you to draw on your God-given energy and to appreciate that its presence in you makes you unique and special. John Bradshaw observes that

> *when we are spiritual, we are in contact with our uniqueness*
> *and specialness. It is our fundamental beingness or I AMness.*
> *. . . My belief is that our I AMness constitutes our core*
> *godlikeness. When a person has this sense of I AMness, he is*
> *one with himself and is self-accepting. . . . The deepest sense*
> *of human spirituality is this I AMness, which incorporates the*
> *qualities of being valuable, precious and special.*

God told Moses: "I am that I am." Thus did God tell us who we are. In recognizing your own individual I AMness, you energize your positive creativity. You are not afraid to doubt or question beliefs or authority; no longer must you run from science, medicine, art, or literature. Rather than avoid or negate who you are, living mired in toxic shame, bereft of the ability to see God in yourself, you rejoice in your creative energy. In that self-acceptance, you find God.

Affirmations.

I rejoice in who I am.

I now discover God in my life.

I reflect my God-energy in my Yes to life.

Love

The concept. Love is essential to any healthy religious and spiritual person. But what is love? It is critical that we look at the specific qualities we attribute to love, for if we talk about a God of love, or say that God is love, we need to know what we really mean.

In *Growing Young,* Ashley Montagu describes love as being modeled for us by our parents:

> *Love is the active process of conferring survival benefits*
> *in a creatively enlarging manner upon the other, the*
> *communication to the other, by demonstrative acts of one's*

involvement in his welfare, giving him the support, sustenance, and stimulation that he requires for the fulfillment of his potentialities for being the kind of human being that you are being to him, that he can depend on you whenever he is in need, that you will never commit the supreme treason of letting him down when he most stands in need of you. It is in this way that one learns to love, simply by being loved, the most powerful of all the developers of one's humane abilities.

In this way, we become what we are shown. Yet the ways in which we manifest love, and how we need others to demonstrate their love for us are different. There is the love of a parent for a child, that of lovers, and that of friends. There is the ethereal agape of a universal and peaceful love as well as the love described in 2 Corinthians: "love is not jealous or boastful. . . ."

Love is all of these and more: What we love, we accept, nourish, delight in, and grow from. We strengthen and sustain ourselves in it—whether we find it in art, music, literature, nature, science, children, parents, lovers, friends, even pets. Whatever we love, however we are loved, there we find God.

Practical application. In your religious addiction, you yearned for and preached about a God of love, while secretly believing in an angry, judging God who found you inherently unacceptable. Thus your actions could never match your words. Believing yourself base and worthless, you treated others as though they were worthless. You were critical, judgmental, and condemning. You relied on outside rituals and dogma to supposedly absolve you of this inborn wretchedness.

In recovery, you no longer look outside to the external trappings of rules, regulations, and platitudes for your self-worth. You find it within. When you can treat yourself with love and respect, you then have no difficulty treating others the same way. Thus love becomes the bridge to healthy relationships. God is love, because you are loving and lovable. You now live what you used to merely preach.

Affirmations.

In my love of self, I discover my love of God and others.

I love through my humanness.

My love is the expression of God's energy.

Acceptance

The concept. Our understanding of God's love and the special relationship that comes with knowing we are God's kids produce self-acceptance. Gone is the frightening, angry, wrathful, critical God who sat majestically enthroned too far away to reach, and whom we approached expecting condemnation and judgment. Instead we find a loving parent to whom we turn for guidance, comfort, and nurture—a playful daddy or mommy, rather than the forbidding father or mother figure whose rules helped create our dysfunctional beliefs.

This shift from the traditional, Old Testament view of God as distant ruler to a more personal relationship with a co-creator nurtures our self-acceptance. We develop personal dignity when we appreciate how God requires our participation in our own redemption. For now we are not passive spectators waiting to be magically saved, but active partners in the exchange of values and behaviors that no longer work for a new set of guidelines to take us on this phase of our journey. In *The Color Purple,* Shug tells Celie:

. . . God love all them feelings. That's some of the best stuff God did. And when you know God loves 'em, you enjoys 'em a lot more. You can just relax, go with everything that's going, and praise God by liking what you like.

Practical application. When you change your belief about yourself and start from the premise that you are born wholly capable of good and a creature of dignity and grace, you accept that God—and everyone else—loves you for who you are. You are able to break the chains of low self-esteem, powerlessness, unworthiness, and sin so that you can take an active role in the creating of your life.

Knowing, as Shug told Celie, that "God love everything you love—and a mess of stuff you don't" lets you shout Yes! to yourself, to life, and to God. In your addiction, you believed that God said No to everything pleasurable. In recovery, you come to believe that what God has created, God also accepts.

Risk becomes easier, knowing you are not going to be eternally damned for failure. You share your feelings knowing they are not bad; they cannot be bad if God made them. This is the "new freedom" spoken of in the A.A. Promises: the freedom to be who you are and to accept others as they are.

Affirmations.

In God's acceptance I claim my divinity.

Knowing that I am accepted frees me to love.

My acceptance of myself is my Yes! to God.

INVITING IN A NEW GOD

I counseled a patient in a treatment center who was struggling to come to terms with personal problems relating to religious addiction and abuse as well as other addictions. We had many talks, listening to each other's views. At the end, the patient turned to me and said, "Father Leo, I've listened to you. Heard you. I want so much to believe you. But what if they're right?"

The question haunted me. Finally, I saw that it was a valid, fearful question only in the context of all that "they" and "being right" means to you. Ask yourself: Who are they? Does the word refer to the authority figures who seek to stay in power by keeping you subjugated in shame and fear? Do they forbid you to question and explore? Do they resist change and insist on rigid dogma? Then perhaps they might be religious abusers.

Certainly, I have asked myself the same question: What if I'm wrong? If I'm wrong, then God is after all an angry, wrathful, unforgiving, bloody tyrant who is definitely to be feared. I cannot, do not, will not believe in such a God. I have abandoned the trappings that might have led me to serve such a God, because believing in that kind of God kept me sick, power-hungry, egotistical, and drunk. I fired that God.

In the passage from *The Color Purple* that I find so moving, Celie has described her God as a bigoted old white man. Shug shares her view of God as It—an entity that depends as much on pleasing us as on our pleasing It. Shug offers Celie a way to find a God she can trust, but Celie's not sure. She says:

> *Well, us talk and talk about God, but I'm still adrift. Trying to chase that old white man out of my head. I been so busy thinking about him I never truly notice nothing God make. Not a blade of corn (how it do that?) not the color purple (where it come from?). Not the little wildflowers. Nothing.*

Shug gives her a suggestion: Whenever that old image comes up, "tell him to get lost. . . . Conjure up flowers, wind, water, a big rock." Celie muses:

> *But this hard work, let me tell you. He been there so long, he don't want to budge. He threaten lightning, floods and earthquakes. Us fight. I hardly pray at all. Every time I conjure up a rock, I throw it.*

Like Celie, before you can say yes to God, before you can invite in new godlike qualities, you have to get rid of the old God who keeps the committee in your head whispering, What if they're right? You must let go of those old attributes that made you fear and hate God. You need to figuratively throw rocks at your image of God as an angry old man. You need to fire that old God.

Earlier, I described techniques for beginning to find a new spirituality that required writing letters to your body, mind, and feelings. When you are ready to let go of your old dysfunctional beliefs, and the God who manifests them, the following exercise may help you move actively into recovery.

Exercise: Write a letter to your old God. Tell him/her/it all of the qualities you once attributed to God that kept you sick and dysfunctional. Describe your behaviors as a result of those beliefs, and how they did not match your professed ideology—how they kept you from practicing what you preached. Include as many of the symptoms as you like. Tell that God how those dysfunctional beliefs made you feel. Try to include negative effects on yourself mentally, physically, and emotionally; also describe what those beliefs did to your relationships. Tell that God that he/she/it doesn't work for you anymore. You are going to interview a new God who will work for you in recovery to help you become positive and creative. Tell your old God what qualities you are now seeking. Then tell that old, dysfunctional God good-bye.

You might want to read your letter aloud to a sponsor, therapist, or friend. I have heard from many people that they find it healing to create a little ceremony, almost like a funeral or memorial service: They burn the letter and then scatter the ashes. You might want to accompany this ceremony with some special affirmations.

Affirmations for letting go of your old, dysfunctional God.

> I release the dysfunctional, negative beliefs of my past and invite healthy, affirming beliefs.

> I let go of that angry and fearsome old God and invite in a loving, accepting, joyful God.

> I release the memories of the shaming God who kept me angry and alone. I bring into my life a God of love, who patiently awaits my Yes to life.

You might find yourself feeling very sad and anxious. Like anything else you let go of, even if only to replace it with something you very much want, there is a natural sense of grief and loss. You should know that this is perfectly acceptable. I encourage you to honor the loss of all the behaviors you let go of in your recovery. In many ways, they were old friends who kept you alive through horrible abuse or dysfunction. It's okay to grieve them. Perhaps the following meditation will help you through the grieving process.

Meditation For Grieving Your Old God
I say good-bye to my magical God of yesterday. At times, I know I will miss you. I know I will be anxious, especially when I want that escaping quick fix.

But today, I know it never worked. Today I understand that I need to be involved in the changes I want to make. Today I have power. I am a part of my new God's Yes to life.

DEFINING ABSTINENCE FROM RELIGIOUS ADDICTION

I'm often asked how one abstains from religious addiction. Alcoholics quit drinking. Drug addicts just say no. For religious addicts, however, as for food addicts and sex addicts, it is not so simple. You are not abstaining so much as you are working toward balance and structure. You can't cut God out of your life any more than food addicts can stop eating or sex addicts can give up having relationships.

Letting go of your dysfunctional God is not always going to be as easy as simply writing a letter. As Celie observes in *The Color Purple,* the old God has been there so long he may not want to budge. Old habits die hard. Addictive, compulsive behaviors and attitudes have a lamentable tendency to pop up in other forms. For religious addicts, there is a danger of not only abandoning your church, scripture quoting, and compulsive crusade attendance but also switching all those addictive patterns to your Twelve Step group. I see it happen all the time, and most people don't realize they've done it. Using some of the tools that follow will help minimize that danger.

You build a foundation for your recovery by creating balance and structure. You cannot become a positive, creative person if you are still using something to numb or escape your feelings. Much of early recovery will focus on simply not using that to which you were addicted. Alcoholics struggle with cravings for drink. Food addicts work through their withdrawal from sugars and flours and learn to use the tools that help them maintain their abstinence.

If you are constantly relapsing and then detoxing and withdrawing from whatever you have abused, it is nearly impossible to build any kind of recovery. The greater the length of sobriety and abstinence from whatever you have abused, therefore, the better able you are to focus on the steps needed for a rich, happy recovery.

Working the Twelve Steps helps you create a framework for your recovery. At the same time, some of the information you discover about yourself and how you functioned in your disease will help you build that solid foundation for your recovery—a foundation consisting of abstinence from the beliefs and behaviors that fed your disease.

For religious addicts, as for food addicts, sex addicts, and those suffering from obsessive-compulsive disorder, defining abstinence requires rigorous honesty and insights into their disease. I have two friends who are food addicts. One is a compulsive overeater who avoids all sugars and any flours that contain gluten—as well as foods like popcorn and mashed potatoes—because they were binge foods. Another friend is a recovering bulimorexic who has no restrictions on what she eats, merely on the quantity. For her, feeling too full can trigger the desire to purge or starve. Part of her recovery is having a team of friends who tell her if she starts losing weight, because she can't see it.

Both of these women call themselves food addicts; yet the ways in which their disease manifested itself are different; therefore, the way they define their abstinence is different. The same holds true for sexual addicts. One woman I know has determined that entering a bar or large party alone can trigger her desire to act out sexually. Other recovering sex addicts find that a certain sexual act sets off their disease. The same dynamics apply to religious addicts.

Several religious addicts have told me that the word *abstinence* can trigger feelings of low self-esteem and a desire to engage in their compulsive religious behavior. Therefore, I suggest replacing it with words like *spiritual sobriety* or *balance,* since these, not total abandonment of religion or God, are the goals of recovery.

To define your sobriety or structure you must first identify how you behaved in your disease. Here the charts and journals you keep as you work the Twelve Steps will also become tools for creating balance and structure. Were you rigid, intolerant, judging? Always quoting scripture? Sending every penny to the church or religious groups such as TV evangelists, crusades, and missions? Spending all free time (and taking time from work) at religious functions? Preaching endlessly to coworkers or to strangers on the streets? Do you still tend to adhere rigidly to rules and ethics? How did your religious addiction cause you to behave? And how were those behaviors harmful to yourself or to others?

Through this self-examination you identify the bottom-line behaviors and beliefs that were key components of your disease. Once these are identified, you must create a structure based on honest self-appraisal. The behaviors and whatever triggers them must be avoided or structured. Some religious addicts, after a rigorous and honest inventory of their behavior, will choose total abstinence from all church attendance, Bible reading, and so forth. Others may find themselves comfortable with structuring a one-day-only attendance at religious services or meetings. Some may have to refine their structure after trying it out, if situations become too dangerous.

These are the same processes used by both compulsive overeaters and sex addicts—identifying binge and bottom-line behaviors and making a commitment to giving up the triggers that lead to self-destructive behaviors. It is important to work with a sponsor, even one in another program, who will help you create a healthy, balanced structure.

Your black-and-white thinking and rigidity may lead you to create an unrealistic structure that is still unbalanced and extreme.

Selecting a sponsor who is willing to learn about your disease and what you need to recover is critical. I suggest that you are careful not to choose someone who is as rigid as you are! Like my friend the bulimorexic, you may need a support team for a reality check periodically.

Sex and love addicts go through an intense period of withdrawal when they cease engaging in sexual compulsions, which they call acting out. Like other recovering addicts, they suddenly start feeling their feelings, especially those of loneliness, isolation, and fear. This may happen to you. During this time, it will be important to have as much support and nurturing as possible.

This is literally a detoxification, which is why it is entirely appropriate for religious addicts to enter residential treatment programs. In most cases, a twenty-eight-day residential program that uses an issues-oriented, all-addictions approach will prove effective. Like other addicts who go through intense withdrawal, you need to be in a safe environment, among people who are trained to guide you through the feelings of anxiety, anger, or panic that often accompany withdrawal.

The process of changing long-held beliefs is very difficult. There is the fear of wondering, What if they're right? There may also be a great sense of emptiness and loss, of wondering what's left. Treatment and ongoing therapy can help you begin replacing your toxic beliefs and attitudes with healthy ones: they can help by allowing you to grieve the loss of your old self. I often think this is why people relapse: They've never finished the grieving process that lets them move on.

At this stage affirmations become critically important. In the place of scripture used as a weapon or drug, religious addicts need affirmations such as:

> I am lovable just as I am.
>
> I am a positive and creative human being.
>
> I am a child of God and am one with the universe.
>
> I rejoice in my specialness.
>
> I release my addict self.

I now allow myself to honor my pain as I let go of my dysfunctional beliefs.

CREATING A BALANCED SPIRITUAL LIFE

In his workbook, *A Gentle Path through the Twelve Steps,* Patrick Carnes developed a worksheet for creating sobriety in any addiction. I have adapted this worksheet and guidelines for use in creating spiritual sobriety.

1. Identify the behaviors that manifest your addiction. If you listed the behaviors that manifested your religious addiction, as suggested in Chapter 6, you may find it helpful to refer to it again. If not, list those behaviors now: for instance, scripture quoting, excessive financial contributions, being judgmental, refusing to question authority, or black-and-white thinking.

SAMPLE BEHAVIORS TO STRUCTURE FOR RELIGIOUS SOBRIETY

- Refusing to think, doubt, or question
- Watching religious TV; excluding other nonreligious viewing
- Refusing to give family religious choices
- Dysfunctional sexual practices/beliefs
- Judging, condemning others with different beliefs
- Rigid adherence to rules
- Excessive financial contributions/tithing

- Obsessive church, crusade, revival attendance
- Proselytizing/witnessing
- Compulsive scripture quoting/Bible reading/praying
- Putting people on pedestals (authority figures always right)
- Eating disorders or other addictions
- Avoiding secular activities (entertainment or education)
- Black-and-white beliefs

Next, list at least one way each behavior hurts you or someone else physically, mentally, or emotionally. For instance, your belief that sex is dirty might have led you to withhold sex from your spouse and to use prostitutes instead. This may have caused emotional shame and fear, mental stress and anxiety, as well as the health risk of catching a sexually transmitted disease that you might have given to your spouse.

This list will serve as a guide as to the severity of your abuse of that particular behavior. Some of you may want to judge everything you did during your addiction with equal harshness. Not every behavior will have affected you in all three ways. You will want to give priority to those that have had the greatest consequences; they will become your sobriety boundaries, as Carnes calls them.

2. Set your boundaries or structure about how you are going to use this behavior. Remember that your goal is balance. You may choose to abandon a behavior, or you may find that you can safely limit it to certain circumstances. You can compare this to food addicts who choose to eliminate certain foods totally but eat measured quantities of other foods in order to structure their behavior.

For example, you may find that you are comfortable with attending morning church services, but that the format of the evening service triggers your religious compulsions about money, crusades, or scripture quoting. Some people who have relied heavily on such rituals as burning incense or chanting certain sayings or mantras repeatedly as part of their meditation process find that they cannot meditate at all without use of these rituals. Others can comfortably replace the formalized meditation process with simply reading a Twelve Step daily meditation book. It will be different for each individual.

One way to tell if you are addicted to something is to recognize the amount of fear that the thought of giving it up produces in you. If you have determined that a certain behavior, such as church going, has been harmful mentally, physically, and emotionally, and if the thought of giving it up produces extreme anxiety, then you have a sign that it is dangerous for you to continue.

You may want to commit to eliminating that behavior for a certain amount of time. Start small; this will reduce the anxiety. Then you can renegotiate the length of time you will continue to refrain from that behavior. After a certain length of sobriety, you may find that you could structure in some limited participation. For instance, some people give up all church participation for a certain length of time in order to work through resulting feelings and issues. Later, they begin to add church activities back in, perhaps seeking affiliation with a more open, affirming church or belief system. In other cases, you may find that you can comfortably structure a balanced way to participate in an activity by limiting the amount of time or circumstances under which you engage in it.

When setting your sobriety boundaries, there are four primary options you might want to consider:

1. Refrain from the activity entirely.

2. Eliminate it for a limited amount of time (for example, three to six months) and then renegotiate.

3. Limit participation under certain circumstances (for example, attending one church service on Sunday or going to church only for special occasions, such as weddings and funerals).

4. Substitute healthy behavior (create affirmations instead of ritualized prayer or scripture quoting).

3. Identify triggers or danger zones that might lead to relapse. Some alcoholics have no problem going to bars; others do. Some food addicts don't mind being around their favorite binge foods; others find that a mere mention of cake can set off cravings. You will also find that there are certain situations or thought processes that can tilt you into relapse. You need to define what these might be. Then you can indicate what action you will take when confronted with these triggers or danger zones. In short, anything that restricts your ability to choose or furthers your victimized belief that you are inadequate is likely to be a signal that you could be heading for relapse.

▲ ▼ ▲

SAMPLE TRIGGERS OR DANGER ZONES

- Preoccupation with or rigid adherence to rules/ethics/rituals (Twelve Step groups, work, new religion, such as metaphysics/New Age)

- Isolating within support groups; not associating with a variety of people

- Inability to question authority figures, putting them on pedestals

- Inability to take credit for achievements or success, saying, God/Higher Power is doing it for you

- Quoting Big Book or other authority texts

- Being judgmental, critical of those not following the rules or doing it right in support groups, work, and so forth

- Obsessing over feelings of inadequacy (saying that you're not doing enough)

- Perpetuating feelings of powerlessness or not having choice, saying that God/Higher Power will show you the way

4. Define behaviors that constitute a slip. Having identified triggers and danger zones, you will be better able to decide what causes a slip or relapse. This is where reality checking with your sponsor and support group is often necessary at first, especially if rigid, black-and-white thinking is a problem for you. Your goal is to learn to develop your own guidelines, which allow for growth and recovery without being so flexible as to permit you to rationalize indulging in your addictive behaviors.

You will rarely be confronted with all-or-nothing choices. You are striving for progress, not perfection. You want to learn to recognize, and live comfortably with, the gray area that lies between the black and white. There is no sense in setting yourself up to fail by creating a structure to which it is impossible to adhere.

5. Use affirming thoughts or behaviors that reflect healthy beliefs to replace dysfunctional ones. Gentle self-nurturing is essential in recovery from any addiction, especially religious addiction and abuse. You have been accustomed to living with self-condemnation, rigid rules, and judgments. As a result, you want to reinforce the idea that you are not giving up God, but are merely replacing that dysfunctional God or belief system with a healthy one that permits spiritual growth. You can do this by creating affirmations or by finding a healthy behavior that replaces the dysfunctional one.

▲ ▼ ▲

SAMPLE AFFIRMING THOUGHTS OR BEHAVIORS

- I am enough.
- My Spiritual Power assists me in making healthy choices.
- I rejoice in my healthy spirituality.
- I am experiencing God's creativity in my life by writing my own personal prayers and affirmations, drawing and coloring my inner child's feelings, learning to play an instrument.
- I am breaking my isolation by socializing after meetings.
- I celebrate my choice to budget my religious contributions.
- I nurture myself by starting my day with at least twenty minutes of quiet time and reading from my daily meditation books.

Jim, a recovering religious addict, is an example of someone setting healthy boundaries. He brought his family nearly to the brink of bankruptcy with his excessive financial contributions. Working with his sponsor, he determined that this was one of his most harmful behaviors. Jim's goal is to become a responsible church member. He realized he was using his excessive financial contributions and heavy involvement in the church to fill his need to feel successful and to gain approval.

His therapist, family, and sponsor agree that his religious addiction was not so abusive as to require him to totally leave his church. So he is working on creating a structured church involvement that allows him to learn to find his self-worth in himself, rather than from his church activities.

Once he creates his sobriety boundary, he commits it to a sponsor or to a support group. His length of sobriety runs from the date that he committed to that sobriety plan. At his group for adult children of alcoholics, he often notes that he has been recovering from this behavior for several months.

Jim's sobriety worksheet for his extreme financial contributions looks like this:

1. Behaviors that manifest my addiction

> Behavior
> Excessive financial contributions

> Abuse Checklist

> Physical: Had to work two jobs; was tired all the time; had headaches

> Mental: Was irritable and depressed; always snapping at people or in a sulk; angry at the family for not understanding

> Emotional: Felt guilty and ashamed; felt inadequate because I couldn't meet my excessive pledges; also inadequate at home because of the financial drain on the family

2. Sobriety boundaries

I will only give one annual contribution to the church, to be broken down into monthly payments. I cannot afford 10 percent of my income. Realistically this year I can only afford to give 3 percent.

3. Triggers or danger zones

Watching religious TV, going to a crusade, reading religious tracts, getting a bonus or tax refund, feeling inadequate and wanting to fix that feeling by giving service or money.

Action to Take:

Refrain from engaging in trigger behaviors for three months, to be renegotiated depending on how I feel. If I feel guilty or ashamed that I'm not doing more, I will call my sponsor or support group members. I will write in my journal and remind myself of the pain my excessive giving caused myself and others. I will give service to my ACA group instead by volunteering to be the coffee person, but I will not get caught up in serving on other committees or in other capacities that make me feel superior and worthy.

4. Behaviors that constitute a slip

Giving more than committed monthly contribution. Trying to atone by giving more service at church, ACA, or the kids' school. Obsessing about money; not talking to my sponsor about feeling guilty or inadequate about having to limit my contributions.

5. Affirming thoughts or behaviors to replace dysfunctional ones and reflect healthy spirituality

My self-worth is not dependent on how much money I am able to earn or give.

I enjoy the free time I now have to spend with my family and friends. Becoming a positive, creative human being is the best contribution I can make to myself, my family, my world, and my God.

WORKSHEET FOR SPIRITUAL SOBRIETY

1. Behaviors that manifest my addiction:

    Abuse Checklist

    Mental:

    Emotional:

    Physical:

2. Sobriety boundaries:

3. Triggers or danger zones:

    Action taken:

4. Behaviors that constitute a slip:

5. Affirming thoughts or behaviors to replace dysfunctional ones
   and reflect healthy spirituality:

ALIVE IN THE MOMENT: SAYING YES TO GOD

The Medal

*A mother could not get her son to
come home before sunset. So she told
him that the road to their house was
haunted by ghosts who came out after dusk.*

*By the time the boy grew up he was so afraid
of ghosts that he refused to run errands at night.
So she gave him a medal and taught him that it
would protect him.*

Bad religion gives him faith in the medal.
Good religion gets him to see that ghosts do not exist.

Anthony de Mello

Creating a balanced spiritual life will take time. You cannot
expect yourself to tackle it all at once. As you gently replace your
dysfunctional beliefs with healthy ones, however, you will find that you
are developing a spirituality that enhances you and frees you, rather
than limits you.

A friend of mine explains why she gets so angry and frustrated
with fundamentalist Christians, by whom she has often been abused:
"They get so hung up on the lamp that they don't see the light. And more
important, they don't see what the light is showing them." To her, the
Virgin Birth, the Resurrection, and the attendant church dogma and
rituals are helpful but not important. Jesus's value to her is in the

message contained in his teachings. "He set down a guide to living in the Sermon on the Mount," she says. "The message of the Resurrection was God's way of telling us to look for a new way of living."

To my friend, the teachings that she received as a child about there being only one right way to worship diminished Jesus, hid the truth, and kept her spiritually stunted. They kept her from using the tools found in Jesus's message. "I used to ask my Sunday school teachers," she told me, "what Jesus was lighting when he said he was The Light. All they could do was quote more scripture at me and tell me how bad I was for asking those questions. I didn't like feeling bad for wanting to get closer to God. I had to leave religion to find my answers."

Today my friend still struggles to reverse the early shaming messages her religious teachings gave her. Although she was raised in what she calls a mainstream Presbyterian church and sang in choirs for twenty years, she still cannot enter a church without instantly feeling worthless and dirty, invalidated and angry. Now she is learning to take her rage and hatred away from herself and from God and to place them on the dysfunctional messages that told her she was worthless. She is learning, step by step, to say No to her dysfunctional God, and Yes to herself.

I believe many of you are on the same path as my friend: struggling to disengage from dysfunctional, shaming messages and beliefs and trying to find a sense of self-worth and the inner peace that comes with it; learning that there are no ghosts by risking a walk in the dark; reclaiming your power by throwing rocks at your personal boogey-man. It is a difficult journey, but before you have traveled long, you will find that most precious gift: yourself. With that gift, you will also find a Spiritual Power more loving, more accepting, and more powerful than you ever imagined.

Religious addiction and abuse kept you so focused on a dysfunctional image of God that you could never appreciate the gifts we were given. You couldn't see the color purple, much less wonder at what makes it so richly beautiful. Using religion as a means to avoid error robbed you of the dignity of choice and left you feeling depraved and worthless. Recovery from religious addiction and abuse allows you to celebrate your unique I AMness.

You were never born wholly incapable of good. That was a lie someone told you, perhaps handed down from generation to generation but still a lie nonetheless. From that lie sprang diseased, stunted spirits that were mired in hopelessness and shame. Healthy, whole spirituality allows you to move toward truth, frees you to discover that you were always meant to be a positive, creative human being.

Your moment has come. Seize it now. Shout Yes! to yourself, to God, and to life.

Appendix I

Intervention:
Helping Others Towarb d Recovery

Sometimes we need a little help from
our friends...

MOST OF THE TIME, life hands us our moments of
intervention: It creates a crisis so great that we are moved to seek
recovery. Other times, we are simply too sick to see what's happening
to us; we are blinded by our addiction and cannot see that there's a
crisis. This is when we need a little help. We need our families and
friends to lovingly yet firmly create our moment for us in such a way
that we want to enter recovery.

When family, friends, and other significant people gather
purposely to create that moment in an addict's life, they are doing what
is known as an intervention. Some of you are reading this book because
you want help for your own religious addiction and abuse. Others are
seeking help for someone else—a parent, spouse, sibling, or friend
whose religious addiction is so destructive to all concerned that some
emergency assistance is required.

I said earlier that it was at one time thought that alcoholics and other addicts had to hit bottom on their own, and that nothing should be done to interfere with the downward spiraling process. Now more people accept that it is possible to intervene constructively—to bring the bottom to the addict rather than wait for the addict to get to the bottom. Many addicts, including religious addicts, might not survive long enough to reach that crisis stage by themselves; they are too near insanity or death to risk waiting.

People are often afraid of doing an intervention. They see it as too clinical or technical for nonprofessional people to attempt. However, an intervention is nothing more than the family and friends of an addict sitting down in an attitude of love and concern, describing the addict's behaviors and then sharing how they feel about those behaviors. An intervention is not a group blame session with the addict as the sacrificial scapegoat. Nor is kidnapping or otherwise forcing a religious addict into involuntary deprogramming centers an intervention. That is merely another form of brainwashing and thus is as unhealthy as the addiction.

An intervention is simply an effective means of communicating; it is a gentle, loving, healthy way to confront addicts with the destructive effects of their compulsive behaviors. What an intervention says, essentially, is: Stop! Look! Change!

An intervention calls a halt to addictive behaviors and points to a different way to look at life and its possibilities. It places the addict squarely in front of reality by using the unmanageability in his or her life to illustrate the destructive results of compulsive behavior and the dire consequences of continuing such behavior. An intervention is tough love in action. It says: "I love you, but I will no longer allow myself to be abused by your behavior. So let's look at our choices and see how we can accomplish this."

An intervention does not so much create a crisis as it merely compiles the little crises in the addict's life so that they loom so frighteningly large that they cannot be denied. This is the method perfected by Vernon Johnson, the pioneer alcoholism interventionist whose techniques have become the model for interventions on addicts of all kinds. In *I'll Quit Tomorrow*, Johnson says,

*we do not invent crisis, . . . it is not necessary to invent it.
Every alcoholic is already surrounded by crises, no one of
which is being used constructively. All we have to do is make
those around the alcoholic knowledgeable enough so that
they can start using the crises. This makes it possible for the
alcoholic to move sooner, and to limit the very real damage
that comes from living with a worsening situation.*

If you are reading this because you have a relative or friend who is
religiously addicted, you already see how religious addiction and abuse
create dysfunction, pain, and unmanageability. You probably are
already in the crisis. What you need to do now is bring your addicted
friend or relative into the crisis so you can get out of it.

Johnson notes that alcoholics (and most addicts) are seldom
confronted by their actions, and most are not even aware of them. He
adds:

*They live with increasing impairment of judgment, and
eventually lose touch with their emotions entirely. They have
conscious and unconscious ways of forgetting painful
experiences. It is a matter of self-survival. If a person is
alcoholic, by definition that person is unable to recognize the
fact.*

A good intervention, then, will help a religious addict recognize
that the discomfort exists, and that it is caused by unhealthy religious
beliefs and behaviors. The key to doing an intervention is found in Dr.
Johnson's statement: "All we have to do is make those around the
alcoholic knowledgeable enough so that they can start using the crises."
Thus the steps to doing an intervention are first to identify the problems,
then to learn how they can be used to create the crisis.

Having illustrated the problems and clarified the existing crises,
next you want to present the solutions. Remember, addicts do not
believe they have choices. The ultimate goal of an intervention is to
place options and choices before the addict that offer the promise of
recovery.

PREPARING FOR AN INTERVENTION

Step 1: Getting the Knowledge

Name the problem. The first step is to make the people around a religious addict knowledgeable. Many people will have recognized the addict's dysfunctional behaviors, but they may not realize that they are seeing the symptoms of an addiction, much less have a clue that this addiction can be treated.

The doctor who treated Cherry Boone O'Neill's anorexia identified some of the religious beliefs and issues that he thought contributed to the illness. He was treating anorexia as the main disease. Today, I hope he would see it as a symptom of religious addiction and abuse.

I spoke earlier of the young woman who became religiously addicted when her son was dying of leukemia. Those around her undoubtedly saw her obsessions escalate and saw her desperately giving her money to any ministry she thought might save him. They did not know to label this behavior as addiction, so no one intervened.

Addictions do not exist in a vacuum. People see the behaviors, such as an elderly widow tithing away her savings in order to assure herself of going to heaven with her husband; they overhear a supposed pillar of the church making bigoted remarks and perhaps think the person is a hypocrite; they see someone stringently adhering to a code of ethics, unable to bend, and may think of the person as rigid or arrogant. Until they are made aware of it, most people don't know how to identify the desperate giving, judgmentalness, and scrupulosity as symptoms of religious addiction.

If you are considering arranging an intervention, you may first want to give this book to all the people whom you think might participate, to help educate them regarding the causes and symptoms of religious addiction and abuse. The members participating in the intervention need to understand that religious addiction is a disease like other addictions. It has its roots in the same sources: self-hate, victimization, codependency, and the need to medicate or escape feelings.

Behaviors and attitudes previously considered irrational will eventually be seen as symptoms of an illness. Family and friends should begin to recognize that the addict's denial, unwillingness to accept criticism or discussion, rigid and narrow interpretation of scripture, black-and-white moralizing, judgmentalness, and condemnation of anybody who thinks differently are all manifestations of the powerlessness and unmanageability created by addiction.

Most important, it is an addiction that can be treated in much the same manner as other addictions. Because of the complexities of the issues surrounding religious addictions, since it usually involves sexual abuse issues and other addictions, I have rarely seen a religious addict who would not have benefitted greatly from residential treatment. So I believe that the goal of the intervention is to move the addict into treatment, then on to recovery. Therefore, the people concerned need to accept that there are viable solutions—that there is a way out of the pain for the addict, and for the family and friends.

Select the participants. It is important that the people who might be involved in an intervention accept that religious addiction is a disease. They must also be people whose opinions and feelings are valued and respected by the addict. You want to have your best chance to be genuinely heard by the addict. The presence of a family member or friend who is likely to anger or irritate the addict could prove counterproductive.

Therefore, an intervention is not limited to immediate family—spouse, children, or parents. Participants may include uncles, aunts, grandparents, cousins, friends, employers, coworkers, pastors, business associates—anyone to whom the addict might listen. Because of the intensity of the information and feelings that may be imparted, it might not be advisable to have pre-teen children participate. However, young children can sometimes reach an addict more effectively than can adults in an intervention. In such cases, I strongly recommend having a psychologist ascertain their ability to cope with the situation, if you think they have an important contribution to make to the intervention.

Some people feel more comfortable having an interventionist—a therapist, social worker, or minister who is trained in interventions or in family counseling—participate in the group in order to help the family maintain objectivity. This is not a requirement. In some cases, an outsider may prove too great an irritant; at other times, an outside authority figure may be able to prevent the addict from physically leaving or simply mentally tuning out. The decision about this should be based on each individual case: You know best under what terms you are likely to be able to capture and maintain the addict's attention.

As you prepare for the intervention by educating people about religious addiction, you need to explore the participants' feelings and beliefs. Some of your family members may also be in denial, not yet ready to see religiosity as a disease or to acknowledge their own pain. These initial pre-intervention meetings may be the first time family members have actually shared their feelings or compared notes about their experiences. Some family members may need time to process the information given or may not feel strong enough to participate in the intervention. They should be treated with understanding and love and given time to decide if they want to be involved.

I participated in an intervention on George Wilson, an extremely disturbed religious addict. His daughter, Marilyn, had been recovering from her alcoholism and overeating for several years. In the process of working through her shame and issues of low self-esteem, she realized that her religious abuse lay at the core of her problems. In the pre-intervention meetings, she was very forthright about expressing her feelings of rage, resentment, and anger. Her younger sister, Amanda, however, was much more reluctant. Amanda, age twenty, was an anorexic; she had attempted suicide while in her teens. She was struggling between her anger at her father and her desire to be Daddy's perfect daughter. As such, she wasn't sure she could tell him how she felt, or that she was strong enough to withstand the onslaught of his righteous anger.

Part of the education process includes allowing participants to voice any doubts or fears they might have that could become obstacles to a successful intervention, as did Amanda in George's intervention. There is often a very real, literal fear of God that makes people hesitate to question someone's beliefs and relationship with God. You will need to explain that the symptoms of religious addiction are signs of a dysfunctional, sick relationship with God, and that recovery can restore the addict to a healthy, healing spirituality.

Remind everyone that the addict is using God or religion as an addict would use a drug. Some family members might begin to use this pre-intervention time to practice seeing behaviors in terms of substance abuse: equating scripture quoting or obsessive proselytizing with shooting up or getting drunk, thus learning to recognize using behaviors, as well as their own victim roles and religious codependency. Taking the time to let the participants grow comfortable with seeing these behaviors as addictive will strengthen their effectiveness in the actual intervention.

In the Wilson family's pre-intervention meetings, George's wife, Maude, gradually began to use phrases like "his addiction to religion . . . to the Bible" as she described his behavior. By the time we did the actual intervention, she really saw herself as the spouse of an addict. She told him, "I feel like an alcoholic's wife."

Another legitimate concern is the idea that you are somehow interfering with someone's constitutional rights to individual religious beliefs no matter how dysfunctional or crazy they may appear. This is a very genuine, healthy concern. There is a fine line between persecuting or punishing someone for having different beliefs and practices, and intervening on behalf of an addict who is self-destructing and hurting others.

Identify concrete incidents and feelings. The next phase of preparing for an intervention involves identifying the behaviors and attitudes that have generated family dysfunction and pain. Understanding is critical at this point. Remember that religious addicts are not bad people, nor is religion bad. The dysfunctional behavior has progressed because of the addicts' belief that they are doing what God expects or demands. They may have been raised with these beliefs and simply may not know how to live differently. They may have grown up in dysfunctional homes that left them vulnerable to religious addiction.

Participants in the intervention must understand that addictions spring from intense inner pain and from feelings of worthlessness, inadequacy, victimization, and despair. Somewhere in their lives, these addicts came to believe that they were sinners who were born depraved or inherently bad. Many religious addicts became addicted in order to avoid or escape from emotional pain in their lives; it may have stemmed from alcoholism, eating disorders, isolation, guilt, shame, sexual abuse, physical disfigurement, poverty, or financial insecurity. Religion made them feel special and made them feel loved. The family must understand that the addict's arrogance, intolerance, judgmentalness, and rigidity are desperate attempts to gain self-worth.

Therefore, interventions must be done in an atmosphere of love and concern. In order to create and maintain this attitude, you might want to recall all that you know about the addict's background and family of origin. What were the parents and grandparents like? Was there alcoholism, physical, emotional, or sexual abuse, extreme poverty, religious addiction? What do you know about the addict's self-image? Some of the participants may already know that this person feels no self-worth and is shame-based and fearful. Others may need help in recognizing these symptoms.

During the Wilsons' pre-intervention meetings, Maude noted that George's mother had been a physically abusive alcoholic who went on religious binges after her drunken rages. Maude had gleaned this knowledge from George's sister; George had rarely talked about his mother's abusiveness. Marilyn immediately recognized the same pattern in her father: Although he was a rigid teetotaler, he had violent rages, for which he would try to repent with pious religiosity. I could see the daughters becoming more compassionate as they learned about their father's past; clearly they had never talked to Maude about their feelings.

This led them to the most important preparatory work in an intervention: identifying their own feelings about George's behaviors. What gets the addict's attention and precipitates the crisis is the creation of pain. An addict in need of an intervention is not in sufficient pain to want to move out of it. You create that added pain by sharing your pain.

The simplest way to identify the effects of religious abuse is to make a chart of the symptoms of religious addiction. In one column list the symptoms; in the next list three or four specific incidents in which the addict has manifested that symptom. In the last column, list your own feelings about those incidents. Were you angry? Embarrassed? Hurt?

▲ ▼ ▲

INTERVENTION PREPARATION WORKSHEET

Symptom:

Behaviors and specific incidents that manifest symptoms, and how I felt about them:

1. Incident/behavior

Feelings:

2. Incident/behavior

Feelings:

3. Incident/behavior

Feelings:

> You may want to use a special notebook or journal to list all the symptoms exhibited by the addict on whom you are doing intervention, so that you have ample room to write all the behaviors, incidents, and your feelings.

Part of Maude's worksheet for George's intervention is shown here.

SYMPTOMS	BEHAVIORS/INCIDENTS	FEELINGS
Compulsive praying, church-going, attending missions or crusades, quoting scripture, and so forth	1. Never listening; bullying us into submission with loud, angry Bible-quoting	Resentment, fear, shame
	2. Went to revival meeting instead of coming to Amanda's school program. Punished her for being upset.	Anger, shame, helplessness, embarrassment
	3. Avoiding discussion of our finances by quoting scriptures about tithing and pretending to pray about my "reluctance to tithe"	Rage, invalidation, fear of bankruptcy, shame at having to avoid creditors

You should think of specific events and incidents (attitudes, actions, conversations) that manifest the symptoms and reveal the dysfunctional behavior or discomfort. Generalizations only allow the addict to express greater denial and rebuttal. Listing specific incidents, and your feelings about them, will give you the greatest chance to work a successful intervention.

Identify solutions and choices. It is important for everyone involved to realize that help is available. One big obstacle to recovery is an overwhelming feeling of helplessness, which sometimes extends to the addict's family and friends. Quite often, in the midst of talking with families who are preparing for an intervention, I see them slide into despair and the feeling that it will never work. In these times, I remain firmly optimistic, pointing out that if the behavior is going to be changed, then something needs to be done.

The goal of any intervention is to open the addict to the possibility of change and to demonstrate that choices exist after all. This means offering concrete solutions. Thus, you might begin to make a list of therapists and/or treatment centers who can treat religious addiction. You may already have such a list, or you might assign one or two family members to gather that information. This serves two purposes: It reinforces the idea that help is truly available; later, during the intervention, having this information can help move the addict swiftly into therapy or a support group.

I know of one intervention in which the addict's bags were packed, plane tickets already reserved, and the treatment center staff waiting to pick him up at the airport. Five hours after the intervention began, he was in his first counseling session, still a little dazed as to how he got there. His family knew him well enough to know that if they left it to him to find out where to go for help, he would never have gone.

There is a growing number of therapists and treatment centers who address religious addiction and abuse. If you cannot find someone in your area, seek out a therapist who specializes in an all-addictions approach. Such a therapist might be open to the idea of religious addiction and abuse and would be able to treat it in the context of other addictions, such as adult children of dysfunction and codependency.

It is also useful to meet someone who is recovering from religious addiction or abuse. You may not choose to have that person attend the actual intervention, but rather have him or her available in case the addict wants to talk to someone who is in recovery.

Ongoing support. Addiction is a family disease. One of the main obstacles to recovery is the belief that no one understands, that we are alone and unique in our depravity. I believe that no intervention will be successful if family members cannot offer support in the form of willingness to address their own codependency and related issues. Part of the solutions and choices presented to the addict should be the promise of support from the family.

Participating members who are part of the immediate family or circle of friends should examine their own willingness to be supportive during the early recovery process. Are you prepared to attend family counseling sessions or to enter your own individual therapy? Would you go to Twelve Step meetings? If you are an employer, are you able to give the addict time off to go to treatment or to attend therapy and support group sessions? All of you must discuss whether it is important to the potential success of the intervention to be able to offer a united support team. You may come to a group decision that anyone who cannot promise continued support should not participate in the intervention. Again, these decisions should be based on each individual case. For some, it might be crucial to know the whole family is behind them; for others, that might not be as important.

Since religious addiction is rooted in codependency, I recommend that religious addicts and family members attend meetings of Adult Children of Alcoholics, or CoDependents Anonymous, as well as any A.A., Al-Anon, O.A., N.A., or other Twelve Step programs that might also apply. I firmly believe that people rarely suffer from only one addiction. Most addicts I have seen are also struggling with codependency, incest, eating disorders, and issues relating to being the adult child of addicts, as well as the primary addiction. I also believe that having religious addicts and codependents in these meetings will help others identify, and begin to deal with, their own issues of religious abuse.

I encourage you to learn where these meetings are held first, so that you may refer the addict to them as part of the choices and solutions you are going to offer; second, so that you may begin to look at your own issues as part of the ongoing support you will offer. I have listed the World Service addresses for the various Twelve Step organizations at the back of this book. You may also find local organizations listed in your phone book.

Step 2: Building the Crisis

You have laid the foundation for the intervention by educating all concerned about the causes and symptoms of religious addiction. Your list of behaviors and feelings will provide the framework of crisis with which you will surround the religious addict. All you need now are a few tools.

An intervention should be created more as a loving encounter than as a head-on confrontation. Because religious addicts usually believe they are inherently bad people, an abusive, blaming approach reinforces their sense of worthlessness, which only increases their resistance.

After you have made your lists of incidents and your feelings about them, you should compare notes and select the ones everyone thinks are the most representative or the most powerful. Try not to overlap, unless you think the particular incident is important enough that hearing everyone's feelings about it could have a strong impact. Be precise about details and events and be even more precise about your feelings.

You want to document the addict's progressive search for a fix and to show the increasing impairment, dysfunction, and pain that resulted. The successful intervention lovingly acknowledges that pain, while showing the addict just how impaired he or she has become, and how that impairment has affected the addict and family members.

Therefore, everyone should be prepared to share how these incidents, occasions, and actions made them feel. Opinions can be argued and challenged, but feelings cannot. This is especially important to remember if the addict is in a great deal of denial and therefore resistant. Keeping the details short, specific, and linked to feelings keeps the interventionists in control. Participants should practice saying, "When you did this . . . I felt . . ." rather than "I think. . . ."

When Marilyn, Maude, and Amanda first began talking with me about the intervention, they weren't sure they could come up with enough incidents. Our meetings and doing the worksheets unleashed a whole flood of experiences, and suddenly they had enough material for ten interventions. Comparing notes, they found one symptom that had affected all of them profoundly.

George was extremely bigoted toward other religions, and refused to socialize with anyone who did not belong to his church. Thus, he effectively picked his daughters' friends. Amanda revealed that she had been sexually abused by the father of one such playmate. George trusted this man implicitly because he was a deacon in the church; he looked up to him and thought it a great honor that Amanda was so frequently invited to sleep over at his house. Amanda decided it was time to tell her father that this man he had trusted without question had abused her.

Similarly, when Amanda fell in love with Patrick, a Catholic, George had delivered an ultimatum: The boy was to convert to George's fundamentalist faith or Amanda would not be allowed to see him. Summing up the pain George's bigoted behaviors caused her, Amanda said, "Patrick's family were real, true Christians, and you never bothered to meet them. If they were Catholic, they were evil. But anybody who went to our church was automatically okay. You were so busy condemning and hating, you couldn't see you were bringing a really bad person into the house when you brought that deacon home. Your religion made you so blind, I couldn't trust you to take care of me!"

George's hypocrisy and outright cruelty to both Patrick and Amanda had outraged Maude. She had kept helplessly silent at the time but was now ready to express her feelings of rage and guilt. "You condemned that boy for doing exactly what you preached a thousand times to your own daughters: honoring his parents by practicing their religion," she told George vehemently during the intervention.

In the course of the pre-intervention meetings, Maude had confronted her own denial about the sterility and barrenness of her marriage. George had once been sensitive and gentle, but as his addiction progressed, he had become so critical, judging, angry, and emotionally withdrawn that he bore no resemblance to the tender youth she had married. She realized that she was ready to end the marriage if he did not seek help. She told him, "You use the Bible to silence me, to keep me feeling helpless and unworthy. . . . I see it now as a mockery of the vows I took. . . ."

As for Marilyn, George's narrow-mindedness and bigotry had set off a rebelliousness in her that had led to her overeating and alcoholism. "Everything you said no to, the rebel in me said yes," Marilyn told him. Worse, his angry, judging behavior left her with an image of God as a mean old man. Struggling with this image was what caused her to come to me for help.

Once the family was able to focus on one or two main symptoms, they were able to select those that had had the most devastating effects on all of them. These were the ones they shared with George in the intervention.

Staying in charge. Be prepared to meet resistance. The addict is likely to be in denial and possibly will lash out in anger and defensiveness. This is why the atmosphere of the intervention should be one of concerned love. When reading your lists, you need to look into the eyes of the religious addict and preface your remarks with a sentence like, "I really need to tell you that I love you and it is because I love you that I share the following concerns . . . I have observed in your religious behavior. . . ."

As you introduce each incident, or if you are interrupted, ask to be heard, with a specific request like, "I know this is difficult for you to hear, but please listen to what I am going to say to you. Please hear me out." This puts the religious addict in the listener role and keeps you in control.

Combating denial. Once a religious addict is allowed to debate or argue, the advantage is lost. In order to avoid facing their own behavior, many religious addicts resort to angry scripture quoting and condemnations of evil behavior. It is critical not to get caught up in that game, which is why all concerned should prepare ahead of time so that they don't get distracted.

In both the religious addict and religious codependent, the biggest obstacle to a successful intervention is likely to be denial. Like all addicts in denial of the powerlessness and unmanageability of their lives, when confronted they are likely to display attitudes or behaviors that are characteristic of denial. Some of the most common symptoms of denial in religious addicts include angrily preaching and shouting scripture to avoid hearing you or using texts to justify, rationalize, or minimize their behavior. Some resort to stony silence or martyred, victimized blaming. Debating, condemning, and interrogating are popular weapons in the religious addict's arsenal.

These kinds of behaviors are used to divert you from the real issues. Because the disease of addiction is cunning, baffling, and powerful, it fights back when challenged like a virus resisting antibiotics. It is important to separate the disease from the person and to view these behaviors as the disease talking. Although it will be difficult, try not to take attacks personally.

Initially, your refusal to be drawn into any of these diversionary tactics might agitate or confuse the addict, especially if you usually give in to such tactics. He or she may step up these behaviors, pull out all the stops, as it were, before finally giving up and just listening. Be prepared for this. Try not to shout. Keep your voices calm and well-modulated. If the addict begins to yell, firmly request to be spoken to civilly and in a cordial tone. Remember to acknowledge the addict's pain. You might say, "I'm not judging you. I know this is painful for you, but I do need you to hear how I feel."

When I was introduced to George, he immediately reacted with hostility, assuming me to be Catholic; he launched into a scripture-laced tirade about not calling any man Father. Instead of arguing, I respectfully suggested he call me Leo. When he tried again to assault me with scripture, Marilyn quietly said, "Dad, this is exactly why I asked Leo to come. I have a problem he's been helping me with, and I need you to help me, too," thus deftly beginning the intervention. When Maude and Amanda shared their feelings about the issue of Patrick, George at first resorted to a martyred, "But I was only trying to do what was best. . . ." Both women acknowledged this, then pointed out that his way of going about it—rigidly choosing people based solely on church affiliation—had been dysfunctional and harmful.

Step 3: Offer Solutions and Choices

Capture the moments. During the intervention process, there will hopefully be some moments of clarity when the religious addict sees not only the pain and dysfunction in his or her own life but also the pain and dysfunction that the disease is causing others. Each recognition of this kind—each time the addict acquiesces—is a small moment of surrender. You are showing the addict the various crises his or her behavior has caused in your lives and, in doing so, building one large crisis, which will be too painful for the addict to remain in without taking action—to decide, hopefully, to get well.

George Wilson was initially extremely resistant to descriptions of his own behavior. Both Marilyn and Maude gently and firmly persisted and did not allow him to rage out of control. They asked to be heard and acknowledged his pain. Thus they created an atmosphere that allowed the crises in George's life to sink in.

Amanda's revelation that a man whom George trusted solely on the basis of his church affiliation was in fact a child molester created the pivotal crisis. His religious obsession had placed his child's life in jeopardy. That his family was too fearful of him to even tell him that Amanda had attempted suicide and was in dire need of help created another crisis. His behavior toward Amanda's boyfriend was described to him as cruel, and the specific attitudes and behaviors supported that. Again, another crisis. His wife threatening to leave him. That created the final crisis.

The intervention worked because he truly cared about his family, did truly love them, and had genuinely believed he was doing the right thing for them. Had the people involved not been as close to him, or if he was so removed from his feelings that they could not be reached, the intervention might not have worked. Because he did love them, the messages he received provided moments of clarity in which he was able to see his behavior in a different light.

Equally important, his family could suggest solutions and answers that showed him the possibility of change. Marilyn had already been in treatment, and George had attended some family sessions then. Marilyn gently suggested that he, too, might benefit from such treatment. When he appeared too resistant to the idea, I suggested he try therapy first, to which he readily agreed. Some months later, he did indeed go into treatment.

In order for an intervention to be fully effective, these moments of recognition and surrender need to be followed by firm and clear directives, such as:

- I know you didn't mean to hurt me. I understand that this is a symptom of your addiction. Will you consider looking at it the same way?

- We want you to receive therapy at a treatment center for your religious addiction. We've already talked with some centers, and we'll help you find a place that is right for you.

- We ask you to go and get counseling. We know there are people in the area who can help you.

- We hope you will go with us to some of the Twelve Step groups that have been recommended.

- If you choose not to get help at this time, we want you to know that we will get help for ourselves, regardless of what you do.

Maybe it's your moment. Religious addicts must not be made to feel that they are the sole cause of the problems. The family should indicate willingness to participate in the solutions, yet family members should be firm in their commitment to get help for themselves, regardless of what the addict does.

An intervention can often benefit the family members more than the addict, as they gain insights into their own dysfunction and resolve to get help. The intervention provides their moments; it also provides an effective way for the family to begin to set boundaries in order to begin to work on their own recoveries. Alcoholics or drug addicts who refuse to get help may be told that they must move, or that the family will no longer pay bills, provide bail, or otherwise continue to enable the addiction.

Families of religious addicts may use the intervention time to serve the addict notice that they will no longer be ruled by the addict's wishes. Family members will now expect their choices and desires to be respected without condemnations. Often, when the family quits enabling and participating in the disease, the addict's discomfort increases to the point at which he or she may decide to get help after all. The intervention still produces results.

Remember, the guides to an effective intervention are:

- Educate about religious addiction as a treatable disease.

- Identify behaviors via specific incidents.

- Approach the addict in an attitude of love and concern.

- Express feelings, not thoughts or opinions, about these incidents.

- Avoid blaming or judging by phrasing feedback in terms of "When you did ___, I felt ___."

- Avoid debating, arguing, personalizing. Request to be heard and to be spoken to politely.

- Offer solutions, choices, and alternatives.

Our moments come in many ways: a car crash, the angry remarks of a significant other, the child who leaves home to escape the relentless religiosity, the gathering of friends and family to share with you the effects your disease has on their lives. In my book, *Spirituality and Recovery,* I explained it this way:

> *For many people, spiritual growth has come with the acceptance of a disease. The acceptance of something they cannot control in their lives. The acceptance of something that will destroy them if left untreated. The acceptance of addiction. This is the moment of a powerful and living spirituality. A. Alvariz says in his book, The Shaping Spirit, "There is a moment at which things come truly alive; the moment at which they are caught in all their subtlety by the imagination. They then take to themselves meaning."*

No matter what the source, our moment is born in pain too excruciating to be tolerated any longer. We must either die or change. From that pain, we are spiritually reborn and able to begin life's adventures anew, no longer victims of religion but positive and creative human beings nurturing ourselves into full blossom.

Appendix II

Treatment:
A Guide for Professionals

THERE'S NOTHING MAGICAL or powerful about religious addiction. That's the mind-game religious addicts play—throwing up the smokescreen of the sanctity of religious beliefs in order to avoid taking responsibility for their lives. Religious addicts are seeking a fix out there that will make them better—just like other addicts.

Treating religious addicts simply requires that you guide these patients out of shame and victimhood into re-empowerment, that you move them from a passive codependency that says, Fix me, God, to a responsible, creative relationship. If you treat any kind of addiction, you can treat religious addiction and abuse, because it, too, is an escape from feelings, a flight from self. If you treat codependency and dysfunctional relationships, you can treat religious addiction and abuse, because it is the ultimate dysfunctional relationship. If you treat shame and self-hate, you can treat religious addiction and abuse, because it is the deepest core of all shame and self-hate issues.

The key to treating religious addiction is in learning to connect the symptoms with the core issues that are common to most addictions, and then using the various therapeutic techniques for addressing those issues. Because healthy spirituality requires mental, emotional, and physical well-being, if you are addressing those three needs in your therapies, you are on your way to developing a program that enhances your patients' spiritual growth.

Probably the most challenging task in working with the religiously addicted patient lies in opening the patient to the idea of a spirituality that is separate from, and even transcends, religion. Religion is created by human beings. Spirituality is God-given. Spirituality is being a positive and creative human being. Religion may be a tool one uses to develop positive creativity, but just being religious—following the rules—is not the same as being spiritual.

Patients may be in denial and could resist this concept, insisting that there is nothing compulsive about their relationship with God or the church. You are likely to be met with a wall of scripture and dogma. Ignore it; don't buy into it. Imagine a drug addict shooting up and ask what the patient is *feeling*, why the patient is medicating. Begin to explore, as quickly as possible, the sources of the guilt and shame that have no doubt propelled the patient into religious addiction.

Using a few of the symptoms of religious addiction as if they were presenting during the course of an intake or psychosocial evaluation, I have listed some of the issues they represent, and some treatment goals for addressing those issues as they might appear in your assessments.

Symtoms	Issues	Treatment Goals
Refusing to think, doubt, or question information or authority	Control, rigidity, validation, fear, perfectionism, isolation, judgmentalness, lack of trust, avoidance of responsibility	Relinquish control, take risks, develop flexibility, elevate self-esteem, identify fears, increase intimacy, develop self- trust, accept own and others' imperfections, take responsibility
Black-and-white, simplistic thinking	Fear, control, magical thinking, perfectionism	Develop self- acceptance, identify fears, relinquish control, accept reality

Symtoms	Issues	Treatment Goals
Magical thinking, belief that God will fix you	Fantasy, distorted reality, codependency, victim stance, fear, shame, perfectionism	Accept reality, increase self-esteem, relinquish control, accept own and others' imperfections, develop healthy concept of Spiritual Power
Scrupulosity: rigid, obsessive adherence to rules, codes of ethics, or guidelines	Fear, control, rigidity, need to feel safe, perfectionism, physical/sexual abuse, inadequacy, victim stance, avoidance of responsibility, shame	Identify fears, relinquish control, develop flexibility, accept imperfections, abandon rules/ritualizing, address sexual abuse, resolve guilt and shame issues, self-empowerment
Uncompromising judge-mental attitudes	Control, perfectionism, validation, fear, anger/ rage, sexual abuse/ dysfunction	Relinquish control, accept self and others, increase self-esteem, identify fears, express rage, address sexual abuse/dysfunction issues
Compulsive praying, going to church, attending missions or crusades, talking about God, quoting scripture	Escape/medicating, obsessive ritualizing, control, shame/guilt issues, validation, sexual addiction/ dysfunction, enmeshment, triangulation	Begin to define religious abstinence and structure, enhance spirituality, resolve guilt/shame, address sexual addiction/dysfunction, elevate self-esteem, relinquish control, disengage from entangling relationships

Symtoms	Issues	Treatment Goals
Unrealistic financial contributions	Validation, fear, control, guilt, shame, perfectionism, low self-esteem, avoidance of responsibility	Increase self-acceptance, identify fears, resolve guilt and shame, relinquish control, learn fiscal responsibility
Believing that sex is dirty, believing that our bodies or physical pleasures are evil	Guilt/shame, self-hatred, incest/sexual dysfunction, lack of intimacy, body image, distorted reality, control, rage	Resolve guilt/shame, elevate self-esteem, address incest/ sexual dysfunction, enhance body image, relinquish control, express rage
Progressive detachment from the real world, isolation, breakdown of relationships	Isolation, withdrawl, fear, avoidance of responsibility, enmeshment with religious groups, reality distortion, dissociation	Socialization, increase imtimacy, accept self and others, take risks, accept reality, stay present, disengage from entangling relationships, begin to appreciate variety

Of course, this list by no means includes all of the issues, and there will be other treatment goals. As you begin to identify religious addiction and abuse issues, you are likely to discover how these issues are tied into larger issues of control, enmeshment, caretaking, triangulation, and other aspects of codependency, as well as issues of body image, sexual identity, and dysfunction.

As you can see from the chart, religious addiction creates many of the same issues as other addictions. Thus the treatment goals are basically the same. Notice that very few of them specifically address God, religion, or spirituality, except in terms of creating structure, defining abstinence, and enhancing spirituality.

Like food addicts and sex addicts, religiously addicted patients will need assistance in creating a structure within which the use of religion can be balanced and healthy. They will also need some cognitive work on the difference between spirituality and religion, especially as it applies to Twelve Step programs.

Many patients go through treatment or therapy without addressing their religious abuse issues, mostly because no one thinks to look for them or recognizes their significance. At a treatment center at which I was consulting, the Aftercare counselor came to me for advice about a patient in her group. The patient was severely codependent. She was ending an emotionally abusive thirty-year marriage in which she was always told she was inferior. She was also extremely enmeshed with her children, constantly rescuing and caretaking.

Although she made some gains in treatment, she was trapped in a sense of powerlessness; her only means of self-worth came from caretaking. During an exercise in Aftercare group, the patient saw that her pattern was to rescue anyone she thought needed help—whether they asked for help or not. "But you're supposed to help people," she exclaimed. "The Church says so!"

This patient had been raised in an extremely Old World Catholic tradition, which taught her that being a good Christian meant unrestrained giving. Moreover, the culture in which she grew up was staunchly patriarchal; women had no value except as mothers and servants to their husbands. The patient was devoutly Catholic and struggled with enormous guilt and shame about divorcing her husband. As they explored the impact that her religious upbringing had had on her, the patient was filled with anger, rage, betrayal, and loss when she recognized that the Church had made her a codependent.

At the time this patient entered treatment, I had not yet begun to work with the staff at that center, and the treatment team was not as aware of religious abuse issues as they now are. Thus, critical information was not recognized that would have allowed this patient to confront her religious abuse during treatment.

The information was there. The staff simply did not realize that the patient's codependency and low self-esteem came as much from her religious beliefs as it did from her dysfunctional family of origin. This illustrates what psychiatrist M. Scott Peck says about the importance of discovering a patient's world-view:

> *In supervising other psychotherapists I rather routinely find that they pay too little, if any, attention to the ways in which their patients view the world. There are several reasons for this, but among them is the notion that if patients don't consider themselves religious by virtue of their belief in God or their church membership, they are lacking in religion and the matter therefore needs no further scrutiny. . . . So I say to those I supervise: "Find out your patients' religions even if they say they don't have any." . . . Patients are often unaware of how they view the world, and sometimes may even think they possess a certain kind of religion when they actually are possessed by a far different kind.*

I also stress that we must seek out the nature of the religious messages or belief systems patients were given in childhood. Peck supports my contention that the actual dysfunctional messages, as well as the ways in which parental behavior reflected or contradicted those messages, shape how a person is going to see the world. Therefore, it is critical to spend some time in the initial intake exploring the complete belief system with which a person was raised, in addition to the behavior of parents and significant adults in a patient's childhood.

GATHERING INFORMATION

In most cases, the tools for gathering information about the addict's worldview are already in place. Many therapists and treatment centers include genograms in or with the psychosocial assessment. When you are tracing the patterns of addictions through a patient's family of origin, ask about religious behavior in the same way that you ask about alcohol or drugs. If Dad was rigid and strict, ask if he was very religious or if his parents were. How did he manifest his religiosity? Was he angry and judging? Was he emotionally and physically absent? Did Mom spend all her time at Mass, saying prayers, totally absorbed in church duties? How did the patient feel about the parents' behaviors?

Since you are looking for sources of guilt, shame, and low self-esteem, also ask about the sexual messages a patient received growing up. Does the patient feel that sex is dirty? Where did he or she learn that? Was it taught in church or somehow validated or confirmed by religious teachings? Patients struggling to come to terms with homosexuality will often have major issues around religion. Ask about them. If a woman seems to have an ingrained sense of inferiority, who other than her dysfunctional family told her she was second-rate? If the patient was Catholic and attended parochial school, ask about the priests and nuns. Were they physically or emotionally abusive? Was the patient subjected to constant humiliation and shaming messages at school? What threats accompanied the religious teachings? What fears did a patient grow up with as a result of religious messages received either in the home or through Sunday school?

Dysfunctional religious messages can contribute to unresolved grief and loss issues. Children are often told it's selfish to mourn a death because their loved one is in heaven. Added to the unresolved grief is the guilt they carry for having grieved. Adults simply may not permit themselves to grieve because of religious messages about the hereafter. Or else they feel guilty for grieving. You will often need to lead patients through a tangle of abusive and dysfunctional messages as you help them uncover and reframe the early teachings they received about why they feel it is bad to grieve.

I recall the case of a woman who had great difficulty becoming intimate with anyone, including her husband and children. Gradually, it was discovered that the only nurturing, caring person in her life had been her grandmother, who died after a lingering illness when the patient was seven. She was initially excited when her grandmother came to live with her family, as she imagined having Gramma's warmth and nurturing full time. No one explained that Gramma was very sick or in any way prepared her for the shock of seeing her beloved Gramma incapacitated and unable to read to her or to play and cuddle as they once had.

Her parents, never very emotionally available or demonstrative, withdrew more as the grandmother's illness progressed. If they noticed the child's sadness at all, it was to irritably tell her to snap out of it.

When her grandmother died, she was told not to cry; no one had time to deal with her, and besides, it was selfish, because now Gramma was in heaven and out of her pain. When she was caught crying, she was spanked.

So the message she received was not to let anyone get close to her because they might inexplicably abandon her and she would be punished for being upset. Additionally, it was wrong to grieve when someone dies; grief was selfish, and a sign that one was telling God it was wrong to take them to heaven. Consequently, she was careful never to let people get so close emotionally that she would grieve if they died. Yet she felt intense guilt because she perceived herself as not caring about her family.

Many Jewish people today were influenced by parents or grandparents who survived the Holocaust or by relatives who carried great guilt and shame at not having spoken out against it. There was such wholesale grief and loss not only of family and friends, but even of an entire culture, that many who lived through it felt their own personal losses were too insignificant. They still carry tremendous burdens of grief and guilt.

Among them, you may find a general tendency to minimize or discount illness or trauma, as well as a deep-seated inability to trust anyone outside their faith or culture. Those issues can have, usually do have, great impact on the survivors—and on the children who were raised by such guilt-ridden parents. I knew of a patient who became extremely paranoid and partially schizophrenic because of her parents' guilt at not having challenged Hitler and because of their obsessive fear of anti-Semitism. This, coupled with a lifetime of being told not to trust anyone, so impaired her that she has spent much of her adult life in psychiatric hospitals.

Ask. You may be amazed at the response. Frequently, patients have never thought about the religious messages they received as having been abusive, or contributing to their shame and inability to accept themselves. Sometimes, their reaction when asked is very dramatic—surprising to themselves. You might hear such answers as, "I never thought about it . . . It never occurred to me . . . That's just the way it is in my religion. . . ."

Adult children of addicts accept the dysfunctional religious message as normal, until someone points out that it's not. That it *was* abusive; that it *has* created or contributed to core guilt and shame issues; that it has blocked patients in the grieving process, adding to the guilt and the loss.

RELIGIOUS ADDICTION AND SEXUAL DYSFUNCTION

Dysfunctional religious messages destroy healthy sexuality. In *The Road Less Traveled,* M. Scott Peck jokingly says the Catholic Church has provided him with a living and notes that he could easily substitute in that statement Baptist, Lutheran, Presbyterian, or other churches. He cites at length the case of Kathy, whose religious upbringing left her with such intense feelings of sin, especially as regarded her sexuality, that she resorted to hypnotic chanting to relieve her chronic fear that she would die. In treating this patient, Dr. Peck had to constantly challenge the religious teachings that had molded this woman's neuroses: "Where did she learn that masturbation was a sin? Who told her it was a sin? How did her informant know it was a sin? What makes a sin? . . ."

It is indeed a painstaking and sometimes arduous task to unravel the threads of religious addiction and abuse from the knots of sexual dysfunction. Sometimes, as in the case of Paul, which follows, the abuse and subsequent dysfunction is fairly easy to spot. Other times, the religious addiction is much more covert, requiring you to be much more attuned to the symptoms and hallmarks of the disease.

PAUL'S STORY

Paul knew from the age of twelve that he was a homosexual, but he kept it hidden. As a child, he had attended church in Marietta, Georgia, and he remembered hearing that being homosexual was the "worst" sin, the unspeakable sin. So he kept his feelings, fears, and questions to himself.

Despite having asthma, he tried to participate in sports. He was not very good at them—but he felt he had to try. He did not want to be considered a sissy, which he thought would give him away. He learned how to act tough, walk butch, and be part of the gang. But always he had homosexual feelings. He had listened to his playmates growing up and watched their interactions. He knew he was different. Finally he had learned that that difference had a name: homosexual. Queer. Fag. Worthy of God's hatred.

He shared with me an incident that was very difficult for him to talk about. When he was fifteen, he was bicycling through a park and stopped to use the restroom. He sensed he was not alone, and as he stood at the stall a young man came and stood at the next stall. Neither of them spoke, but he felt the excitement of sexual tension. He realized that the young man was masturbating and Paul immediately became erect. He was nervous and scared—and yet excited. He looked away but felt himself being drawn into the activity. Soon, he was showing himself to the other man. A noise outside the restroom scared the other man and he left. Throughout this encounter not a word was spoken.

Paul learned two things from this experience: that he was not alone, and that he liked what had happened. He needed to talk things over with someone but didn't know where to go. He needed to check his perceptions of how his family would react. One night when his family was entertaining their minister at dinner, Paul made up a story that was loosely based on the incident. He described what had happened as if he had been an innocent bystander, just minding his own business in the restroom when the two men came in and the incident occurred. He said he immediately left. What did it mean?

The minister, incensed, exclaimed, "These people are the lowest of the low. They are the scum of the earth. They defame the sacred image of God. They are an abomination. Their punishment will be the unquenchable fires of Hell!" His parents told him not to go to that park again. The minister later formed a citizens' protest to make the police crack down on what he called "them queers." Paul was consumed with shame and fear. That night he asked Jesus to remove his dirty feelings and forgive him.

All through high school and college Paul kept his sexual feelings to himself, but they never left. Then he went with some friends to one of Jimmy Swaggart's crusades. Swaggart thundered and railed against homosexuality; in his tearfully pious fashion he prayed that the Holy Spirit would heal all those afflicted by this disease of Satan.

When Swaggart called for all who wanted to renounce Satan to come forward and be healed, Paul tearfully went forward to embrace the Lord, believing he would be healed of his homosexuality. From that crusade on, religion became a drug to him. He could not get enough prayer, crusades, fasts, missions, and personal witnessing. He became rigid, dogmatic, judgmental—and viciously homophobic. Homosexuality became his own personal crusade. He made statements like: All queers are going to hell; homosexuals are child molesters and spread disease; gay teachers should be removed from schools; and only Jesus could cure homosexuality.

Paul became an elder in the church. He married a young woman who belonged to the Assembly of God, but they had no children. All the time he was preaching against homosexuality, he was still burying his homosexual feelings. He rationalized it as his personal battle with Satan: Satan was trying to get him.

I met Paul after he attempted suicide following his arrest for so-called lewd behavior in a restroom. He told me he had never forgotten the excitement he had experienced as a youth in the park. Sexually, his marriage had been dead for years—if it was ever alive. His wife had been brought up to believe that sex was dirty and they had slept in separate beds for years. He felt guilty for feeling relieved that he was not required to perform his marital duties often; sex with a woman felt unnatural to him. He felt doubly dirty.

Today, Paul has become an Episcopalian and attends my Spirituality Masses. He has separated from his wife and has been in therapy since he was in treatment. He is still struggling with his sexuality, both in terms of his homophobia and his own homosexuality. He occasionally attends meetings of

Integrity (a support group for gay members of the Episcopal church) in order to begin integrating his sexuality with his Christian beliefs.

When Paul came to treatment, he was very overt about his Christianity. Despite his arrest and subsequent suicide attempt, he remained loudly homophobic. Initially, he tried to maintain that Satan caused his lewd behavior. He actually said that the devil made him do it. His religious magical thinking had so distorted his reality that he truly believed he had no responsibility in the act. Satan had caught him off guard when he was tired. It wasn't his fault.

Gradually, the treatment team worked its way through the religious bombast to the childhood issues. When he would attempt to quote scripture, his therapists and fellow patients stopped him and requested that he share his feelings, rather than his religious thoughts. It was difficult at first; Paul literally could not converse on the most simple basis without quoting scripture or religious platitudes: He would say "Bless you" if someone passed him the salt.

Through intense experiential therapy, he reached the feelings of fear, anger, and shame he had buried as long as he could remember. Slowly, he came to accept that he had been religiously abused: The religious context in which he grew up had not allowed him to ask questions about his feelings and sexual confusion; it had caused him intense guilt and shame.

Paul became aware that he had been acting out sexually much more than he knew. The pressures from the guilt and shame would grow so intolerable that he would literally dissociate so that he could act out sexually. It was the only way to avoid the consuming shame that conscious knowledge of the act produced. His only other outlet had been his rage at homosexuals, which, when he couldn't vent it at crusades and missions, he channeled into compulsive exercising.

During treatment, his therapy focused on his overall judgmentalness and harshness, first of himself and then of others. He had created many little rituals for himself to atone for his sinful thoughts. To replace these, it was suggested that he find affirmations that would elevate his self-esteem and enhance a healthy spirituality.

Instead of his punishing exercise regime, he was assigned to go out with the slowest group of walkers. During the walk he was to note how his body felt—the sensation of his feet in his shoes hitting the pavement, his breathing, the feel of the sun. This new regimen was to help him learn to stay present and not to escape via rigorous exercise or obsessive religious thoughts. His therapists were careful not to present him with absolute rules, because he was likely to try to use them against himself.

Paul completed treatment with much work ahead of him, yet he had made a very good start. He acknowledged his religious addiction and abuse and his homosexuality. He was able to recognize his abusiveness to himself and others. Most important, he was willing to consider developing a different spirituality—one that would foster self-respect and acceptance.

Patients like Paul are easy to identify as religious addicts. But some, like Charlotte, deny ever having been either religiously addicted or abused.

CHARLOTTE'S STORY

Charlotte's father was an alcoholic; her parents were divorced when she was very young, and her father would make sporadic reappearances in her life. She spent summers with her maternal grandmother—a rigid, controlling woman who had never approved of Charlotte's mother—and made this abundantly clear to Charlotte. All her life, she was caught between her mother's values and her grandmother's. In addition, when her mother remarried, she found herself caught between her mother, father, stepfather, and stepsister.

Trapped in endless emotional triangles, Charlotte desperately tried to keep everybody happy. Early on, she realized that all these people had different sets of rules. If she could find out the rules, she'd be safe from criticism and the terror of rejection and punishment. Charlotte was also sexually and physically abused by her stepfather, as well as being emotionally abused by her father, mother, and grandmother. Staying safe became an all-consuming, but totally subconscious, endeavor.

As a result, Charlotte lived by rules. She always worked either for the government or in a company that had rigid dress codes, ethical guidelines, and clearly defined standards. She was judgmental and critical of those who did not follow rules to the letter. Indeed, much of her self-worth came from her pride in following rules. Beneath this lay an overwhelming terror of what would happen to her if she bent or strayed from the rules. Consequently, she was unable to truly evaluate situations or people on any basis other than whether they fit into her narrow structure. She was lonely and isolated; her rigid judgmentalness kept people away from her.

Thus, Charlotte presented most of the symptoms of religious addiction. Her early abuses caused her to avoid organized religion: She knew she had already violated most of the rules about sex. When she was introduced to Twelve Step programs and New Age metaphysics, she became one of those who always gave her Higher Power credit for anything she achieved. She used the metaphysical belief that there are no accidents as a means to avoid taking responsibility for her actions. She had a history of addictive relationships, which she dismissed as the result of past lives. All of her rules and beliefs, all the effects of her scrupulosity were a desperate attempt to avoid error—a pursuit that ultimately so limited and stunted her that she suffered a breakdown, which led to treatment.

Although she had been in therapy for years, no one had examined her scrupulosity as a symptom of an addiction. Many of its symptoms—control, rigidity, and perfectionism—had been addressed, but until she was identified as a religious addict and treated as such, she was not able to gain insight into, much less relinquish, much of that behavior. Today, she has recognized how she made a religion out of all the rules and guidelines; she has made great strides toward creating a balanced structure in her life. Risk taking is still difficult and frightening, but she is more and more able to use rules as guidelines to healthy choices, rather than as sole dictators of her actions.

These cases illustrate the difference that awareness of religious addiction and abuse can make in a patient's therapy. By recognizing that Paul was medicating himself with his religiosity and by not allowing him to engage in this type of behavior, his therapists were able to focus on the issues underlying his external behavior. In contrast, Charlotte's earlier therapy had been unsuccessful, since her therapists were essentially trying to treat symptoms without recognizing the underlying disease that caused them.

RELIGIOUS ADDICTION AND MULTITRACK PROGRAMS

People often ask me if there should be specific groups and lectures (a separate track) for religious addicts. After weighing the advantages and disadvantages of this, I have decided that it is most beneficial to all the patients to treat religious addiction and abuse alongside other addictions.

Religious addicts typically seek a way to feel superior, chosen, and special. Separating them into their own track only enables that arrogance and false sense of specialness to flourish and serves to further isolate them. Mainstreaming them with other patients helps break down those barriers.

Patients frequently get in touch with such issues as incest and emotional abuse by hearing other patients share their experiences. I believe that having religious addicts or victims of religious abuse working through their issues with a group of patients whose addictions may vary can help those patients examine their own issues around religion. It will also help those working through religious abuse issues to see that they are truly not alone. Many religious addicts, moreover, suffer from other compulsions and addictions, such as eating disorders and sexual addiction. I believe these addictions are linked and should be treated alongside each other.

I would like to say a word about dual-diagnosis patients. I believe that traditional A.A. did a great disservice, and still does, by putting down people who take antidepressants, making them feel guilty and ashamed, as if they aren't working a good enough Twelve Step program. I also see this in some substance abuse treatment centers, which often do not test alcoholics and addicts for organic depression.

Many patients suffer from a clinical, endogenous depression, which hinders the effectiveness of their therapy and their ability to practice the Twelve Step program. Manic-depressives especially have little or no emotional floor or ceiling. Their mood swings are so high and so low that living on such an emotional roller coaster is exhausting. The struggle against the depression itself takes so much energy that there is little left to give to therapy or the Twelve Step program.

My experience has shown that with time, good therapy, and the support found in Twelve Step programs, many dually diagnosed patients eventually work out of their organic depression and no longer need medication or at least need only very low dosages. Certainly, therapists and treatment teams need to carefully evaluate patients who may have clinical depression. I do not advocate treatment methods that use antidepressants as a matter of course, but I do recognize, and support, the need for chemical therapy when it is appropriate.

In addition, our psychiatric hospitals are full of deeply disturbed, sometimes psychotic patients who express their mania through religious obsession. Many psychiatrists see patients suffering from acute Obsessive-Compulsive Disorder (OCD) whose ritualizing centers on religion. Dr. Judith Rapoport, in her book *The Boy Who Could Not Stop Washing,* described three such patients. One was a little girl just approaching her church confirmation; another was a young woman in her twenties, also Catholic. The third was a young Jewish boy. In each case, the obsessions had begun earlier in childhood when the children began to believe that they weren't doing it right, that somehow they had sinned, failed, or were evil. Their obsessive rituals were frantic attempts to avoid doing something wrong.

Without wanting to second-guess the diagnosis, I cannot help but wonder if these young people would have developed full-blown OCD if they had not been exposed to the more abusive, dysfunctional forms of their respective religions. Dr. Rapoport notes that religions that use rituals, especially those of penance and purification, seem to "work well as a vehicle for compulsions." I wonder if she, and other physicians, have connected the early shaming messages with the obsessive behaviors used to escape the resulting fear and shame. Perhaps, if religious addiction and abuse become more widely recognized and treated earlier, patients like those Dr. Rapoport described would not become so desperately sick and would not suffer so needlessly for so long.

A TREATMENT PLAN

How then do you treat religious addiction alongside other addictions? What modifications, if any, should be made to the curriculum to accommodate issues of religious abuse? I repeat that many of you have nearly all of the tools in place. It is merely a matter of placing them in context, of addressing spirituality as being different from religion, and focusing on the mental, emotional, and physical wellness that promotes healthy spirituality.

Most treatment centers combine lectures, medical education, family therapy, and recreational therapy as well as individual and group therapy sessions. Lecture topics should address all obsessive-compulsive behaviors, including religion. If you teach patients how to identify symptoms of addiction—any addiction—they are more likely to recognize addictive behavior when they see it, no matter what substance or process is being abused.

The following is a treatment plan that addresses the needs of those in a treatment center who have religious addiction and abuse issues among others.

Lectures. A series of lectures on a variety of topics relating to addiction and compulsive behavior should educate patients about the nature of addictions and begin to teach them how to recognize when they are behaving addictively or compulsively, no matter which substance or process they are abusing. Lecture topics might include:

- Overview of obsessive-compulsive behaviors/addictions, including religious addiction/abuse
- Medical aspects of addictive behavior
- Psychological aspects of addictive behavior

- Family rules and family roles
- Changing life-styles in recovery
- Spirituality in recovery—difference between spirituality and religion
- Increasing self-esteem
- Adult children of dysfunctional families
- Codependents in treatment
- Relapse

Educational films. Religious addicts will benefit from seeing a mixture of educational videos and popular films. Viewing such programs as "It Will Never Happen to Me," or my videos on spirituality and recovery, in tandem with popular films, such as *Nuts, Agnes of God,* or *Elmer Gantry,* often serves as an effective means of getting patients in touch with their issues and feelings.

Nutritional/exercise programs. Keeping in mind that many religious addicts view their bodies as evil, and thus may have neglected or outright abused themselves physically, it is important that they begin to change that thinking by learning to take better care of themselves. Some of these patients may have entered treatment for help with an eating disorder, so they will doubly benefit from lectures on nutrition and exercise.

Sexuality, too, is frequently an issue, so I suggest a series of lectures or groups focusing on healthy sexuality and body image therapy. Many treatment centers use body movement work as a way to heal. When used in combination with affirmations and journaling, bodywork and movement therapy can help patients begin to enjoy their bodies and feelings of sensuality.

Writing a letter to their bodies provides a powerful tool in helping patients begin to nurture and accept their bodies. Patients who are having sexual identity or sexual dysfunction problems benefit from learning to open a dialogue with their "disowned parts"—the needs and feelings they have tried to escape.

Spirituality groups. Careful distinction should be made from the outset that there is a difference between religion and spirituality. The treatment team should also be aware that patients with religious abuse issues may react strongly to having chaplains, ministers, nuns, or hospital outreach teams arbitrarily visiting the unit. I can usually tell who these patients are: When I come into a treatment center, many patients greet me lovingly and enthusiastically; the religiously abused who do not know me hang back, fear and suspicion clearly written on their faces when they see me in clerical garb.

Bear in mind that religiously abused patients view ministers, priests, and other religious people as perpetrators. They will react as strongly as if you put a rapist in a room full of rape survivors. One patient nearly left a treatment center before she finished checking in because religious tracts had been left in her room. "I came here to feel safe," she said. "How can I feel safe when you let them in my room?"

I know it is still the practice in many hospitals to allow chaplains or religious lay visitors almost free access to patients. I have seen such people bearing down on a new patient, religious tracts and New Testaments in hand, totally unaware that the person was a survivor of religious abuse and quite hostile. If such practices are still in place in your facility, I recommend that you limit such visits and services to patients who request them. I know of some units that have discontinued the practice of placing Bibles in bedside tables and no longer allow religious tracts and literature to be placed on the unit. It is disrespectful of those who are of different faiths or no faith, and it is abusive to religious abuse survivors, as well as a trigger for religious addicts.

The goal is to create an environment that nurtures a healthy spirituality. The day should start with a spirituality group that focuses on developing self-love and self-acceptance. The group should also encourage love and acceptance of others—especially those who come from different cultures and religions, or from a nonreligious background. Mindful of the fact that some patients may have religious addiction and abuse issues, the meditations should be neutral and nonreligious, taken perhaps from some of the daily meditation books currently used by the various Twelve Step groups.

Alternatively, a group leader may choose a theme, such as love, personal power, or honesty, and have patients describe the feelings that the theme evokes or describe how it applies to their recovery. This opens the door to connecting spirituality with feelings, as well as stimulating creativity. It also allows patients to begin to see how they may take responsibility for their recovery and for their personal development.

I also encourage the use of affirmations and find them especially effective when patients create their own, based on their knowledge of their own needs and issues. Suggested affirmations include:

- I am a positive and creative person.

- I am capable of changing.

- I deserve to be loved by myself and others.

- I take responsibility for my recovery.

- I have choices today.

I especially advocate journaling and using the letter-writing techniques; these can be effective tools for helping patients recognize how they have abused themselves and thereby take the first steps toward self-acceptance and reparenting.

As patients begin to explore their addictions, guilt, and shame, I suggest that they be encouraged to write about early religious messages. This will help you identify which patients might have religious addiction and abuse issues, and it helps them get in touch with sources of shame they may not previously have considered. Some of the questions they could cover include:

- What were the religious messages you received in childhood?

- Was the majority of religious education given in the home or at church/synagogue?

- Was the behavior of your parents or other role models congruent with their beliefs—did their actions more or less match their words?

- How did these messages affect you as you were growing up?

- How do those messages still affect you today?
- How would you describe the God of your understanding today?

You are looking for the worldview that is described by M. Scott Peck as so essential to identifying and diagnosing issues and compulsions. Cognitive group therapy can then focus on helping patients gain insight into how these messages and beliefs shaped their self-image and led to addictions. When I conduct such groups, I continually challenge black-and-white, noncritical thinking. Such questioning sets off powerful emotions. The idea that we have choices, that we can be responsible for our spirituality, that we can re-create our image of God as a partner and guide can be explosive when heard for the first time. I'm told that the therapists get as much of a workout as the patients after such groups, because they produce such strong reactions.

Inner-child play therapy. Many of the treatment methods described earlier in this book are often used in conjunction with inner-child play, which has become a vital part of many treatment programs. It seems to be a matter of course in many workshops these days for participants to be handed paper and crayons and invited to draw or color some childhood experience and feeling. This works especially well with the use of writing and drawing with the nondominant hand.

Have patients draw their earliest image of God. Ask them to dialogue with that image: Where did it come from; Did they acquire it through formal religious education, or was it absorbed from watching parental behavior, or from playmates?

Next, you might want to have the patients draw their current image of God. Most people still see God the way they did as a small child, just as they carry many other childhood assumptions and beliefs with them as adults. You might also have them draw the image of God that they would like to have if they were inventing God all over again. This works well with patients who are preparing to let go of their old God.

There are several guided visualizations that ask people to journey to their childhood bedrooms and houses. These are easily adapted to help find the origins of religious guilt, shame, and fear. In visualizations that ask them to look at their earliest feelings about their parents, you can have them invite God into the room and thus to begin dialoguing with the dysfunctional beliefs.

Be creative. The more imaginative you are in adapting or devising tools for inner-child work, the more you begin to teach patients how to discover their own creativity. In the process, you bring them closer to healthy, whole spirituality and a happy co-creatorship with God.

Family treatment. As we have already discussed, religious addicts usually profoundly affect their families. If possible, it is important for family members or significant others to be involved in treatment. Remember, many religious addicts are children of religious addicts or may have children of their own. In these cases, parents and children need to be included in the family therapy.

Communication and the setting of boundaries is very important, especially if the family has been forced to attend church with the addict or has been routinely subjected to the addict's obsessive behavior. Family members, particularly those who want to attend a different church or none at all, must be permitted to set boundaries concerning their own religious expression and growth. While the religious addict is responsible for defining what their abstinence will look like, family members may have boundaries they wish to have set concerning respect for their beliefs.

Teaching the family members to express their feelings healthily will, as usual, be the biggest challenge. No doubt, the family members will, in self-defense, have acquired many of the guilt, shame, and blame tactics employed by the addict. They will need many sessions to learn to disengage from the dogmatism, scripture quoting, and proselytizing. They need to learn to remind the addict gently but firmly of the particular boundaries that may have been set and to state their need to have that boundary respected. Some may find it beneficial to be a bit confrontational. For example, saying, "Mom, you're quoting scripture again. Are you trying to tell me how you feel about this subject?" In time, each family will find its own methods of healthy communication. I encourage family counseling on a regular basis, at least once a month if not more, for a good six months following treatment and longer if the abuse was extremely severe.

Support groups. It will be especially helpful if religious addicts and religious codependents attend outside Twelve Step support groups with other patients. Again, the likelihood of multiple addictions makes it probable that patients would need to attend Twelve Step groups for codependency, substance abuse, and eating disorders, as well as sexual addiction and incest survivor groups. Being among people who share similar feelings, regardless of the substance or process abused, helps end that sense of isolation and being different. Others in those meetings might also benefit from hearing the experiences of religious addicts and religious codependents.

As I stated earlier, there are no specific groups for religious addicts and their codependents. I hope that will change. In the meantime, sending the addict and family members to relevant Twelve Step support groups will be of great help. Perhaps, if there is enough interest, the treatment center might begin to facilitate such support groups.

Ongoing support. Last, but certainly not least, treatment for religious addiction must include ongoing support. I hope that one result of this book will be the creation of a Twelve Step program designed for religious addicts, based on the Steps as revised for religious addiction. As more people begin to talk about their religious addiction and abuse in other Twelve Step meetings, I believe that they will find a nucleus from which to form Religious Addicts Anonymous, and, perhaps, even Religious Codependents Anonymous.

Many patients may have been treated for years for some of these symptoms, as was the case with Charlotte. In some instances, these patients make some progress if their related addictions are addressed. I do not believe any religious addict can build a strong recovery if the religiosity is not identified and addressed as its own disease. Treating the symptoms is rather like putting salve on boils caused by a virus. Until you treat the virus, the boils will keep coming back—so will the patients, time and again, in relapse—until their religious addiction is treated. That bedrock of shame remains untouched until religious issues are addressed.

As more of you begin to identify and treat religious addiction, I hope you will begin to network with one another and with me. My office receives calls daily from people who desperately want help with religious addiction and are seeking a therapist who can help them. I know they are out there. I see them everywhere I go. They are in desperate need of help. I hope you will be there for them.

Appendix III

Support

THE TWELVE STEPS OF ALCOHOLICS ANONYMOUS

1. We admitted we were powerless over alcohol—that our lives had become unmanageable.

2. Came to believe that a Power greater than ourselves could restore us to sanity.

3. Made a decision to turn our will and our lives over to the care of God *as we understood Him.*

4. Made a searching and fearless moral inventory of ourselves.

5. Admitted to God, to ourselves, and to another human being the exact nature of our wrongs.

6. Were entirely ready to have God remove all these defects of character.

7. Humbly asked Him to remove our shortcomings.

8. Made a list of all persons we had harmed, and became willing to make amends to them all.

9. Made direct amends to such people wherever possible, except when to do so would injure them or others.

10. Continued to take personal inventory, and when we were wrong, promptly admitted it.

11. Sought through prayer and meditation to improve our conscious contact with God *as we understood Him,* praying only for knowledge of His will for us and the power to carry that out.

12. Having had a spiritual awakening as a result of these steps, we tried to carry this message to alcoholics, and to practice these principles in all our affairs.

TWELVE STEP SUPPORT GROUPS

**ALCOHOLICS ANONYMOUS
WORLD SERVICES**
P.O. Box 459
New York, NY 10017
212/870-3400

AL-ANON FAMILY GROUPS
P.O. Box 862
Midtown Station
New York, NY 10118
212/302-7240

**CODEPENDENTS
ANONYMOUS**
P.0. Box 33577
Phoenix, AZ 85067-3577
602/277-7991

OVEREATERS ANONYMOUS
4025 Spencer, #203
Torrance, CA 90503
213/542-8363

**ADULT CHILDREN OF
ALCOHOLICS**
P.O. Box 3216
Torrance, CA 90512
213/534-1815

**NARCOTICS ANONYMOUS
WORLD SERVICE OFFICE**
P.O. Box 9999
Van Nuys, CA 91409
818/780-3951

**SEX AND LOVE ADDICTS
ANONYMOUS**
P.O. Box 1964
Boston, MA 02105
617/625-7961

DEBTORS ANONYMOUS
General Service
P.O. Box 20322
New York, NY 10025-9992
212/642-8220

**GAMBLERS ANONYMOUS
NATIONAL SERVICE OFFICE**
P.O. Box 17173
Los Angeles, CA 90017
213/386-8789

**OBSESSIVE-COMPULSIVE
ANONYMOUS**
P.O. Box 215
New Hyde Park, NY 11040
515/741-4901

**12-STEP SUPPORT GROUP FOR
RELIGIOUS ADDICTION &
ABUSE**
1926 W. 18th Street
P.O. Box 119
Houston, TX 77008

Notes

CHAPTER 1: SIN, SHAME, FEAR, AND CONTROL: THE ROOTS OF RELIGIOUS ADDICTION

19. "The question is . . ." Erich Fromm, *To Have or To Be?* (New York: Harper & Row, 1976), 135.

19. "Not necessarily . . ." ibid., 135.

21. "A child who is early taught . . ." William James, *The Varieties of Religious Experience* (New Hyde Park: University Books, 1963), 83.

21. mutually enlivened . . . *Père* Teilhard de Chardin, *The Phenomenon of Man* (London: William Collins, 1959), 68.

22. sin as diminishments *Père* Teilhard de Chardin, *Le Milieu Divin* (London: William Collins, 1960), 58.

22. "the realistic acts . . ." Wayne E. Oates, *The Psychology of Religion* (Waco, Tex.: Word Books, 1973). 203.

22. "sin as alienation . . .", ibid., 211.

23. search for truth William James, *The Varieties of Religious Experience* (New Hyde Park: University Books, 1963), 605.

23. "I also object to original sin . . ." Sam Keen, "Original Blessing, Not Original Sin," *Psychology Today* (June 1989), 56.

25. "there were nineteen billion years . . ." ibid., 57.

26. the consequences of that disobedience . . . Erich Fromm, *To Have or To Be?* 122–24.

26. carefully documented overview . . . Erich Fromm, *The Dogma of Christ and Other Essays on Religion, Psychology and Culture* (New York: Holt, Rhinehart and Winston, 1955), viii.

26. "have the double function . . ." ibid., 20.

30. "We are eternal consumers . . ." ibid., 178.

31. From 1984 to 1987, the Bakkers . . . David Brand, "An Outrageous Ministry" *Time* 129, no. 18 (May 4, 1987), 82.

32. Swaggart spent less than 10 percent . . . Kenneth Woodward with Mark Miller, "What Profits a Preacher?" *Newsweek* (May 4, 1987), 68.

32. "There's times I just have to quit thinking . . ." Jean Seligman, "The Inimitable Tammy Faye," *Newsweek* (June 8, 1987), 69.

32. "I do not call it a mistake . . ." Richard N. Ostling, "Now, It's Jimmy's Turn," *Time* (March 7, 1988), 46.

33. "I thought [Swaggart] . . ." Joanne Kaufman, "The Fall of Jimmy Swaggart," *People* 29, no. 9 (March 7, 1988), 37.

CHAPTER 2: WHEN GOD BECOMES A DRUG: THE STAGES OF RELIGIOUS ADDICTION

37. progressive relationship . . . Craig Nakken, *The Addictive Personality: Understanding Compulsion in Our Lives* (San Francisco: Harper & Row, 1988), 3–4.

38. "forms of nonverbal . . ." Wayne E. Oates, *The Psychology of Religion* (Waco, Tex.: Word Books, 1973), 143.

44. in a cover story on support groups . . . Charles Leerhsen et al., "Unite and Conquer," *Newsweek* (February 5, 1990), 50.

45. how we label . . . Jean Kinney, M.S.W., and Gwen Leaton, *Loosening the Grip: A Handbook of Alcohol Information* (St. Louis: The C. V. Mosby Company, 1978), 45.

45. defends the disease model . . . George E. Vaillant, *The Natural History of Alcoholism: Causes, Patterns and Paths to Recovery* (Cambridge, Mass.: Harvard University Press, 1983), 19.

46. self-inflicted . . . E. M. Jellenik, *The Disease Concept of Alcoholism* (New Haven: Hill House Press, 1960), 49.

46. With proper self-care . . . Jean Kinney, M.S.W., and Gwen Leaton, *Loosening the Grip*, 47.

CHAPTER 3: WHERE DOES IT HURT? THE SYMPTOMS OF RELIGIOUS ADDICTION

56. "do not express healthy striving . . ." N. S. Xavier, M.D., *The Two Faces of Religion: A Psychiatrist's View* (Tuscaloosa, Ala.: Portals Press, 1987), 46.

58. "Healthy spirituality enlightens . . ." ibid., 26.

67. "Even if Jim and Tammy did everything . . " David Brand, "God and Money," *Time* 130 (August 3, 1987), 49.

68. "indoctrination, rewards, punishments . . ." Erich Fromm, *To Have or To Be?* (New York: Harper & Row, 1976), 78.

68. "Suppose we told him . . ." Bertrand Russell, *Why I Am Not a Christian* (New York: Simon and Schuster, 1957), 28–29.

69. creation of taboos . . . Erich Fromm, *To Have or To Be?*, 80.

69.   rampant sexual abuse by . . . Katy Butler, "Encountering the Shadow in Buddhist America," *Common Boundary* (May/June, 1990), 14–22.

85.   "a restricted, undemonstrative . . ." Judith L. Rapoport, M.D., *The Boy Who Couldn't Stop Washing* (New York: E. P. Dutton, 1989), 227.

CHAPTER 4: RELIGIOUS ADDICTION: A FAMILY DISEASE

104.   Kelley describes Green . . . Ken Kelley, "Cruising With Anita," *Playboy* 25, no. 5 (May, 1978), 97.

104.   "independent spirit . . ." ibid., 232.

106.   "an emotional . . ." Robert Subby, *Co-Dependency: An Emerging Issue* (Hollywood, Fla.: Health Communications, Inc., 1984), 26.

107.   "protective stance adopted . . ." Marie Schutt, *Wives of Alcoholics: From Codependency to Recovery* (Pompano Beach, Fla.: Health Communications, Inc., 1985), 2.

110.   desperate attempts wives of . . ." ibid., 7.

110.   rules of caretaking described . . . ibid., 23.

CHAPTER 5: SUFFER THE CHILDREN: THE CONSEQUENCES OF RELIGIOUS ADDICTION AND ABUSE

116.   The hero is the one who takes charge . . . Sharon Wegscheider-Cruse, *Another Chance* (Palo Alto, Calif.: Science and Behavior Books, Inc., 1981), 104.

116.   The Scapegoat feels rejected . . . ibid., 117.

116.   The Lost child also feels . . . ibid., 131.

116.   Like the hero . . . ibid., 140.

120.   M. Scott Peck describes . . . M. Scott Peck, *The Road Less Traveled* (New York: Simon and Schuster, 1978), 187–191.

129.   describes virtually all . . . Cherry Boone O'Neill, *Starving for Attention* (New York: Dell Publishing, Inc., 1982), 22–35; 34–39

135.   "It is a simple psychological fact . . ." James M. Wall, "Swaggart's Confession: There's Room to Mourn," *Christian Century* (March 9, 1988), 235.

136.   "the excessive emphasis . . ." ibid., 235.

137.   "I have read that interest . . ." ibid., 235.

138.   Cherry Boone O'Neill writes . . . Cherry Boone O'Neill, *Starving for Attention,* 76–79.

141. one viewer, who contributed . . . Richard N. Ostling, "TV's Unholy Row," *Time* (April 6, 1987), 67.

CHAPTER 6: RECOVERY:
THE TWELVE STEPS TO BREAKING YOUR CHAINS

155-156. "We can have faith . . ." Alcoholics Anonymous, *Twelve Steps and Twelve Traditions* (New York: Alcoholics Anonymous World Services, Inc., 1953), 35.

158. "The very distinction . . ." Martin Israel, *Precious Living* (London: Hodder & Stoughton, 1976), 95.

163. Patrick Carnes . . . suggests . . . Patrick Carnes, Ph.D. *A Gentle Path through the Twelve Steps* (Minneapolis: CompCare Publishers, 1989), 136–137.

165. clear away the wreckage . . . Alcoholics Anonymous, *Big Book of Alcoholics Anonymous* (New York: Alcoholics Anonymous World Services, Inc., 1955), 164.

CHAPTER 7: TOWARD A HEALTHY SPIRITUALITY

173. "Before ever a Yes . . ." Alan Ecclestone, *Yes to God* (London: Darton, Longman & Todd, 1976), 58.

174. "Thus, our religious . . ." Erich Fromm, *To Have or To Be?* (New York: Harper & Row, 1976), 135–136.

177. "when we are spiritual . . ." John Bradshaw, *Homecoming* (New York: Bantam Books, 1990), 38.

177-178. "Love is the active . . ." Ashley Montagu, *Growing Young* (New York: McGraw-Hill Book Company, 1981), 92–93.

179. "God love all . . ." Alice Walker, *The Color Purple* (New York: Pocket Books, 1982), 203.

180. "God love everything . . ." ibid.

181. "Well, us talk . . ." ibid., 204.

187. Worksheet for creating . . . Patrick Carnes, Ph.D. *A Gentle Path through the Twelve Steps* (Minneapolis: CompCare Publishers, 1989), 201–204.

195. "A mother could . . ." Anthony de Mello, *The Song of the Bird* (Garden City: Image Books, Division of Doubleday & Company, 1984), 61.

APPENDIX I: INTERVENTION: HELPING OTHERS TOWARD RECOVERY

204. "we do not invent crisis . . ." Vernon Johnson, *I'll Quit Tomorrow* (San Francisco: Harper & Row, 1980), 4.

204.   "They live with increasing . . ." ibid., 5.

217.   "For many people . . ." Father Leo Booth, *Spirituality and Recovery: A Guide to Positive Living* (Deerfield Beach, Fla.: Health Communications, Inc., 1985), 43.

APPENDIX II: TREATMENT: A GUIDE FOR PROFESSIONALS

224.   "In supervising other . . ." M. Scott Peck, *The Road Less Traveled* (New York: Simon and Schuster, 1978), 186.

227.   "Where did she learn . . ." ibid., 202.

234.   religions that use rituals . . . Judith L. Rapoport, M.D. *The Boy Who Couldn't Stop Washing* (New York: E. P. Dutton, 1989), 159.

Bibliography

Alcoholics Anonymous. *Twelve Steps and Twelve Traditions*. New York: Alcoholics Anonymous World Services, Inc., 1953.

Booth, Father Leo. *Spirituality and Recovery: A Guide to Positive Living*. Deerfield Beach, Fla.: Health Communications, Inc., 1985.

Bradshaw, John. *Homecoming*. New York: Bantam Books, 1990.

Brand, David. "An Outrageous Ministry." *Time* 129, no. 18 (May 4, 1987).

———. "God and Money." *Time* 130 (August 3, 1987).

Butler, Katy. "Encountering the Shadow in Buddhist America." *Common Boundary* (May/June, 1990).

Carnes, Patrick, Ph.D. *A Gentle Path through the Twelve Steps*. Minneapolis: CompCare Publishers, 1989.

de Chardin, *Père* Teilhard. *The Phenomenon of Man*. London: William Collins, 1959.

———. *Le Mileu Divin*. London: William Collins, 1960.

Fromm, Erich. *The Dogma of Christ and Other Essays on Religion, Psychology and Culture*. New York: Holt, Rhinehart and Winston, 1955.

———. *To Have or To Be?* New York: Harper & Row, 1976.

Hudson, Rock, and Sara Davidson. *Rock Hudson, His Story*. New York: Avon Books, 1987.

Israel, Martin. *Precious Living*. London: Hodder & Stoughton, 1976.

James, William. *The Varieties of Religious Experience*. New Hyde Park: University Books, 1963.

Jellenik, E. M. *The Disease Concept of Alcoholism*. New Haven: Hill House Press, 1960.

Johnson, Vernon. *I'll Quit Tomorrow*. San Francisco: Harper & Row, 1980.

Kaufman, Joanne. "The Fall of Jimmy Swaggart." *People* 29, no. 9 (March 7, 1988).

Keen, Sam. "Original Blessing, Not Original Sin." *Psychology Today* (June 1989).

Kelley, Ken. "Cruising With Anita." *Playboy* 25, no. 5 (May, 1978).

Kinney, Jean, M.S.W., and Gwen Leaton. *Loosening the Grip: A Handbook of Alcohol Information*. St. Louis: The C. V. Mosby Company, 1978.

Leerhsen, Charles et al. "Unite and Conquer." *Newsweek* (February 5, 1990).

Nakken, Craig. *The Addictive Personality: Understanding Compulsion in Our Lives.* San Francisco: Harper & Row, 1988.

O'Neill, Cherry Boone. *Starving for Attention.* New York: Dell Publishing, Inc., 1982.

Oates, Wayne E. *The Psychology of Religion.* Waco, Tex.: Word Books, 1973.

Ostling, Richard N. "TV's Unholy Row." *Time* (April 6, 1987).

———. "Now It's Jimmy's Turn." *Time* (March 7, 1988).

Peck, M. Scott. *The Road Less Traveled.* New York: Simon and Schuster, 1978.

Rapoport, Judith L., M.D. *The Boy Who Couldn't Stop Washing: The Experience and Treatment of Obsessive-Compulsive Disorder.* New York: E. P Dutton, 1989.

Russell, Bertrand. *Why I Am Not a Christian.* New York: Simon and Schuster, 1957.

Schutt, Marie. *Wives of Alcoholics: From Codependency to Recovery.* Pompano Beach, Fla.: Health Communications, Inc., 1985.

Seligman, Jean. "The Inimitable Tammy Faye." *Newsweek* (June 8, 1987).

Subby, Robert. *Co-Dependency: An Emerging Issue.* Hollywood, Fla.: Health Communications, Inc., 1984.

Vaillant, George E. *The Natural History of Alcoholism: Causes, Patterns and Paths to Recovery.* Cambridge, Mass.: Harvard University Press, 1983.

Wall, James M. "Swaggart's Confession: There's Room to Mourn," *Christian Century* (March 9, 1988).

Wegscheider-Cruse, Sharon. *Another Chance.* Palo Alto, Calif.: Science and Behavior Books, Inc., 1981.

Woititz, Janet. *Adult Children of Alcoholics.* Hollywood, Fla.: Health Communications, Inc., 1983.

Woodward, Kenneth, with Mark Miller. "What Profits a Preacher?" *Newsweek* (May 4, 1987).

Xavier, N. S., M.D. *The Two Faces of Religion: A Psychiatrists View.* Tuscaloosa, Ala.: Portals Press, 1987.

Leo Booth

He's a different kind of priest who says you don't have to be religious to be spiritual. The dynamic Englishman is a spiritual 'rebel with a cause': He wants to bring spirituality back into religion, and help the essence of being real and human. An energetic mix of Charlie Chaplin with a touch of Dudley Moore, he's an Episcopal priest who's as likely to quote The Velveteen Rabbit as often as the Bible. He's not afraid to tweak the noses of religious and psychotherapy establishments to get his message across, but once he's heard, he treats his listeners with warmth, dignity, compassion and insight.

For over 17 years he has focused on helping people reclaim their spiritual power. A recovering alcoholic and certified addictions and eating disorders counselor, he is a national consultant to treatment programs and organizations. Rev. Booth is an active Episcopal priest in the Diocese of Los Angeles. He is the author of many books on the issues of spirituality and recovery.

BOOKS BY LEO BOOTH

THE ANGEL AND THE FROG

In this charming spiritual fable, Cedric the Frog and the residents of Olde Stable Farm meet an angel named Christine and discover the Spiritual Process.

SCP Limited

HEALING THOUGHTS:

Reflections

This is a wonderful, spiritually provoking book that speaks directly to our feelings—always offering a positive response to whatever is challenging us.

SCP Limited

THE GOD GAME: IT'S YOUR MOVE:

Healing the Wounds of Religious Addiction and Abuse

This ground-breaking book is an invitation to move beyond the unhealthy religious beliefs and messages that for too long have held you hostage from attaining healthy spirituality.

SCP Limited

SAY YES TO LIFE: *Daily Meditations*

365 daily meditations on issues relating to alcoholism, chemical dependency, eating disorders and codependency.

SCP Limited

MEDITATIONS FOR COMPULSIVE PEOPLE

In this collection of meditations in verse, Leo the poet meets Leo the theologian. Revised, with worksheet and process questions.

SCP Limited

SPIRITUALITY AND RECOVERY

One of the most popular of Father Leo's works, this book is a guide to crating healthy spirituality in recovery. It explains the difference between religion and spirituality, and suggests ways in which to become a positive, creative person.

SCP Limited

OTHER MATERIALS FROM LEO BOOTH

40 INDIVIDUAL AUDIOS
and AUDIO ALBUMS (4 titles per set)

Individual audios and album sets on spirituality, religious abuse, self-empowerment, drug and alcohol abuse, codependency, relationship and life issues.

VIDEOS

An excellent addition to your personal recovery library, or for treatment programs, hospitals, alcohol and drug councils. Each approximately 55 minutes running time.

V1 Say Yes To Life
V2 Meditations For Compulsive People
V3 Spirituality and Adult Children of Alcoholics
    Recovery
V4 Creating Healthy Relationships
V5 Recovery From An Eating Disorder
V6 Intervention: Creating an Opportunity to Live
V7 Overcoming Religious Addiction and
    Religious Abuse
V8 An Evening With Father Leo

ANNUAL SPIRITUAL EMPOWERMENT CONFERENCE CRUISES AND RETREATS

Each year, Leo Booth presents conference cruises and retreats. During these fun-filled days, you'll explore all aspects of healthy spirituality, from the morning "Attitude of Gratitude" meeting to the evening dancing and play. Themes include manifesting your life's dreams, achieving goals, claiming spiritual power and healing spiritual wounds of addictions or other issues. Dates and itineraries vary from year to year. Space is limited and fills up quickly, so early reservations are recommended.

CONFERENCES * WORKSHOPS * INSERVICES * CONSULTANCIES *

Leo Booth works with a variety of groups and organizations, from treatment centers and therapists, to the general public, teaching how to create healthy spirituality. The Spiritual Concepts staff will help you with any phase of the event, from choosing a topic to suggesting marketing strategies and creating ads and copy. If you would like to share his wit, wisdom and zest for life with your program or organization call Spiritual Concepts.

For a catalog and information call:

Spiritual Concepts
(800) 284-2804
(8:00 AM - 4:00 PM Pacific time Mon.- Fri.)
2700 St. Louis Avenue
Long Beach, CA 90806
Internet: www.fatherleo.com
E-Mail: frleo@deltanet.com